# POPe
# Francis

Life *and* Revolution

# POPE Francis

## Life *and* Revolution

*a biography of* Jorge Bergoglio

ELISABETTA PIQUÉ

Foreword by Cardinal Seán Patrick O'Malley, O.F.M. Cap.

LOYOLAPRESS.
A JESUIT MINISTRY
Chicago

## LOYOLA PRESS.
### A JESUIT MINISTRY

3441 N. Ashland Avenue
Chicago, Illinois 60657
(800) 621-1008
www.loyolapress.com

Originally published as *Francisco. Vida y revolución* by Elisabetta Piqué
(Buenos Aires, Argentina: Editorial El Ateneo, 2013). The exclusive world
rights for the Spanish language are held by Editorial El Ateneo, an imprint of
Grupo ILHSA S. A.

Translated by Anna Mazzotti and Lydia Colin

Cover art credit: Vatican Pool/Contributor/Getty Image News/Getty Images
Back cover author photo, L'Osservatore Romano.

**Hardcover**

ISBN-13: 978-0-8294-4213-7
ISBN-10: 0-8294-4213-8

**Paperback**

ISBN-13: 978-0-8294-4217-5
ISBN-10: 0-8294-4217-0
Library of Congress Control Number: 2014948226

Printed in the United States of America.
14 15 16 17 18 19 Bang 10 9 8 7 6 5 4 3 2 1

*For Gerry*

# Contents

# Foreword

"I am the same as I was in Argentina." Pope Francis told me this recently in a conversation over lunch at the Casa Santa Marta. For the world Pope Francis is the man of surprises, but for Elisabetta Piqué he is a reincarnation of Padre Jorge, the Jesuit Archbishop of Buenos Aires. She was quick to realize that his choice of a name was in itself a program to recover the essential values of the gospel: to overcome one's own sinfulness; to be on the side of the poor; to dialogue with everyone, even those of other faiths or of no faith; to go to the periphery carrying the light and the joy of the Gospel.

Elisabetta Piqué has produced a most compelling description and analysis of Pope Francis. Pope Francis's revolution is like that of Saint Francis of Assisi, whose mission to rebuild the Church really began the day he kissed the leper. Being able to accompany Pope Francis last October 4 on his pilgrimage to Assisi was indeed a spiritual experience. The Holy Father began the day at the Istituto Serafico where he embraced a hundred severely handicapped children, their families, and their caregivers. He reminded us that when the Risen Christ appears to the Apostles, the first thing he does is show them his wounds, those wounds that he carries with him when he returns to the right hand of the Father. In kissing these children, the Holy Father is kissing the glorious wounds of Christ. All of this is but a continuation of a vocation that stirred in his heart when Jorge Bergoglio was a young man in Buenos Aires.

In some ways this biography reminds me of George Weigel's biography of John Paul II, which demonstrates the clear connections of the priestly ministry of the young Karol Wojtyla and the themes of John Paul II's pontificate. Betta Piquè shows us how Francis was the parish priest of Buenos Aires before becoming the parish priest of the world, with the same love for the poor and the marginalized, the same desire to reach those on the periphery with Gospel joy.

What we have in our Holy Father is a Pope who has embraced the vocation of being a follower of Ignatius, who once declared that he wanted to be a saint like St. Francis of Assisi. Bergoglio is thoroughly Jesuit, thoroughly Ignatian, right down to the fascination with St. Francis. Shortly before his ordination, the thirty-two-year-old Bergoglio wrote a short "credo." He has kept that piece of paper as a reminder of his core convictions. It is a clear indication of the habit of self-reflection so deeply ingrained by his Jesuit formation.

In his credo, he speaks of his own history and says that on a spring day of September (in the Southern Hemisphere!) "The loving face of God crossed my path and invited me to follow Him." He often hearkens back to that September day, the day of his own spiritual awakening and conversion on the Feast of St. Matthew that found him breaking away from his friends to go to church to receive the sacrament of confession. It was there that he first felt called. Later, he shared that his favorite painting in Rome is Caravaggio's *Calling of St. Matthew*, where Jesus is pointing at the tax collector. Bergoglio said that when he looks at that painting he feels that Jesus is pointing at him. It is not surprising that Father Bergoglio, when appointed Bishop, chose the phrase *Miserando atque eligendo*—"having mercy and calling me"—from the homily of the Venerable Bede on the Feast of St. Matthew, the publican converted and called to be an apostle.

That experience as a seventeen-year-old was, in his words, "the astonishment of an encounter . . . of encountering someone who was waiting for you. . . . God is the one who seeks us first." The Holy Father views morality in the context of an encounter with Christ that is "triggered by mercy"; "the privileged locus of the encounter is the caress of the mercy of Jesus Christ on our sins, and thus a new morality—a correspondence to mercy—is born." He views this morality as a "revolution"; it is not a titanic effort of the will but simply a response to a surprising, unforeseeable, and "unjust mercy." Morality is not a "never falling down" but an "always getting up again." The Holy Father's emphasis on mercy helps us understand why the author of this book has chosen to include "revolution" in the title.

In keeping with his own Jesuit formation, Pope Francis is a man of discernment, a practice that at times results in freeing him from the confinement of doing something in a certain way because it was always thus. There are many indications that Pope Francis is very comfortable in his own skin and does not feel constrained by practices of pontificates in the past. But to me one of the most striking examples of this clarity of vision and confidence is his decision to celebrate the Holy Thursday Mass during the first two years of his pontificate outside the traditional Rome basilica. He chose to celebrate Mass at a residential rehabilitation center for the disabled this past year, and the year before he celebrated it in a Rome prison for juvenile offenders.

On Holy Thursday, Jesus washed the feet of the Twelve. They were shocked and unhinged by the experience. St. Peter rebelled at the thought and capitulated only when Jesus insisted. For most of us, it has become a rather stylized liturgical gesture that is but a weak reflection of what the original foot washing entailed. Pope Francis replicated the surprise and the shock of the apostles even as he dismayed those who preferred the stylized liturgy in a basilica.

This was not an innovation for Pope Francis, for as Archbishop of Buenos Aires, he had been doing this each Holy Week. While many were surprised that the Holy Father did not opt to celebrate the Holy Thursday Mass as other popes had done in the Basilica of St. John Lateran, the Holy Father was jostling our imaginations because we have grown so complacent that we can no longer see beyond the familiar custom to glimpse the challenging truth. With a simple gesture, the pope was challenging core assumptions about power, authority, and leadership. As he told the prisoners, this is a symbol, it is a sign. "Washing your feet means I am at your service," he said.

In a world that is so often polarized and divided, Pope Francis's message has brought hope into people's lives and enticed many people to look at the Church again. The field hospital imagery is more compelling than that of the museum or the concert hall.

Most Catholics have felt energized by the focus on God's love and mercy and on the clarion call to embody the ideals of the Church's social gospel in our relations with others, especially the most vulnerable and forgotten. The Holy Father has made us more aware of Lazarus, covered with sores, who is on our doorstep suffering alone while we are absorbed in our pursuit of entertainment and creature comforts. *Evangelii Gaudium* reminds us: "Sometimes we lose our enthusiasm for mission because we forget that the Gospel responds to our deepest needs, since we were created for what the Gospel offers us: friendship with Jesus and love of our brothers and sisters."

In the pages that follow, you will come to know Pope Francis better. One of God's greatest gifts is this Jesuit pope who follows closely the path of St. Ignatius by wanting to be like St. Francis of Assisi. In doing so he is helping the whole world rediscover the Joy of the Gospel.

And all this *Ad majorem Dei Gloriam.*

Cardinal Seán O'Malley
July 20, 2014

# 1

# The Vigil

It's pouring rain. He wakes up very early, as usual. Today is March 12; it's four o'clock in the morning and still dark outside. Kneeling with his eyes closed, concentrating, he prays silently, as he does every morning. He asks St. Joseph and St. Teresita (Thérèse of Lisieux) in particular to enlighten him. He asks God to forgive him his sins and Jesus to allow him to serve, to allow him to be his instrument.

It's a special day. This afternoon the conclave that is to elect a successor to Benedict XVI is to start. And he is one of the 115 electors who will be locked in the Sistine Chapel to carry out this mission.

It's cold. From his big room in the Casa Internazionale del Clero Paolo VI, a Vatican guesthouse for priests, on Via della Scrofa, where he usually stays when he is in Rome, he can hear the rain falling on the cobblestones. The people here know him; he has been here several times during the past ten years, and they always book the same room for him, No. 203.

Although he doesn't like coming to Rome, or rather, to the Vatican—where one risks losing one's faith with all that intrigue, pomp, and circumstance—he feels at ease in this room, with its high ceilings, austere on the whole in spite of its period furniture and damask upholstery.

He's an organized man, careful, methodical—he "doesn't take a step without thinking about it first," as the people who know him say—and the night before he had prepared a small suitcase. Not being interested in material things, he won't take much with him to the Casa Santa Marta, the Vatican guesthouse where he is to lodge with the other cardinals for the duration of the conclave. A conclave that will not last long, he hopes. As in 2005, when he took part in the election to choose John Paul II's successor, he is convinced that a long election, one lasting more than two days, would—given the world of media and information technology we live in—give the impression of a divided Church. That is why, at the 2005 conclave, when he happened to be the second most-voted-for Cardinal after Joseph Ratzinger, he took a step back, so as not to impede Ratzinger's election. After John Paul II's nearly twenty-seven years as pontiff, it was not easy to replace a giant like him, charismatic until the end. The candidacy of Ratzinger (former right-hand man of the Polish pope, kindly, sensible, and had filled a key role as the dean of the College of Cardinals during the preconclave meetings and was supported by a conservative lobby) had been the easiest card to play.

That time, the conclave had been not only a new experience—the first time in Jorge Bergoglio's life that he had entered the Sistine Chapel to elect the successor of St. Peter—but also a somewhat traumatic one. A conclave is a very secret event, but messages, emotions, and even information always leak out, and the cardinals who had taken part in the 2005 election had seen, during the first vote count, Cardinal Jorge Mario Bergoglio, Archbishop of Buenos Aires, age sixty-eight at the time, nearly distraught as he gradually gained vote after vote. He had even surpassed Cardinal Carlo Maria Martini, like him a Jesuit and very *papabile*, the candidate of the progressives but no longer a possibility because of illness.

"I remember that after the 2005 conclave he came back from Rome very distressed," an old friend of Bergoglio's recalls. "He called me up and said, 'Doctor, you can't imagine how I suffered.' He felt that he had been used by some who were losing out and had been put forward to block Ratzinger. He returned much affected by this fact."

Padre (Father) Jorge, as he prefers being called, because he feels himself to be a simple priest, a pastor, finishes putting away his things in his room on Via della Scrofa. Eight years have passed since that first conclave, when, thanks be to God, "he had got off"; in other words, he had been saved. Those eight years were undoubtedly difficult for Benedict XVI, who on February 11 had turned the tables and become the first pope to give up his mandate in more than six hundred years. Bergoglio defined this gesture as "courageous and revolutionary."

The Argentine Cardinal looks out the wide window of his Roman room. It is six thirty in the morning, and there is not a soul on Via della Scrofa. He has had a light breakfast, as he does every morning, in the breakfast room of the Casa Internazionale del Clero Paolo VI. He has exchanged a few words about the bad weather, about the rain and the cold, with the few priests he meets in the room. A few of them go so far as to wish him luck, hinting at that afternoon's conclave.

Because of the rain and his suitcase, he won't be able to walk to the Vatican, as he usually does when in Rome. It's a walk that relaxes him; as he walks, he prays and admires the beautiful little alleys of the Eternal City, passing through Via dei Coronari with its antique shops. Further on he never fails to stop and pray to the Madonna dell'Archetto in an old passage-way that leads to the Via dell'Arco dei Banchi. Here this splendid fresco of the Virgin is painted on the wall, a special image among the thousands to be found in Rome. After praying there, Padre Jorge, like any passerby (he doesn't like showing off his scarlet cardinal's robes, which he usually hides under a black coat or a raincoat) crosses the Vittorio Emanuele II bridge over the Tiber River and presses on toward the Vatican.

He has taken this walk many times, peaceably, alone, because, even though he has thousands of friends, he is essentially a solitary man. Every step thinking and praying, thinking and praying, something he never stops doing, even when he is asleep. This walk is one of the few things he enjoys in that splendid city, Rome. He is well aware that behind all this sacred beauty, these monuments, churches, and ancient temples, a nest of vipers is often concealed.

He doesn't want to think that he might never take this walk again. But his mind betrays him. Since the day he heard about Benedict XVI's resignation, on February 11 when a friend from Rome called him at eight o'clock in the morning to inform him (it was noon in Rome), he has had the feeling that his life could change unexpectedly. Even if his deeply rooted rationality tells him that he cannot possibly be elected because he's already a pensioner (he had handed in his letter of resignation as Archbishop when he turned seventy-five), his intuitive part, his heart—even more deeply rooted—warns him that it isn't impossible.

He hasn't forgotten a telling conversation, on the morning of February 11, with Father Alejandro Russo, Rector of the Cathedral of Buenos Aires, whom he had invited into his office to talk about the breaking news.

"Oh my God, what a situation with this story of the vacant see!" commented the Cardinal. "You know that I was thinking that in March we could start the procedure for the succession here in Buenos Aires. . . . Now we'll have to put everything off for two or three months."

"Or else anticipate things," suggested the rector.

"Do you think the new pope will send me home at once?"

"No, I didn't mean that. I was thinking that the new pope might be you."

"But no, Alejandro! I've just handed in my resignation. I'm seventy-six years old. It's not possible!"

It's still raining. He looks at the black plastic watch he wears on his right wrist; he is very punctual, he doesn't like being late. Calling from the phone on the desk in his room, he asks reception to call him a taxi, "please." "Right away, Your Eminence," a humble, submissive voice replies. He hates being called "cardinal" or "eminence" with the obsequious tone of voice used in Rome when talking to high-ranking prelates. But he is used to it. And his Jesuit sensibility sees to it that his aversion does not show.

He goes down to the reception desk, accompanied by Father Fabián Pedacchio, a young Argentine priest. There he greets the people behind the counter with a shy smile. It's a quarter to seven in the morning. "Good luck, Your Eminence," they wish him very courteously, escorting him to his taxi with an umbrella. "See you soon," the Argentine Cardinal salutes them. In spite of premonitions and the intuition he feels deep inside, Bergoglio is calm. In contrast to the 2005 conclave, his name has not appeared among the *papabili* (possible candidates) mentioned in the Italian media. The Vatican correspondents who have included his name on the lists of candidates in the troubled preconclave period can be counted on the fingers of one hand. Most of them believe that the only Argentine *papabile* is the other one who is taking part in the conclave, Leonardo Sandri, age sixty-nine, Prefect of the Congregation for the Oriental Churches and substitute for general affairs at the Vatican's Secretariat of State toward the end of John Paul II's pontificate.

It will be a "match" between Italy and Brazil, several Italian Vatican correspondents have written, using soccer terminology to illustrate their prediction of what will happen during the first vote of the afternoon. They think that most of the 115 votes will be shared between two favorites: Angelo Scola, Archbishop of Milan, and Odilo Pedro Scherer, Archbishop of São Paulo. Among the main candidates are also mentioned the Canadian Cardinal Marc Ouellet, Prefect of the Congregation for Bishops, and the American Seán O'Malley, Archbishop of Boston, a likable friar with sandals and a long beard. They are all younger than Bergoglio: Scola is seventy-one; Ouellet and O'Malley, sixty-eight; Scherer, sixty-three. The mantra heard repeatedly from the day of Benedict XVI's resignation until today, the first day of the conclave, is that the future pope must be between sixty-five and seventy-five years of age. That is why Bergoglio is calm. Yet he also knows that it's not the media that decides what will happen at the conclave. He knows that there is much indecision and that the situation is very complex, because in reality the conclave is marked by the lack of a single great favorite, as Ratzinger was in 2005.

When he leaves the hotel, the Archbishop of Buenos Aires doesn't think for a moment that it might be his turn to take the baton. He is quite sure he will be able to use his return ticket to Argentina, booked for March 23, which he has left at the Casa Internazionale on Via della Scrofa.

His room at the Casa di Santa Marta is 207. It was assigned to him by lot the day before, during the last general congregation of cardinals before the conclave. It is a small, simple room, furnished only with what is strictly necessary—a bed, a chest of drawers, a desk, a crucifix on the wall, a bathroom—the way he likes it. It's eight o'clock in the morning. Although strictly speaking the seclusion *cum clave* (with a key) has not yet begun, isolation has already started. No more phone calls, no more reading of the daily papers, no more contact with the outside world—only with the other 114 cardinals from the five continents, who have the tremendous responsibility of electing the new pope at a truly turbulent time in the history of the Catholic Church.

Bergoglio knows all the cardinals from the preconclave meetings. He is a great friend of some of them, less so of others. There's a laugh when, in the small bus that is taking them to St. Peter's Basilica for the Mass *pro eligendo Romano Pontefice* (for the election of the Roman Pontiff), a very popular American Cardinal confesses that he feels he is missing something: he has had to leave behind his cell phone and the tablet he uses to send e-mails, tweets, and other online updates; these things have by now become appendages of his body. Bergoglio understands hardly anything about such things. He has never had a cell phone. He has always managed with the aid of his brain or his little black notebook, where he jots down everything in minute handwriting. Or with his landline phone, dialing the number he needs directly, without an intermediary.

It is still pouring rain in Rome while, with the other cardinals, Bergoglio attends the Mass transmitted live on television. The homily by the dean of the College of Cardinals, Angelo Sodano, who calls heartily for unity, is accompanied by thunder and lightning, which could almost be taken for a divine message.

"And we must all collaborate in building the unity of the Church, because to achieve it we need to be 'joined and knitted together by every ligament' [referring to Ephesians 4:16], every member's energy," says the influential former Secretary of State. "All of us, therefore, have been called to cooperate with Peter's successor, the visible foundation of this ecclesiastical unity," stresses Sodano, a great diplomat and godfather of a conservative group of the Curia who never approved of the Archbishop of Buenos Aires. He alludes to the eight years of Benedict XVI's pontificate, marked by avoidable crises, intrigues, and internal strife.

Sodano, who will not take part in the conclave because he is eighty-five (once cardinals reach the age of eighty, they cannot participate in a conclave), also sketches the profile of the next pope: "The fundamental mission of every good shepherd is to give his life for his sheep. This is particularly true for Peter's successor, pastor of the universal Church. Because the higher and more universal is the pastoral office, so much greater must be the charity of the pastor," he declares. Some interpreted these words as a veiled criticism of Joseph Ratzinger, who had unsettled the world with his unexpected resignation. The dean of the College of Cardinals, who presided over the preconclave meetings, also stresses that mercy must be an essential part of the next pope's agenda. He does not realize that he is being prophetic.

"The mission of mercy binds every priest and bishop, but it binds even more the Bishop of Rome, pastor of the universal Church," he goes on. "The greatest task of charity is actually evangelization. . . . We implore the Lord that through the pastoral concern of the cardinals he may soon grant his holy Church another good shepherd." And he concluded: "We pray that the Lord grant us a pope who shall carry out this noble mission with a generous heart."

The setting is impressive, as is the organ music and the choir of the Sistine Chapel. The Argentine Cardinal seems absorbed. Once more, he prays to St. Joseph and St. Teresita, and he still believes it impossible that it might be his turn to become the new head of the Catholic Church.

However, the thunder echoing loudly within St. Peter's immense basilica like a divine warning seems to foretell that fate might have a surprise in store for him. As has happened before in other circumstances, perhaps now God also wants him to be the one to take the helm of St. Peter's boat in the middle of the storm.

He has already been a leader in times of crisis twice before. The first was when he was appointed Provincial Superior of Argentina's Jesuits in 1973, at only thirty-six years of age (the youngest of all Provincial Superiors) on the eve of the dictatorship and in the turbulent period after the Second Vatican Council. The second was when he became Archbishop of Buenos Aires in 1998 upon the death of Antonio Quarracino, the Cardinal who had called Bergoglio back from his "exile" in Córdoba. At that time the financial scandal of the Banco de Crédito Provincial's bankruptcy, involving the Archdiocese and an alleged gap of ten million dollars, exploded in Bergoglio's hands. In addition, he was attacked by former enemies who came out with old, unfounded accusations of complicity with the dictatorship.

As a deeply religious man who prays and listens to what God wishes to tell him and who, in his prayers, refers to everything that happens to him, Bergoglio overcame these two trials. With regard to these crucial challenges, the Cardinal Primate, who knows very clearly who he is and what he wants, proved himself to be a man with strong nerves who knows how to govern. A man of power who has suffered rejection and won support; a man who has sometimes made mistakes, as happens to all of us; a man with many friends but also some enemies; a man who has faced hostility and emerged from those battles initiated by his adversaries with his head held high—he is a man of great interior strength who is not easily demoralized.

Outside the storm still rages; there is even hail. Is it the wrath of God? And yet the organ music in the basilica attempts to cover the sound of nature turned unexpectedly furious. The Mass is broadcast live to the whole world; viewers see Bergoglio advancing in procession with the other cardinals—whose average age is roughly seventy-one years and ten months—toward St. Peter's high altar to bow before it and kiss it. His face is marked by concern, as are the faces of the other 114 cardinals of the

Church, framed from a distance, one by one, by the television cameras of the Vatican Television Center.

When the Mass is over, Bergoglio, who looks calm, is approached by a European Cardinal who is considered a kingmaker, so to speak, because his opinion will guide many others; this Cardinal campaigned openly for the Archbishop of Buenos Aires in 2005 and also backs him now. He has the feeling that the Argentine Cardinal has accepted, in the depths of his heart, the possibility of becoming pope. The Cardinal feels that this time the Archbishop won't draw back. "Watch out, now it's your turn," he says, half seriously and half joking, as if to defuse the situation. Bergoglio responds with a look and a shy smile.

After the first group lunch at the Casa di Santa Marta, during which the Argentine Cardinal tries, diplomatically, to avoid any approach by the many lobbies, tension becomes the common denominator among the cardinal-electors. As laid down by ancient ritual, in the afternoon they move in procession from the Pauline Chapel to the Sistine Chapel. It's half past four.

With their scarlet vestments, in an atmosphere of great solemnity, the cardinals advance singing "Veni Creator Spiritus," the hymn that invokes the help of the Holy Spirit for the crucial election. They take their places behind the long tables under the awesome images of Michelangelo's *Last Judgment*. And then, one by one, reading a Latin text, their right hands resting on the Gospels placed on a lectern in the middle of the chapel, they swear to maintain absolute secrecy with respect to everything regarding the election of the pope.

According to the Italian media, Scola is the great favorite, but he cannot count on the backing of the majority of the other twenty-seven Italian cardinals; he is visibly nervous. His alleged rival, the Brazilian Odilo Scherer, of German origin and the candidate of the "Roman" party of the curia—those who do not want any change—appears deep in concentration. According to many experts, the other favorite, the Canadian Ouellet, who could become the candidate of compromise between reformists and curia supporters, looks more at ease. Ouellet works for the curia but is believed to be "clean," or outside the ferocious internal fights that were revealed last year by the Vati Leaks scandal, the unprecedented leaking of confidential documents from the office of the pope himself.

Not much notice is being taken of the Cardinal Archbishop of Buenos Aires, Jorge Mario Bergoglio, and the serenity on his face is striking.

It is thirty-four minutes past five. The master of pontifical liturgical ceremonies, Monsignor Guido Marini, announces in an almost shy voice the *extra omnes*—"everyone out"—which decrees the departure from the Sistine Chapel of everybody who is not taking part in this most secret election. The Maltese Cardinal Prospero Grech, who is older than eighty, offers a last meditation to illuminate the electors. At its close, he and Marini leave the Sistine Chapel. Under the frescoes and in a filmlike atmosphere—perhaps Nanni Moretti's *We Have a Pope*?—the silence is interrupted by the sound of the pens now touching the elegant sheet of paper that every cardinal has in front of him. For the first time, the 115 cardinals write on their sheets of paper the name of the person they believe to be the right one to succeed Benedict XVI. They write on the line beneath the words: *Eligo in Summum Pontificem* ("I elect as Supreme Pontiff").

As the Cardinal scrutineer reads out, one by one, the written names, expectation in the Sistine Chapel is overwhelming. The acoustics are not good, but as he hears his first and last name over and over again, Jorge Mario Bergoglio—serious, his eyes attentive—begins to realize that the intuition he has never taken seriously is being fulfilled. It is true; he is in danger.

# 2

# Black Smoke

"After having repeatedly examined my conscience before God, I have come to the certainty that my strengths, due to an advanced age, are no longer suited to an adequate exercise of the Petrine ministry," says Benedict XVI on February 11, 2013, announcing his abdication during a consistory for the canonization of several persons who already were beatified.

"I am well aware that this ministry, due to its essential spiritual nature, must be carried out not only with words and deeds, but no less with prayer and suffering," he declared. "However, in today's world, subject to so many rapid changes and shaken by questions of deep relevance for the life of faith, in order to govern the barque of St. Peter and proclaim the gospel, both strength of mind and body are necessary, strength which in the last few months has deteriorated in me to the extent that I have had to recognize my incapacity to adequately fulfill the ministry entrusted to me." The whole world is touched by the timid German pope. He announces that his resignation shall become effective as of February 28, at eight o'clock in the evening. That moment will mark the start of the "vacant See" (*sede vacante*), during which the conclave to elect the new pope must be convoked.

It's past six o'clock in the afternoon. At the 2005 conclave, the first smoke signal, obviously black, appeared at 8:04 p.m., as Father Federico

Lombardi, Vatican spokesman, recalled in one of the lengthy press conferences preceding the conclave.

I take a taxi to St. Peter's Square. I can't miss the first smoke signal of this 2013 conclave, the first one convened while a former pope is still living. It's an accurate reflection of this fascinating event ("the papal transition," or "the papal event," as the main American television networks call it), which is keeping the whole world waiting with bated breath. Next to the taxi driver's steering wheel, a small television screen is transmitting, minute by minute, pictures of the Sistine Chapel's chimney, right now the most watched spot in the world.

It's already dark, and it's cold in St. Peter's Square. The temperature has dropped sharply since the morning's torrential rain. It's drizzling, but there are thousands of people waiting for the first smoke signal. A colorful carpet of umbrellas covers the square, framed by Bernini's majestic colonnade, witness once more to a unique event. Although everybody knows that the first smoke signal is certain to be black, expectation is great and the atmosphere has a mystical feel. Groups of faithful recite the rosary with lit candles, among them many priests, monks, and nuns. "We are accompanying the cardinals with our prayers, because we are a great family," says Sister Maria Aylesford, age twenty-five, from Mendoza, Argentina, who belongs to Servants of the Lord and the Virgin of Matará, the female branch of the Religious Family of the Incarnate Word. "We are keeping vigil," adds another sister, Maria della Pietà, twenty-three. She assures me that the nationality of the future pope is not important. "It doesn't matter if he's a Latin American or an African. The important thing is that he should love the Church and guide it like a real father," she says with conviction.

Those words remind me of the man who passed the whole of yesterday morning standing opposite St. Peter's Square with a prophetic placard: "Francis I—Pope." I took a picture of him—later a huge success on Twitter—and asked him if he wanted the next pope to be an Italian again. "I don't care about his nationality. The important thing is that he should be inspired by a figure like St. Francis," the man replied. His name was Saverio, and he came from Urbino.

Now it is 7:41 in the evening. From the intensely watched chimney of the Sistine Chapel—also visible on the many huge screens in St. Peter's Square—fitful spurts of black smoke finally emerge. There are exclamations of disappointment and even one or two whistles of disapproval.

Exactly as expected, none of the 115 cardinal-electors has obtained the seventy-seven required votes, equal to a two-thirds majority, to be elected successor to Benedict XVI and the 266th head of the Catholic Church.

I go home. I start writing my story for the next day, convinced that there will have been a white smoke signal by then. In 2005 it came on the second day, after the fourth count. Of course there is more indecision this time; no single candidate looks as strong as Joseph Ratzinger did then, but my intuition tells me that's how it will go.

My husband, Gerry, comes in: he's an Irish Vatican correspondent, hired by a Canadian television broadcaster to cover the conclave. He's freezing after working to transmit the smoke signal live from a terrace overlooking St. Peter's Square. The Canadians are excited, on edge at the idea of a compatriot of theirs, Cardinal Ouellet, becoming pope.

"Tomorrow Bergoglio could be pope," declares Gerry, coming into the study. I sit frozen in front of my computer. Since before the 2005 conclave, Gerry has been convinced that Bergoglio could become pope. "But he's seventy-six, he had his chance in 2005, he didn't take advantage of it, and now it's no longer his moment," I reply, repeating the usual arguments of the Vatican correspondents who didn't include him in their lists of *papabili*. I start getting nervous, or rather, hysterical. If Bergoglio becomes pope—I've known him since he was created Cardinal, in February 2001—my life, as a journalist and otherwise, will change radically.

Gerry's opinion doesn't express a wish or an intuition. It's the result of concrete information, of verified facts. He is the only Vatican correspondent who, on the eve of the conclave, was able to talk face-to-face with a number of cardinals from all the continents. He held several interviews, which were published in the "Vatican Insider" section of *La Stampa*'s website and in other media, but he also had many conversations off the record.

He worked out the numbers, time and time again, and he is sure that Padre Jorge—as we call the man who always brings *alfajores* (Argentine cookies) as a present for our children—entered the conclave with a good number of votes. "There are twenty-five or thirty cardinals who will definitely vote for him," Gerry assures me, more seriously than ever.

I immediately get in touch with my daily paper, *La Nación*, of Buenos Aires, for which I am working as a correspondent in Italy and the Vatican. "Watch out. Tomorrow Bergoglio could be the new pope." "What? Are you sure, Betta?" and "Isn't it just wishful thinking?" ask Inés Capdevila and Gail Scriven, my bosses and friends.

No, it's not just wishful thinking. These are mathematical calculations with additions and subtractions made personally by Gerry, concrete facts, firsthand information. During the past few weeks, both of us have talked off the record with cardinals from different continents taking part in the general congregations, the preconclave meetings. And according to Gerry's last-minute checks, with updated calculations, Bergoglio is a very strong candidate, stronger than people realize.

I manage to convince my bosses that we must do something. They ask me to write a piece, unfortunately just a paragraph, which turns out to be prophetic. I've entitled it "Bergoglio Could Be the Surprise of the Conclave."

Why? Forty-eight of the other 114 electors already know him from the preceding conclave. As for the other cardinals, Bergoglio startled them with his three-and-a-half minute contribution at the general congregation of Thursday, March 7. Several cardinals, including the *papabile* Scola, approached him to compliment him on his speech, short but intense and crystal clear. The Archbishop of Buenos Aires spoke about evangelization, the raison d'être of the Church, which must come out of itself and go toward the peripheries. Not just geographical but existential peripheries: the ones that stand for the mystery of sin, pain, injustice, ignorance, lack of faith, and every form of poverty. He criticized "a 'self-referential' Church, sick with narcissism, which breeds the evil of spiritual worldliness [according to the Jesuit theologian Henri de Lubac, this is the worst evil that can befall the Church] and of living for mutual glorification." "There are two images of the Church: the evangelizing Church, which comes out of itself, the Church of God's word, which listens to it and proclaims it faithfully; and the worldly Church, which lives in itself, by itself, for itself. These considerations should illuminate the changes and reforms to be achieved for the salvation of souls," he declared, according to what Cuban Cardinal Jaime Lucas Ortega y Alamino, Archbishop of Havana, revealed later—but by then he had papal authorization.

But that's not all. In contrast to other *papabili* regarded as favorites, the Argentine Cardinal—known for his low profile, his trips by subway or bus in his beloved Buenos Aires, his austere lifestyle, and his commitment to the poor—has no organized group or faction lobbying for him; in other words, he has no propaganda campaign.

There was, however (and this did not please many cardinals from the Third World, who are often ignored when they arrive in a Eurocentric Vatican), a bloc supporting the candidature of another Latin American, the Brazilian Scherer. A group of curia cardinals from the diplomatic old guard, including the Italians Giovanni Battista Re and Angelo Sodano, thought to propose Scherer. This would be in appearance, though not in reality, a radical change: the first Latin American pope, native of the country with the greatest number of Catholics in the world, but who would likely change nothing in the highly criticized Roman Curia. There is another aspect to the scheming of those wanting Scherer to be pope, those who feared being swept away by the cleanups that might well be undertaken by Benedict XVI's successor: an Italian and conservative Secretary of State would be imposed to accompany Scherer's candidacy. Those mentioned for this post are Cardinal Mauro Piacenza, Prefect of the Congregation of the Clergy, and the Italo-Argentine Leonardo Sandri, Prefect of the Congregation for the Oriental Churches and substitute of the Secretary of State (that is, the right-hand man of the influential Sodano) between the end of John Paul II's pontificate and the beginning of Benedict XVI's.

But on March 2 the "Scherer operation" begins to founder. That day, my husband, Gerry, and Andrea Tornielli, Vatican correspondent of the daily *La Stampa* and a friend of ours, reveal the scheme in an article published in "Vatican Insider." Despite this and according to the press, Scherer is still one of the favorites on the eve of the conclave. In actual fact, in Brazil everyone has gone crazy at the idea of a Brazilian pope, as I'm told by the correspondent of *La Nación* in Rio de Janeiro, my friend Alberto Armendáriz, who is already anxious at the possibility. But every time we talk about it I tell him to keep calm. I'm convinced that Scherer won't be elected, not so much on his own account but because the plot behind his candidacy has been revealed.

There are more journalists than faithful at the Mass celebrated by Cardinal Scherer, Archbishop of São Paulo, on the eve of the conclave on Sunday, March 10, at the Church of St. Andrew's at the Quirinal, designed in 1658 by Gian Lorenzo Bernini and a masterpiece of baroque architecture. At half past ten in the morning, the church (which is just opposite the Quirinal Palace, former summer residence of the popes and now home to Italy's president) is besieged by legions of reporters from all over the world, armed with stools, television cameras, and very long telephoto lenses.

German in origin, Scherer, who worked in the Congregation for Bishops of the Roman Curia from 1994 to 2001, speaks perfect Italian. The Cardinal seems hardly bothered by the noisy media: "I salute you journalists as well. Today all the churches of Rome are resonating with the presence of their titular cardinals, who invite you to pray for the conclave." And he adds, "As Benedict XVI said, the Church is in the hands of the Lord, and we invite you to pray for the Church to perform its role well at this difficult but joyous time."

I attend Scherer's Mass as part of my work. But it is Sunday, and I take communion from the hands of Scherer himself, so I see him up close. Something inside me tells me that he will not be the next pope.

Back at home, I call Padre Jorge in his room at the Casa Internazionale to find out how he is. I ask him if, like the other cardinals, he celebrated Mass at the Church in Rome of which he is titular since he was ordained Cardinal, dedicated to St. Robert Bellarmine, a Jesuit like himself. No, he didn't go. Faithful to his low profile, he preferred to avoid the assault of the media, though there would probably have been fewer journalists at his Eucharistic celebration than there were at Scherer's Mass.

Showing how important friendship is to him, Bergoglio went to lunch with an old friend, as he does every time he comes to Rome. She's the ninety-two-year-old sister of Monsignor Ubaldo Calabresi, who had been papal nuncio in Argentina for nineteen years. During that time Calabresi had lived through a crucial period for the country, marked by the conflict with Chile over the Beagle Channel, the Malvinas-Falklands War, the two visits of John Paul II, and the restoration of democracy. On June 27, 1992, Bergoglio was ordained Bishop in the cathedral of Buenos Aires by Calabresi, Cardinal Antonio Quarracino—his predecessor in the Archdiocese—and the Bishop of Mercedes-Luján, Emilio Ogñénovich.

Judging from his voice, Padre Jorge is calm. I tell him that the Italian papers are still talking about Scola and Scherer as the great favorites, even if my intuition tells me that neither of them will be elected. I also tell him that I was at Scherer's media-saturated Mass, and that in my opinion, his style seems more Germanic than Brazilian.

Padre Jorge is aware that the situation is difficult, unclear. As always, he asks me to pray for him. We agree to talk again, before he is locked up *cum clave*. But in any case we'll meet on my birthday, March 15.

Neither he nor I imagine that God has other plans.

# 3

# *Habemus papam*

Cardinal Bergoglio gazes to his left at Michelangelo's *Last Judgment*. He is focused and prays in silence. The first ballot, the one that resulted in black smoke, has just finished. Despite all the predictions, more than ten names came up in this scattered first round of voting. Bergoglio is one of those who have garnered the most votes, second only to the Italian Cardinal Angelo Scola. Bergoglio has twenty-five votes. Scola, however, has reached nearly thirty. But Scola, who is visibly on edge, is not the most convincing of candidates.

"He needs a translator when he speaks," murmur some cardinals critically. Perceived as one of the great intellectuals of the Catholic Church, Scola is the son of a socialist truck driver, a member of the Communion and Liberation movement (a lay Catholic movement founded by an Italian priest, don Luigi Giussani after the Second Vatican Council), and has been friends with Joseph Ratzinger since 1971, when they founded the high-profile theological journal *Communio*, together with Henri de Lubac and Hans Urs von Balthasar. He has written many books and articles that are profound and erudite but not particularly accessible. He was formerly the Rector of the Pontifical Lateran University and in 2004 started the Oasis International Foundation, which seeks to foster understanding between Christians and Muslims. He was the patriarch of Venice for several years before Benedict XVI designated him Archbishop of Milan, the largest diocese in Europe. This was a signal, experts said, that Scola was Benedict's chosen successor.

When I interviewed Scola in February 2011 at the spectacular Patriarchal Palace in Venice, next to St. Mark's Basilica, I liked him because he seemed human. He became very angry when I asked about the "double moral standards" of the Catholic Church toward Silvio Berlusconi, whose government had always passed laws that favor the Church in return for its support. "That's not true! It's just not true!" he exclaimed, expounding on the issue for a good ten minutes. When I said, "I'm sorry, I didn't mean to make you angry," Scola replied, "Not to worry. I get all worked up about things like this. It's just the way I am."

In answer to my question about him being *papabile*, when I reminded him of the other patriarchs of Venice who rose to become pontiffs—in the twentieth century, Pius X, John XXIII, and John Paul I—Scola said, laughing, "That's all nonsense. It's just the papers. It's got nothing to do with the real world. Anyone who has inside experience of a conclave, which is secret, will realize that all these predictions melt into thin air when you're actually in the room. It's true that the pope is chosen by the Holy Spirit. I really think that the Holy Spirit guides the Church and puts human pettiness—I mean the *cordate* and *controcordate* [factions and counterfactions]—to good use. At the end of the day, the Church's wisdom stretches back two thousand years. So many factors have to come together for a pope to be elected that no one can appreciate them all in advance. That's where the Holy Spirit steps in and makes his choice." Prophetic words. Two years later, during the 2013 papal conclave, Scola was supported by several Italian newspapers that were clearly campaigning on his behalf. But he was not backed by the other Italian cardinals—numbering twenty-eight, they were the largest group from a single country. Several among them detest Scola, although he is appreciated by other cardinals from Europe (including Spain, Germany, and Poland), the Middle East, and the United States.

Staunchly pro-Ratzinger, Scola has difficulty communicating in simple terms, his Achilles' heel. Moreover, quite a few cardinals are unenthusiastic about the idea of another pope who is a theologian, like Benedict XVI.

Scola's relationship with the Communion and Liberation movement does not go down well either, with cardinals or the general public; the

Catholic movement is very influential in Italian politics, and its name has been stained by corruption scandals involving some of its leaders, such as the former governor of Lombardy, Roberto Formigoni.

And after the uproar caused by "Paoletto"—Paolo Gabriele, Benedict XVI's butler who leaked documents to the press—and the intrigues of Vati Leaks, feelings among the foreign cardinals were decidedly anti-Italian.

"I don't know where it comes from and I'm not part of it, but an anti-Italian sentiment arose among the cardinals, even the Italian ones themselves," admitted Peruvian Cardinal Juan Luis Cipriani Thorne, Archbishop of Lima and a member of Opus Dei, in an interview with "Vatican Insider."

During the first count of the 2013 conclave, two other firm favorites, the Brazilian Odilo Pedro Scherer and the Canadian Marc Ouellet, also reap votes, but so does the American Cardinal Seán O'Malley. Another dozen or so cardinals are mentioned in the ballots, as is normal in the first round of voting. The first count always brings up names of those who have no chance of sitting on the Throne of St. Peter, but people vote for them as a token of respect and gratitude or because they have shown courage in difficult situations.

As at the 2005 conclave, at the 2013 conclave Bergoglio sits next to the Brazilian Cardinal Cláudio Hummes, an old friend, and the Portuguese Cardinal José da Cruz Policarpo. The table, in the second row on the left-hand side, facing the main altar of the Sistine Chapel, is covered by one burgundy cloth and another beige one.

All around the room are stirring frescoes by Michelangelo, Botticelli, Perugino, and Ghirlandaio, and the atmosphere is tense. The cardinals acting as scrutineers are sitting at a table in front of the altar. After the vote, the first thing they do is shuffle the ballots. They go on to count them, to check if there are as many votes as cardinals present. Then the first scrutineer draws a ballot, unfolds it, looks at the name written on it, and passes it to the second scrutineer. That Cardinal verifies the name and passes it to the third, who reads it aloud so that the cardinal-electors can note down the results themselves.

When all the ballots have been counted, the scrutineers add up the votes for each candidate and make note of them on a separate piece of paper. As the last of the scrutineers reads each ballot, he makes a small hole in each by punching through the word *Eligo* with a needle and threads them together to keep them safe. When all the names have been read out, the two ends of the thread are tied together, and the ballots, thus joined, are placed in an empty container on one side of the table. This is followed by the third and final stage, also known as post-scrutiny, which includes recounting the votes, checking them, and burning the ballots. The scrutineers tally the votes for each candidate, and if no candidate has reached a two-thirds majority, there is no new pope. After being checked, all the ballots are burned by the scrutineers. Two furnaces are used: one for the fire and the other for the chemicals that are used to color the smoke black or white, depending on the result. Some of the smoke during the 2005 conclave was a confusing grayish color, but this time they use an electronic cartridge containing five nontoxic chemicals, harmless to both Michelangelo's frescoes and the cardinals themselves while leaving no doubt as to the outcome.

That first count is the only one held that afternoon. It serves to get things started and indicate what the next round might bring, as is set out in the *Ordo rituum Conclavis*, the book of guidelines for cardinals that explains in detail the rites for papal election. Once the first vote is over, the 115 cardinals say vespers. Bergoglio's face is serious, and he seems deep in concentration.

Outside, the drizzle falls. Several buses are ready to take the cardinals from the Apostolic Palace to the Domus Sanctae Marthae, or Casa Santa Marta, a five-minute drive away on the other side of St. Peter's Basilica. Bergoglio wants to walk, which is permitted, but the drizzle and cold prevent him from doing so. He needs a breath of fresh air, to think. He knows, he feels, somehow he senses, that this time the danger of his having to stay on in Rome is much greater than it was in 2005. But he still thinks the possibility is rather remote.

It is past eight in the evening. In the dining hall at Casa Santa Marta, the evening meal is ready, the first to be shared by the 115 cardinals who are in seclusion *cum clave*. The Archbishop of Buenos Aires eats with fellow Argentine Leonardo Sandri. They've known each other since they were young. Bergoglio was Sandri's Prefect at the seminary in Villa Devoto, Buenos Aires, before he decided to join the Jesuits. The two have had very different careers—Bergoglio's pastoral and Sandri's diplomatic, as he has spent nearly all his life in the Roman Curia—and they have had serious differences in the past. It's no secret. But they act as if nothing has happened.

"Come here, sit next to me, let's have dinner together," Bergoglio says to Sandri, according to the latter. The menu for the evening is *zuppa di verdure*. Sandri is not well. He has pharyngitis, and his eyes are watering. Bergoglio, who has a background in chemistry, looks at the antibiotic that Sandri is taking and tells him how many milligrams of some other substance he should take to get better. Also, they can't help talking about the conclave, which is the reason they are sitting together in the dining hall at the Casa Santa Marta, the mediocre cooking standards of which are cause for complaint among the *buongustai* Italian cardinals, with their discerning palates.

"Get ready, my friend," says Sandri to his compatriot, who has understood that there is a steadfast group of cardinals, including Latin Americans, Asians, Africans, and a few Italians, all ready to catapult him onto the Throne of St. Peter. The name of the Archbishop of Buenos Aires—who tendered his resignation from his position on December 17, 2012, when he turned seventy-five—is on everyone's lips.

That night, the last night, Bergoglio does not sleep much. Although there are cardinals who talk late into the night about the next day, "D-day," Bergoglio stays inside room 207 and doesn't take part in any of these gatherings. All he wants to do is pray, to commend himself to Our Lady of Luján, to St. Joseph, to St. Teresita, to God. They know what they do.

On Wednesday, March 13, breakfast at the Casa Santa Marta is between 6:30 and 7:30 a.m. The cardinals are wearing forced smiles. *Buon giorno, Eminenza*, they say to one another, strained. The corridor is filled with the smell of freshly brewed coffee and *cornetti* (croissants) that have just come out of the oven. The clinking of cups and cutlery mingles with the murmurs of the cardinals—sixty Europeans, fourteen North Americans, nineteen Latin Americans, eleven Africans, ten Asians, and one Australian—as they prepare for a memorable day. Outside, it's still raining.

At 7:45 a.m., as scheduled, the buses transfer the cardinals to the Apostolic Palace. There, they celebrate Mass in the Pauline Chapel. It is the most intimate place of worship in the Vatican. Even more than the Sistine Chapel, this chapel has been called on to portray the mission and fate of the universal Church. It is dedicated to the holy apostles St. Peter and St. Paul, patrons of the Catholic Church and the city of Rome.

Half an hour later, after another prayer, the second vote begins. The cardinals write the names of their chosen candidates on their ballots before getting up from their tables in the order assigned to them in the College of Cardinals. Catching one another's eyes, ballots in hand, they make their way toward a ballot box standing opposite the altar, beneath the *Last Judgment*. The suspense is enormous.

Father Federico Lombardi, SJ, director of the Vatican Press Office, surely worthy of overnight sainthood for the infinite patience he has shown the six thousand reporters from all around the world who ask a relentless stream of improbable questions, including whether or not there is wine at the Casa Santa Marta, explains that there will be two rounds of voting that morning, the second day of the conclave.

If the first round of voting is negative, those ballots will be burned with the ones from the second round, so there will be smoke of one color or another around midday. As on the night before, crowds begin to fill

St. Peter's Square. The devout are there to pray for the new pope; curious tourists want to be there when history is made. There are Argentines carrying their flag. Once again, the weather is bad. It's raining, but no one minds. Everyone is waiting for the wisps of smoke from the chimney. Expectations are high on Twitter, too; people are asking me at what time the smoke will be released, a question that is impossible to answer.

Within the four walls of the spectacular Sistine Chapel, the cardinals may well be feeling this mounting global pressure. This might be why the vote is speedier than at the 2005 conclave. After two counts, at 11:39 a.m., black smoke billows from the chimney for the second time. No one has reached the magic number of votes: seventy-seven.

Bergoglio, however, has taken the lead. In both the second and third ballots of voting that morning, he has received more votes than any of the other *papabili*—more than fifty in the third ballot. It's clear that Scola is no longer a likely candidate. Nor are the chances picking up for the Canadian Ouellet, the American O'Malley, or the Brazilian Scherer, whom Vatican insiders indicated was the favorite of the anti-reform block.

In the end, the match isn't Italy versus Brazil, as had been slated in the Italian press, but Italy versus Argentina.

The cardinals go back to the Casa Santa Marta for lunch. During the three-and-a-half-hour break, they realize that there is no turning back; it becomes clear that by afternoon, for the first time in the history of the Church, the papacy will cross the Atlantic. The dynamic in favor of Bergoglio is unstoppable, and the snowball effect is inevitable.

Bergoglio, who realizes that his moment has come, has lunch with Honduran Cardinal Óscar Rodríguez Madariaga and others from Europe and the United States. He doesn't eat much; his nervousness about what's to come has taken away his appetite.

During the meal, even though it's clear that the die is cast, ploys to torpedo the Argentine Cardinal are still rife: a lobby against him spreads the rumor that he has only one lung. The story is false; he is missing only the upper lobe of his right lung, which was removed in 1957 after he suffered a serious lung infection, from which he made a perfect recovery.

According to stories published by the Italian media, during lunch Scola imitated Bergoglio's supposed "retreat" during the 2005 conclave so as not to block the election of Joseph Ratzinger. Scola realizes that he is never going to scrimp together more than the forty or so votes he has managed so far. He lets the other cardinals know that he doesn't want his candidacy to cause divisions, and he invites them to work toward unity.

Argentina is four hours behind Italy: at 11:39 a.m. in Rome, it is 7:39 a.m. in Buenos Aires. But many people are up, following the conclave as though it were a World Cup soccer match. On Twitter, things are reaching a frenzy. Many people are commenting, asking questions, wanting to know what's going on. I tweet the story that I had written for the paper the day before, with the headline "Bergoglio Could Be the Surprise of the Conclave," which starts generating comments. The most extraordinary of all is from an anonymous follower, Mina, who tweets that she had fallen asleep, hadn't seen the black smoke, and had dreamed that Bergoglio had been elected pope. Caught between euphoria and hysteria, I reply, "Your dream might come true."

At a midday Vatican press conference, in which everyone's nerves are on edge, Father Lombardi insists that it is totally normal for there to have been two incidences of black smoke. It doesn't mean that the cardinals are divided, he says. To slake the thirst for information, to calm the hungry lions in the press conference, which lasts an hour and forty-five minutes, Lombardi goes into details about the size of the ballots and the chemical components used to make the different colors of smoke. He reminds the press that the chosen candidate can choose his own name, a very personal decision. He even reveals that Benedict XVI's private secretary, the handsome Archbishop Georg Gänswein, known as "the Vatican's George Clooney," has said that the Pope Emeritus has been following the conclave attentively on the television and praying from the papal summer residence at Castel Gandolfo.

It is four in the afternoon. According to the timetable, after lunch and a brief siesta the cardinals have returned from the Casa Santa Marta to the Apostolic Palace. The fourth round of voting begins at 4:50 p.m. During the 2005 conclave, the white smoke appeared after the fourth count, the first one after the lunch break. That year, the smoke floated out at 5:50 p.m. and the *Habemus papam* announcement came some forty-five minutes later.

I remember it well. I was outside in the square, six months pregnant with my first child, Juan Pablo. But there was no Twitter. This time, though, in 2013, many of my followers from Argentina are betting on the Brazilian Odilo Pedro Scherer. "I don't think it's going to be him," I reply. I can't explain in 140 characters that Scherer, the favorite of the Roman Curia, has little chance in the conclave. The cardinals who realize that he would be "a domesticated pope"—a puppet for a group of anti-reformers—are looking elsewhere.

It's still raining. People keep arriving at St. Peter's Square. I don't remember there being so many in 2005, when the conclave took place in April, when it didn't get dark so early, and when it wasn't raining. I look at my watch. The cardinals are already voting, and there's a feeling of expectation in the air.

A seagull rests on the chimney of the Sistine Chapel and is immortalized by photographers, becoming the star of the evening, the news story of the day. Some say the seagull was drawn by the warmth of the chimney. Others say it's a sign, and others that they'd like to become a gull to be able to hear what's going on at the bottom of the chimney, inside the Sistine Chapel. On Twitter, the hashtag #habemusbird begins to circulate. Within minutes, the gull has a Twitter account called @SistineSeagull and several thousand followers.

It's six in the evening, and still no sign of smoke. This conclave is now definitely longer than that of 2005, and it's clear that the cardinals are getting ready to vote a fifth time; my intuition tells me it will be the last one. In the betting pool organized in my section of the newspaper, I bet on the new pope being chosen on Wednesday, March 13.

The seagull (no one knows if it's the same one or a different one—they all look the same) perches on the chimney again. Once again, Twitter explodes. Does it mean that white smoke is imminent? Is the gull carrying a microchip to spy on things? Saying that people are getting anxious is quite an understatement.

There's plenty of suspense in the Sistine Chapel, too. During the fourth round of voting, Bergoglio, his expression serious but serene, was very close to getting the seventy-seven votes. It's crystal clear that he is well on his way to becoming the next pontiff. And now, in the fifth round, he's about to reach and surpass the magical threshold of seventy-seven votes. But something unexpected happens: after the voting but before the ballots are read, the scrutineer mixes them up inside the box but then realizes as he counts them that there is one extra, 116 instead of 115. It seems that one of the cardinals accidentally put two ballots in the box, one with his choice of pope and a blank one that got stuck to the actual ballot. These things happen.

There's nothing to be done. The round of voting is immediately annulled, the ballots will be burned later, without being counted, and a sixth round of voting will take place immediately. Tensions are sky-high by now.

Sandri, who is opposite Bergoglio, teases him each time he passes by to place his vote in the ballot box. "Your turn!" he signals. The Archbishop of Buenos Aires raises his eyebrows and shakes his head, resigned.

"He was sitting right opposite me, and I could see on his face that he was accepting the will of God and obeying the Lord's wishes. He knew, as we all did, that the Lord had chosen him, and he wasn't going to shy away from the cross he was being offered," says Cardinal Oswald Gracias, Archbishop of Bombay/Mumbai.

During the counting of the votes, which seems to go on forever, Bergoglio can't stop thinking about that last conversation he had with Father Alejandro Russo, Rector of the Metropolitan Cathedral in Buenos

Aires, on Tuesday, February 26, before leaving for the airport to travel to Rome, a journey that would turn out to be one-way. A specialist in canon law and an interdiocesan tribunal judge, the "Big Guy," as Russo's known, had come to say good-bye and sort out some last-minute matters with Bergoglio.

"I hope the conclave isn't too rushed. The Church needs to be given time to reflect after what happened with Benedict. That's why I wanted to tell you that tomorrow I'm going to send out a statement to the entire Archdiocese with forms of prayer for the period of the conclave, including a particularly important one: that they pray for the Archbishop of Buenos Aires, who has the vital duty of taking part in the conclave. I want you to know, when you're voting, that the entire Archdiocese is praying for you. You'll see, when they say, *Eminentissimo* Bergoglio, seventy-five; *Eminentissimo* Bergoglio, seventy-six; *Eminentissimo* Bergoglio, seventy-seven. And the applause breaks out!" said Russo, with his usual sense of humor.

"Can't you give that story a rest?" answered Bergoglio, getting up from his desk and going to pick up his suitcase.

"Don't forget article 86 of the Apostolic Constitution," said Father Russo, giving Bergoglio a hug. He was referring to John Paul II's *Universi Dominici Gregis*, which addresses the vacancy of the Apostolic See and the election of a new Roman pontiff and reads: "I also ask the one who is elected not to refuse, for fear of its weight, the office to which he has been called, but to submit humbly to the design of the divine will. God who imposes the burden will sustain him with his hand, so that he will be able to bear it. In conferring the heavy task upon him, God will also help him to accomplish it and, in giving him the dignity, he will grant him the strength not to be overwhelmed by the weight of his office."

"All right, Big Guy, that's enough!" said Bergoglio, looking straight at him before going down the corridor toward the elevator, laughing.

Just as "Big Guy" Russo predicted, when Bergoglio's vote count reaches seventy-seven, enthusiastic applause breaks out in the Sistine

Chapel—applause that releases tension and pent-up emotion. The first one to embrace the Cardinal from Buenos Aires who has been elected pope is his friend sitting next to him, the Brazilian Cardinal Cláudio Hummes. "Don't forget the poor," he says, a phrase that sinks into the heart and mind of the first Argentine pope, the first from Latin America, and the first who is a Jesuit.

As the applause continues and various cardinals come over to congratulate Bergoglio, the scrutineer goes on counting the ballots with the name of the Archbishop from Buenos Aires, which number far more than the established threshold. The election of the new pope, by almost ninety votes, has ended up being a landslide.

As required by ritual, Cardinal Giovanni Battista Re, another old acquaintance of the Argentine Archbishop, asks him: "Do you accept your canonical election as Supreme Pontiff?"

"I am a great sinner, but trusting in the mercy and patience of God, with suffering, I accept," he replies, certain of himself.

"What name do you take?" asks Re.

"Francis."

The acoustics in the Sistine Chapel are not very good. Some cardinals have not heard the name. "Did he say Francis?" others ask. The incredulous faces of many of the cardinals reveal more than many words would. No one had ever dared to pick a name like that, a name containing a firm, clear, and direct message, a plan of government even.

Although some prefer to think the name is a homage to Francis Xavier, a Jesuit missionary who traveled to Asia, those who really know Bergoglio—the priest who always visited Argentina's slums, who has always been on the side of the poor, and who renounced all luxuries—realize that he is thinking of Francis of Assisi, known as Il Poverello, the poor friar who dared to criticize the luxuries of the Roman Church during the Middle Ages.

Accompanied by the master of ceremonies, Bergoglio shuts himself away in the "Room of Tears" (*stanza delle lacrime*), the small sacristy of the Sistine Chapel. He isn't weeping, though; he is calm, and he has accepted the cross. With help, he gets dressed. The famous papal tailor, Gammarelli, has made three full-length habits in different sizes. Bergoglio chooses the medium. When he emerges dressed as pope, all in white, the cardinals are once again astonished because he's wearing his usual cross and silver ring and has turned down the gold papal pectoral cross. Nor does he put on the red *mozzetta* that his predecessors have used to greet the world for the first time. "No, thank you," Bergoglio says to the assistant who is helping him dress. "It's not carnival time," he adds jokingly, according to unlikely stories circulated by the Italian press. Nor does he let them take off his black orthopedic shoes. He will never be able to wear the blood-red shoes he is offered. From the very first minute, the new Argentine pope is firm. He knows exactly what he wants and what he doesn't want.

In St. Peter's Square, the atmosphere is electric. Delighted applause and shouts resound at 7:06 p.m. when smoke begins to drift from the chimney. Night has already fallen, and the smoke at first appears black but after a second reveals itself to be white. To ensure that there is not the slightest doubt, the huge bells on St. Peter's begin to ring out, along with those of all the churches in Rome. A pope has been chosen, but who is it? During the 2005 conclave, forty-five minutes went by between the white smoke and the *habemus papam* announcement that told the world Joseph Ratzinger had been elected. The sixty-six minutes this takes during the 2013 conclave seem to go on forever.

Twitter is on fire. Someone asks me to give a name, to put it out there on the social network who I think has been chosen. So I go out on a limb: Bergoglio.

As I wait for the Cardinal Protodeacon to announce the new pope in Latin, I think that "Jorge" translates as "Georgius." But at the same time, all sorts of rumors start circulating madly. Someone says that Angelo Scola's Twitter account has been closed, a sign that he is the new pope. The fact that church bells are also ringing out all over Milan seems to confirm the news.

The *Habemus papam* announcement is taking a long time because there's still plenty of action going on in the Sistine Chapel. When Bergoglio emerges from the Room of Tears dressed in white, he catches everyone off guard. Instead of going to the altar, as the protocol demands, he heads quickly for the way out. He even trips on a step and stumbles, because the new snow-white habit is too long for him. "We didn't know what he was doing," one of the cardinals would later say.

The first thing the new pope does is go straight to talk to a Cardinal who is in very bad health, confined to a wheelchair, and who has taken part in the conclave with some difficulty. The man in question is the Indian Ivan Dias, Archbishop Emeritus of Bombay/Mumbai and former Prefect of the Congregation for the Evangelization of Peoples. The new Argentine pontiff's first gesture, humble and spontaneous, makes a great impact on the princes of the church.

The rite then indicates that after a reading from one of the Gospels and a prayer, the cardinals must file by, one by one, to show Francis their obedience.

"Don't make me cry," says a kneeling, emotional Sandri when his turn comes.

Bergoglio, who hates being treated like an emperor, continues to surprise them all. When the cardinals from Vietnam and China, seventy-nine-year-old Jean-Baptiste Pham Minh Man and seventy-two-year-old John Tong Hon, try to kiss his ring, he stops them. Instead, he, the pope, kisses their hands, an act without precedent. Tong is the only Cardinal to present him a gift: a small bronze statue of Our Lady of Sheshan, whose shrine is on the outskirts of Shanghai. The Chinese Cardinal had been carrying the statue in his pocket since the lunch break, when he realized that the final act of the drama would come about that afternoon.

After the gift is given, the cardinals sing the "Te Deum," a hymn of thanks. The atmosphere is incredibly moving.

Before emerging onto the central balcony of St. Peter's Basilica, where there's already a certain amount of activity and on which all the world's television cameras are now focused, the new pope also stops to pray before the Blessed Sacrament in the Pauline Chapel. Pope Francis isn't sure if what's happening to him is a dream, a nightmare, or even real.

People continue to pour into St. Peter's Square. The rain has stopped—a sign from above? A group of Vatican musicians arrives, along with a formation of Pontifical Swiss Guards, who line up under the balcony. A *carabinieri* (police) band also arrives. They play the Italian national anthem, then that of the Vatican. The crowd is in a state of overwhelming anxiety. Shouts of "*Viva il papa!* Long live the Pope!" ring out, as if to release some of the tension. Flags from all over the world flutter in St. Peter's Square, many of them Argentine. Even the Via della Conciliazione is filling up with people.

The red velvet curtains twitch on the loggia, the central balcony of St. Peter's Basilica. It is 8:12 p.m. The Cardinal in charge of protocol, the Frenchman Jean-Louis Tauran, appears on the balcony. He reads a Latin phrase that will go down in history for the faithful the world over, and particularly for Argentines: "Annuntio vobis gaudium magnum; habemus papam: eminentissimum ac reverendissimum Dominum, Dominum Georgium Marium Sanctae Romanae Ecclesiae Cardinalem Bergoglio qui sibi nomen imposuit Franciscum."

I freeze. My fingers aren't working properly. I start tweeting in capital letters, to make my enormous excitement totally clear: "THE NEW POPE IS JORGE BERGOGLIO!" I'm so beside myself that he's the new pope that I miss his choice of name: Francis, a revolution, no less.

Ten minutes later, Padre Jorge, dressed in white, comes out onto the balcony. He doesn't seem to believe what he's seeing either; an ecstatic sea of people fills St. Peter's Square. He remains silent, astonished. He starts his papacy brilliantly, simply being himself. "Brothers and sisters, *buona sera*," he says timidly, prompting thunderous applause and immediately connecting with the people gathered below.

"You know that the duty of the conclave was to provide Rome with a Bishop. It seems my brother cardinals went to the end of the world to fetch him," he says in perfect Italian, with an Argentine accent. Once again, the crowd explodes into applause. "But here we are. I thank you for your welcome. The diocesan community of Rome now has its Bishop: thank you!" Francis continues humbly. His seventy-six years, which many experts thought an impediment, seem to have evaporated, and he suddenly seems rejuvenated.

Considerate and correct, he goes on to pay homage to his predecessor. "First of all, I would like to offer up a prayer for our Bishop Emeritus, Benedict XVI. Let us pray for him together, that the Lord may bless him and that Our Lady may protect him," he says simply. Francis does not refer to his predecessor as Pope Emeritus but as Bishop Emeritus. It is a signal of change. There is more applause, and the new pope begins the Our Father, then the Hail Mary, and then the Glory Be, accompanied by a chorus of the faithful, amazed by how different this new pope is—so human, so simple.

"And now, we set off on this journey together: Bishop and people. This journey of the Church of Rome, which leads all the churches in its charity. A journey of brotherhood, love, and trust among us. Let us always pray for one another," he continues, surely giving everyone present goose bumps. "Let us pray for the whole world, so that there may be a great spirit of brotherhood. I hope that this journey of the Church that we set out on today, and in which my Cardinal Vicar, here beside me, will assist me, will be fruitful for the evangelization of this beautiful city."

When the time comes for the "Urbi et Orbi," addressed to the city and the world, after putting on his stole, the new pope continues to astonish those gathered. "And now I would like to give you a blessing, but first I want to ask you for a favor: before the Bishop blesses the people, I ask you to pray to the Lord to bless me—a prayer by the people, asking for a blessing for their Bishop. Let us say this prayer in silence, your prayer for me."

In a gesture that once again leaves viewers the world over speechless as they watch, live, a sight they've never before seen, Bergoglio leans forward and bows his head before the thousands of people in the square below. This is another unprecedented gesture, loaded with symbolism. The silence that follows is absolute. The new pope, who refers to himself as a

"Bishop," then blesses all those present and "the whole world, all men and women of goodwill," raising his right arm and setting off yet more cheering below.

"Brothers and sisters, I take my leave. Thank you so much for your welcome. Pray for me, until we meet again. We'll see one another again soon. Tomorrow I wish to pray to Our Lady, for her to watch over all of Rome. Good night and sleep well," he finishes. In St. Peter's Square, but also all over the world, wherever people are watching television, astonished by what is taking place live in Rome, the sensation is that Francis, with his new, down-to-earth style, has opened up a new phase, one of reform and hope for the Catholic Church.

I don't sleep that night. In fact, it's the longest night of my life. My phones don't stop ringing. I get calls from radios, press agencies, and TV channels. Suddenly everyone wants to know who Bergoglio is. But I need to focus on the paper I work for, *La Nación.* I have to get to work, but I'm too stunned. Inés Capdevila, my boss, calms me down.

"Take it easy. We're going to close late today, so calm down." As well as my report, I need to write an eight-thousand-word profile on Padre Jorge. Me? "Yes, you. You're the best person for the task," says Inés, very sure of herself. I have no idea where to begin. I'm too overwhelmed. I decide to put my phone on silent because it doesn't stop ringing. I pick up only if I see that it's a call from the paper. Gerry gets home after midnight, but I don't have time—or the words—to talk with him about what has happened. He makes me a sandwich that I bolt down as I type, breathless. Somehow I manage to concentrate and finish the articles on time.

I go to bed at four in the morning, but I find it hard to sleep with my mind so busy thinking about Padre Jorge becoming pope. Finally, I sleep for three hours. I take my daughter, Caroline, to kindergarten in the morning. On my way home, I stop by the hotel where Luisa Corradini is staying. *La Nación*'s Paris correspondent, she has come as backup. Mariano de Vedia, the paper's political editor and an expert in church matters, is on his way and will get to Rome the next day to strengthen the team during this historic time for Argentina.

Luisa's hotel is near the Trevi Fountain. "She's in the dining room," they tell me at reception. When I find her, we give each other a big hug, excited and still incredulous. When she had dinner at our house a few weeks earlier, Gerry had already suggested that even though Bergoglio's name didn't come up in the media, he could still surprise us all.

I'm so on edge that I can't eat a thing. But I need a cappuccino. My cell phone keeps ringing; the calls are from Italian television producers who are desperately hunting me down. I can barely cope with them all. But I feel I have to go and tell them what I know about Padre Jorge. I'm also aware that I have to go out and defend him from the accusations that have already started to circulate, just as in 2005, about his supposed involvement in Argentina's most recent military dictatorship. I know perfectly well that they're false accusations, based on nothing, as I state categorically the next day on the RAI's famous *Porta a Porta* program, presented by Bruno Vespa.

At 9:55 a.m. I get the umpteenth call to my cell phone. The number doesn't show; it's private, like lots of production companies. I almost don't pick up, fed up with the sudden media bombardment. But I do answer.

"Hello, Elisabetta?" The voice is unmistakable. I can't believe it, but it's him, Padre Jorge, the pope. I knew that he would call sooner or later; in fact, I'd already been wondering how I was going to address him now because I didn't think "Holy Father" would come naturally.

I never imagined he'd call so quickly. Padre Jorge, Francis, hasn't changed a bit. I'm delighted.

# 4

# The First Steps

Sunday, May 26, 2013. In Buenos Aires, autumn is dressed in sunshine. My niece Paola, my brother Enrico's daughter, has asked me to be godmother at her confirmation. I've been crazy enough to grant her wish and have made the long journey from Rome to Buenos Aires for a few days.

The last time I went to Argentina was in December 2012, for Christmas. With Gerry, my husband, I had lunched with Padre Jorge in the curia. Delicious Patagonian lamb, with baked potatoes and salad, washed down with a fine red wine—a classic menu of our meetings. The meal had been cooked by the nuns whom we greeted and thanked together with the Cardinal when we would go to the kitchen after clearing the table, as we did every time. When we were leaving, Padre Jorge had escorted us to the main door: "That's how I'm sure you'll leave," he had joked, as always. And he had said good-bye with the traditional "Pray for me."

Everything has changed since that quiet lunch. Now Padre Jorge is Francis and lives in Rome, where he has set in motion a revolution that no one could have imagined only a few months ago. And I'm writing—I still can't believe it—a book about him, about the pope.

Buenos Aires, too, has changed: the city has been invaded by his pictures. Not only in the churches, which are overflowing again with the faithful, proud to be the pope's compatriots, but also in the streets of the city he loved to walk, without attracting attention, when he was still a Cardinal. The giant poster on the Banco Ciudad building, a few meters from the Obelisco, symbol of Argentina's capital, is the most impressive. With a white and blue banner as background, this is an enormous photo of Francis, dressed in white and with his familiar silver cross. Under the portrait are the words: "The city celebrates Pope Francis with pride and happiness."

I decide to join the recently started Pope Tour, a free service offered by the municipality of Buenos Aires to inform people about the places where the Argentine pope was born, took his first steps, and grew up.

Zoraya Chaina, a guide for more than twenty years but still as enthusiastic as when she started, asks many questions of the passengers in the coach painted in the Vatican colors, to find out how much we know. There are many people from Flores and other parts of the city, several Colombians, and a couple of foreign journalists. I'm there as an ordinary tourist with Paola and Isabella, my twin nieces.

If Jorge Bergoglio was a little-known figure before March 13, now every Argentine has a story to tell. "The lady from Paraguay who works in my home has some photos with him; he married her and christened her children"; "He found work for the son of a friend of mine's brother-in-law"; "My neighbor traveled with him on the underground and saw him confessing a woman." These are the tales of the passengers on the coach, where there is no one who doesn't know the main events of the pope's life.

The son of Piedmontese immigrants—Mario Bergoglio, first a railway worker and then the proprietor of a stocking factory, and Regina Sivori, a homemaker—and the first of five children, Jorge Bergoglio was born in the Flores district, in the heart of Buenos Aires, on December 17, 1936.

Zoraya points out the house at 531 Membrillar where Pope Francis spent his childhood. It's a quiet, tree-lined area, with low houses, now famous throughout the world. The Pope Tour goes on for a couple of blocks till it reaches the Basilica of San José de Flores, on Avenida Rivadavia, number 6950. Built in romantic style, inaugurated on February 18, 1833, this church is not only the church of Jorge Bergoglio's childhood and adolescence. It is much more. As the pope himself recounted on the eve of Pentecost, May 18, 2013, it was there that he heard God's call, on September 21, 1953. "I was nearly seventeen. It was Students' Day, which for us is the first day of spring. Before going to the party, I went to my parish church, found a priest I didn't know, and felt the need to confess. For me, this was the experience of a meeting. I found someone who had been waiting for me for a long time. After confession I felt that something had changed. I was no longer the same person. I had really heard a voice, a call: I felt that I had to become a priest. We say that we must look for God, go to Him and beg His forgiveness, but when we go, He is waiting for us—He's there first! In Spanish, we have a word that explains it well: 'The Lord always *primerea* us'; He arrives first, He's waiting for us."

On that day in the spring of 1953, Bergoglio "el Flaco" (the thin one) as his friends call him, doesn't reach Flores Station to go and celebrate the holiday. He goes home to reflect. Several years go by, but another journey has already started.

Before being *primereado* by God, Jorge Bergoglio is a boy like so many in the district: courteous, intelligent, with a great sense of humor, who likes playing football with his friends. Like a good eldest son he's very responsible and studious, besides being a great reader. His family is not a poor one. But because there are so many of them at home—he has four younger siblings, Óscar Adrián, Marta Regina, Alberto Horacio, and María Elena (the only one still living in 2014)—resources are not unlimited and must be managed with thrift.

Born in a typical Italian immigrant family, where the Piedmontese dialect is still spoken and where he considers it a duty to improve himself, Jorge Mario has a very special relationship with his grandmother Rosa. This is his father's mother, who lives around the corner and not only looks after him when necessary—the five children are very close in age and their mother isn't always able to look after them—but also instills in him a profound religious faith. The faith, says the pope, that only women—mothers and grandmothers—pass on. A faith that shows the way.

"I always remember that on Good Friday evenings she would take us children to the candle procession, and when the 'dead Christ' arrived at the end, grandmother would make us kneel and told us: 'Look: he's dead, but tomorrow he will rise again.'" "That's how faith came in," Francis tells us on the eve of Pentecost, May 18, 2013.

His detachment from material things is due in great part to what he learned from his grandmother, the pope admits during his first Palm Sunday Mass, when he condemns the greed for money. "My grandmother used to tell us children, 'A shroud doesn't have pockets!'" he recalls.

Originally from Piana Crixia, a country village in the province of Savona, Rosa Margherita Vassallo is a brave woman. In search of new horizons, Rosa had decided to move to Turin, the big industrial city of northern Italy. The same step is taken by Giovanni Bergoglio, her future husband and the grandfather of the pope, born in Valle Versa in the province of Asti.

In 1908, after getting married, Rosa gives birth to Mario José Francisco Bergoglio, father of the present pope, at Portacomaro Stazione on the hills near Asti. The pope's grandfather owns a grocery store and also works as a barman and a porter at a nursing home.

Rosa and Giovanni climb the social ladder, join the middle class, and decide that their son Mario should go on studying, a rare thing at the time for the son of peasants. Mario graduates as an accountant in 1926. Three years later the Bergoglio family, wishing to further improve their condition, decide to emigrate to Argentina. It is February 1, 1929.

Mario chooses Argentina not only to "discover America"—in contrast to the majority of migrants, they are not badly off—but also because in 1922 three brothers of his emigrated to Argentina, where they set up a big flooring enterprise at Paraná, in the province of Entre Ríos. They even built a four-story building in that city, as the Cardinal himself recounts in the book *The Jesuit*, a series of conversations between the future pope and the journalists Sergio Rubin and Francesca Ambrogetti, published in 2010. (This book has been retitled *Pope Francis: Conversations with Jorge Bergoglio: His Life in His Own Words* [Penguin, 2013]). He also recalls in that book that after the 1932 crisis, the family lost everything.

Today, on the tour coach, Zoraya tells us the well-known story of Grandmother Rosa. By a quirk of destiny, the grandmother of the first Latin American pope decides not to board the ship *SS Principessa Mafalda*, which sinks north of Brazil, but a few months later boards the *Giulio Cesare* in the port of Genoa. Rosa disembarks in a torrid Buenos Aires at the height of austral summer in her coat with its fox-fur collar; she keeps the family savings hidden in the lining!

The Pope Tour now crosses the Almagro neighborhood, because Pope Francis is a fan of the Club Atlético San Lorenzo, a football team founded in 1907 by the Salesian father Lorenzo Massa in honor of St. Lawrence Martyr. But that isn't the only reason. It is in this neighborhood that the pope's parents, Mario José Francisco Bergoglio and Regina María Sivori, met in the Salesian Oratory of St. Antony in 1934 and later married in the Basilica of María Auxiliadora and San Carlos, on Calle Bocayuva No. 1444. Here, too, the infant Jorge Mario Bergoglio was baptized on Christmas Day, 1936.

Another Italian immigrant who arrived in Argentina in 1906, Don Enrico Pozzoli, a Salesian missionary from Senna in Lombardy, christens Mario's and Regina's firstborn. Don Enrico will become an important figure for Jorge and a model of priestly life. In 1982, in his prologue to his *Meditaciones para religiosos* ("Meditations for Religious"), the future pope remembers Don Enrico as "an example of ecclesiastic service and religious consecration" and for having had "a strong influence" on his life.

The Pope Tour also stops opposite the Institute of Our Lady of Mercy on Avenida Directorio, where in 1940 Bergoglio started kindergarten and then took his first communion. At the institute, directed by the Daughters of Our Lady of Mercy, they still remember little Jorge. "He learned to do multiplications by going up and down the stairs. That was his method; the other children learned from a sheet of paper or by counting on their fingers, but he created his very own method," Sister Maria Ilda told *L'Osservatore Romano*. "Even when he was little he didn't like being shut up in a classroom; he preferred the open air as he often says in his homilies," she adds.

Because the institute doesn't have a primary school for boys, Bergoglio attended School No. 8, Coronel Ingeniero Pedro Cerviño, at Calle Varela No. 358. At the age of thirteen he joined the Salesian college Wilfrid Barón de los Santos Ángeles in Ramos Mejía as a boarder for a year, together with his brother Óscar.

Faith was strongly present in the family. "We were taught to love God since we were small. We went to Mass together, and when he came home Dad used to recite the rosary. Dad and Mom brought us up in the faith since the day we were born and taught us by their example," says María Elena Bergoglio, Pope Francis's younger sister. "The day we liked best was Sunday, when we all went together to the parish church for Mass and then home for lunch. . . . Jorge liked pasta and a good meat stew. As in every Italian family, on Sunday there had to be pasta," she adds. And then she confesses, laughing, that because there were twelve years between her elder brother and her, she was the "little doll of the house" while he was "the big one."

"As a child I didn't live long with Jorge. When I reached the age of reason he had already joined the seminary . . . But during the time we spent together he was very protective because our father had died young, at fifty-one, on account of a heart problem that probably could have been solved today . . . He was a good companion, warm, cheerful, a normal boy," María Elena remembers.

The pope himself recalls the religious faith of his family during a Mass in the chapel of Santa Marta, on May 8, 2013, stressing the changes in the lifestyle of the Church. "I remember that when I was a child, in Catholic families like mine you could hear them say: 'No, we can't go to visit them because they weren't married in church.' They were excluded. We really couldn't go! It was the same thing if they were socialists or atheists. Now, thank God, we don't say that anymore. It was a kind of defense of the faith, but with walls; now, however, the Lord has built bridges."

When María Elena was born, mother Regina was paralyzed for a year. The family wasn't helpless; they set to work and collaborated. Upon returning from school, Jorge and his brothers started cooking supper, as if it were a game, following the instructions of their mother, who had already peeled the potatoes and prepared the food for the meal. That was how the future pope learned to cook.

During the 1940s Flores was a popular neighborhood, with big houses usually inhabited by more than one family and where everyone knew and greeted everyone else. The bell of Cerviño School rang at eight o'clock in the morning. To get there, Bergoglio, accompanied by his mother or grandmother, walked five blocks. From his house in Calle Membrillar—an ordinary two-story house with the living room and kitchen on the ground floor and the bedrooms upstairs—he walked toward the Avenida Directorio. There he turned left and continued for three blocks to Varela. Half a block from there was his school, where he was a good student.

"Jorge was always very tidy and came to school well dressed, but when it was time to play soccer in the little Herminia Brumana Square, he would take off his overalls and start playing," says Ernesto Mario Lach, a school friend of his.

"His father used to take him to the stadium and that's how he became a San Lorenzo fan. But Jorge wasn't good at soccer, he was a dead loss!" confesses another friend of Jorge Bergoglio's childhood and adolescence, Hugo Morelli. "We also played basketball. We weren't very good at that either, but we still enjoyed ourselves."

"He was good, polite, kind. He came to play in the square like everybody else in the neighborhood. But later, as he grew up, we noticed that he was different from the others. He studied more and always had a book in his hands," says Rafael Musolino, Jorge's neighbor for many years.

Jorge was ten years old when General Juan Domingo Perón—founder and leader of Justicialism, which still is the main political force in Argentina—was elected president for the first time, in 1946. Even though legend has it that the pope is a Peronist (after the pope's election, Buenos Aires awakened covered with posters with Pope Francis's picture and the words "Francis I, Argentine and Peronist"), Morelli categorically refutes this version. "He wasn't a Peronist at all. If anything, I was the Peronist, and we were always quarrelling about it. He tended to be anti-Peronist, a conservative. And that story about him coming to school one day with a Peronist coat of arms—it's not true . . . We and the others used to say that we don't know who invented such a thing. It never happened."

Julio Bárbaro, a Peronist leader educated by the Jesuits who has met with Bergoglio all his life, is of the same opinion. "We both belong to a story that is always misinterpreted. Bergoglio was interested in ideologies in so far as a person can be who is concerned with people living in the real world; he entered the real world by sharing the thoughts of the people who surrounded him, and we were Peronists. Bergoglio was clearly a militant of religion, but never of politics."

Bergoglio himself remembers the radical tradition of his mother's family (in support of the social democrat Unión Cívica Radical, the first Argentine political party, founded in 1891). "My maternal grandfather was a carpenter, and once a week a gentleman with a beard came to sell him paints. They would stop in the courtyard, chatting for some time while my grandmother served them tea with wine. One day my grandmother asked me if I knew who Elpidio, the paint seller, was. It turned out that he was Elpidio González, who had been vice president [from 1922 to 1928]. I was struck by the image of that former vice president earning his living as a salesman. It was an image of honesty. Something has happened to our politics; we have lost ideas, proposals. Today the image counts more than what is being proposed," commented Jorge Bergoglio in *On Heaven and Earth*, a book of dialogues with his friend Rabbi Abraham Skorka.

In 1950 Jorge, age fourteen, began secondary school at Technical Industrial School No. 12 (now No. 27) at Calle Goya No. 351, in Floresta. Before he started, during the summer holidays, his father sent him out to work. "It's something I am very grateful to him for, because work has been one of the things that did me most good in life," said Bergoglio in *The Jesuit*.

Since childhood, Jorge is not accustomed to taking holidays. He started working in the stocking factory where his father dealt with accounts. For the first two years Jorge did the cleaning, and during the third he dealt with the administration.

Then he started working in a laboratory with an unusual boss, Esther Ballestrino de Careaga, from whom he learned that work must always be taken seriously. Esther was a Paraguayan and a communist sympathizer; years later, during the dictatorship, her daughter and son-in-law were kidnapped, and then she herself was abducted together with two French nuns, Alice Domon and Léonie Duquet, *desaparecidas*. Later she was murdered by the military.

Bergoglio's gifts as leader became evident early on. "He was very intelligent, but not because he was a bookworm, spending all his time studying, but because he understood everything very fast. His intelligence was clearly superior to ours. He was always a step ahead of all of us. He was a kind of leader. During the whole of his time at secondary school he was reprimanded only twice, and once it was for a collective action. There was a new teacher of Spanish who imposed herself on us very severely. We didn't like her at all, we rebelled and wrote on the blackboard that we wanted our old teacher back, and we all signed, including Bergoglio. That's how we got the collective reprimand," Hugo Morelli relates.

Technical Industrial School No. 12, which specialized in nutrition, was rather special. "In the morning we had two lessons on theory and in the afternoon plenty of practice. Sometimes we even butchered and processed the pork on site. In the end only ten of us got the diploma, and today six of us are still alive: three in Buenos Aires, two in Córdoba and one—well, one is in the Vatican," says Óscar Crespo, former schoolmate and still a friend of Bergoglio's.

"We shared everything that can be shared at that age ... We always met in a bar at the intersection of Avellaneda and Segurola, where we played billiards. On weekends we had 'assaults,' which is what we called our get-togethers, in the home of one of us, or went dancing at the club of the Chacarita neighborhood because there were many girls ... Jorge was engaged to one of them from the neighborhood," he recalls.

The story of twelve-year-old Jorge's fiancée, Amalia Damonte, is well known. She was the daughter of Bergoglio's neighbors. One day Jorge declared his love and warned her that if she didn't accept him he would dedicate his life to God. "He said to me, 'If I don't marry you, I shall become a priest.' But these were childish things. Even if, luckily for him, he didn't marry me and now has actually become the pope," recalls Amalia Damonte today, age seventy-six, always with a smile on her lips. "He gave me a letter with a drawing of a little white house with a red roof and had written: 'This is the house I'll buy when we get married.'" The story ends with a problem between Jorge's family and their neighbors: when the parents of "Juliet of Flores" found the love letter, her father was furious, her mother tore up the letter, and both of them forbade the two young ones to continue seeing each other.

As soon as he is elected pope, this interrupted love story with Amalia becomes news in all the magazines and newspapers of the world. But the identity of Bergoglio's real girlfriend, a more serious relationship with a girl who belonged to the group of friends he went dancing with, is still unknown. Why did that story end? "I discovered my religious vocation," Bergoglio recalls in *The Jesuit*.

Jorge Bergoglio—who, like John Paul II, became a seminarian when he was an adult—had normal relations with his women friends, to the extent that one of them even made him doubt his vocation. "When I was a seminarian, I was dazzled by a girl I had met at the wedding of an uncle of mine. Her beauty, her intellectual radiance surprised me . . . [I]n a word, I was confused for some time, she kept on coming into my mind," Bergoglio himself confesses in *On Heaven and Earth*. "When I went back to the seminary after that wedding, I couldn't pray for a whole week, because when I wanted to do so, this girl appeared in my head. I had to reconsider what I was doing, I was still free because I was a seminarian; I could simply go back home. I had to rethink my decision. I went back to choosing the religious path—or let myself be chosen."

"It's something that comes from inside," says Bergoglio about the tango, confessing that when he was young, when it came to dancing, he preferred the *milonga*. He adored Juan D'Arienzo's orchestra and never stopped listening to Carlos Gardel, Julio Sosa, Ada Falcón (who would later become a nun), and Azucena Maizani (to whom later he would impart extreme unction). But he was also open to more modern experiences; he admired Astor Piazzolla and Amelita Baltar. He also admits to having an ear for opera, which his mother used to play to the three older children, sitting around the radio every Saturday at two o'clock in the afternoon. At the age of ten, Jorge also took piano lessons.

Besides music, dancing, soccer, and his group of friends, Jorge's religious vocation was beginning to come out clearly. "There's a story that makes it clear. During his second year, in 1951, Catholic Religion was a mandatory subject at school. Zambrano, the teacher who taught this subject, asked which of us had not taken first communion. I and another student stood up, and then he started a discussion. It was clear that he had already talked to Jorge because he told us, 'Your classmate Bergoglio has offered to be your godfather in the San José de Flores Church.' On the Sunday of that same week we took communion and then Jorge treated us to dinner in his house. At fourteen he already had the vocation of catechizing!" says Óscar Crespo.

So it was not a surprise when his friend finally joined the seminary of Villa Devoto in 1957. "I remember that much earlier, in 1952, Jorge and I went to work for four months in the Hickethier-Bachmann laboratory between Santa Fe and Azcuénaga. There we spent many hours together and chatted a lot. One day he told me, 'I'll finish secondary school with you, but I will not be a chemist. I'll be a priest. And not a basilica priest. I'll be a Jesuit, because I like going to the shantytowns, to the peripheries, being with people.' And that's how it was! For years I used to drive him personally in my car, because he has never had one, to the shantytowns. I stayed outside; he would go in as if there wasn't any risk."

Apart from one interruption, Óscar always stayed in touch with the future pope. This is how he tells the story: "We used to go and visit him, and we'd eat roast beef at San Miguel. Once, when he was head of the Jesuits, we talked till something like four o'clock in the morning . . . Then I lived abroad for many years and we lost touch. When I came back I didn't contact him because I'd heard that he was now a Cardinal and I didn't know how to treat him . . . A neighbor insisted that I go to see him, and one day she took me to the intersection of Triunvirato and Cullen, to the Iglesia del Carmen, at Villa Urquiza, where he was to say Mass. When he saw me, Jorge, who was arriving on foot because he had got off the bus and had a very simple briefcase with him, ran to meet me. 'Óscar!' he cried and embraced me. He didn't stop talking, insisting that I join the group again, so much so that the priest of the church had to remind him that Mass was about to begin. From that moment on we have kept in touch and never stopped seeing each other."

Óscar's last meeting with Bergoglio before he was elected pope took place on a Saturday. "Jorge called up a catering service, we ate cannelloni and drank wine, and it was a party full of comradeship. We recalled some stories from our school days. It got quite late and the catering [workers] had already gone home. As we were going away he said, 'Guys, are you going to help me clear the table?' We just missed having to wash up! That's what he's like, a unique human being. For someone who has got where he has, he has never lost his humility."

When in 1957, at the age of twenty, Jorge announced that he wanted to be a priest and join the seminary at Villa Devoto, reactions at home were varied. His father approved his decision without hesitation. "My father was the happiest from the very first moment," says Jorge's sister, María Elena. His mother, Regina, reacted negatively. She told him that she didn't see him as a priest. She didn't hide the fact that she had other expectations. Indeed, when he traveled to join the seminary, she did not accompany him and didn't accept his decision for years.

"When Jorge completed secondary school, Mom asked him what he wanted to do, and he told her that he wanted to study medicine. Then Mom arranged a room just for him so that he could study in peace and quiet. One day she went there to clean and found books of theology and Latin. Mom didn't understand and asked him, 'Son, what are these books? Weren't you going to study medicine?' and he answered: 'Yes, but the medicine of the soul,'" recalls María Elena.

"When I told my grandmother, she already knew but pretended that she didn't and answered me, 'Well, if God calls you, so be it!'" Bergoglio once recalled, speaking to Rubin and Ambrogetti. "But she added at once, 'Please don't forget that the door of home is always open and no one will reproach you if you change your mind.'"

His four siblings chose other ways of life, giving the future pope many nephews and nieces. Óscar Adrián worked as a teacher for a few years, then became an administrative clerk; he married and had three children: Sebastián, Mauro, and Vanesa. Alberto Horacio, a salesman of automotive parts, also had three children: Virna, Teseo Emanuel, and Ariadna; he died in June 2010. Marta Regina, who died in 2007, chose teaching and had two sons: Pablo and José Luis Narvaja, who decided to become a Jesuit like his uncle. María Elena, a homemaker who lives in Ituzaingó, has two sons, Jorge Andrés, the pope's godchild, and José Ignacio. His namesake nephew tells stories that confirm once more Francis's sense of humor. "It was he who taught me my first swear words . . . My parents have told me that when, as a baby, I started crying, he would wet my comforter with wine or whisky to calm me down."

In the seminary of Villa Devoto in Calle Cubas—which the Pope Tour also passes, and the guide doesn't forget to point out that in the neighboring Devoto prison the future pope celebrated Mass and visited the inmates hundreds of times—Jorge lived with many seminarians whom he will meet again as priests during the course of his life. One of them is Leonardo Sandri, today a Cardinal. Recalling Bergoglio, Sandri says, "He used to be my Prefect and woke us up in the morning, ringing the bell to make us get up on time. He was a very keen seminarian, exemplary, pious, serious, but he also had a sense of humor, which he has kept to this day."

After a few months at Villa Devoto, which was a diocesan seminary run at the time by the Jesuits, he was destined to live through another fundamental experience: he was stricken with a serious form of pneumonia, which brought him to death's door. The upper part of his right lung had to be removed. Fear, a very high fever, and acute pain accompanied the terrible days he spent in the Syrian-Lebanese Hospital in Buenos Aires. Only Sister Dolores, a nun who had prepared him for his first communion, spoke to him words that marked him like a brand: "With your pain you are imitating Jesus."

It was then that Don Enrique Pozzolli, his spiritual guide, advised him to spend a few days at Villa Don Bosco, a Salesian residence in the Tandil hills. In this period of convalescence, attracted by the spirit of the Society of Jesus, Jorge decided to leave the seminary at Villa Devoto and become a Jesuit. He was determined to be a missionary, and the Order founded by St. Ignatius in 1540 is famous for being first in this field.

On March 11, 1958, at the age of twenty-one, Bergoglio entered the Society of Jesus in Córdoba as a novice. Thus began a course of study lasting fourteen years; it included not only theory—the humanities, Greek, Latin, literature, history of art, psychology, and obviously, theology—but also practice, work in the field, and ongoing contact with the faithful and their suffering.

At the end of the first two years he took the vows of poverty, chastity, and obedience. In 1960 he began Humanities Studies in Chile. There, while he lived in Casa Loyola—the Jesuit residence with three floors and ninety rooms in the rural community of Padre Hurtado, fourteen miles from Santiago del Chile—he began to have a vision of the Church that cares for the lowest, a vision that will mark his life.

This comes out clearly in a typewritten letter dated May 5, 1960, to his sister María Elena:

> I teach religion, the little boys and girls are very poor, some of them come to school barefoot. Often they have nothing to eat and in the winter they feel the cold in all its harshness. You don't know what this means, because you have never missed something to eat, and when you feel cold you just sit nearer the stove. I'm telling you this to make you think. . . . While you are content, there are many children who are crying. While you are eating, many of them have nothing but a piece of bread, and when it's raining and cold, many of them are living in tin shacks and sometimes they have nothing to cover themselves with.

The other day a little old woman said to me: "Dear Father, if only I could have a blanket, how happy I should be! Because at night I'm very cold." And the worst thing is that they don't know Jesus. They don't know him because there is no one to teach them about him. Now do you understand me when I tell you that we need many saints? [And he suggests to his sister, who at the time was only eleven]: I'd like you to become a little saint. Why don't you try? We need so many saints . . .

# 5

# A Friend and Master

It's the year 1964. Jorge Bergoglio is not yet a priest; he is a Regent. That is the name given to students of the Society of Jesus who have studied philosophy and are teaching in one of the schools of the Order, in his case the Institute of the Immaculate Conception of Santa Fe, a paradigm of religious and upper-class education in Argentina.

Founded in 1610, the institute welcomes male boarders and day students from the fifth grade of elementary school to the fifth grade of secondary school, a kind of Latin American Oxford. High-ranking names, future governors, and illustrious intellectuals have passed through this aristocratic place of learning.

The institute occupies a block on May 25 Plaza, next to the palace of the provincial government and opposite Santa Fe's court of justice. It also owns another property nearby, which houses the Ateneo Club, with two covered swimming pools; a football and rugby field; facilities for basketball, fencing, and judo; and apparatus for gymnastics, among other sports. After the expulsion of the Jesuits from the Americas in 1767, the building was taken over by the Mercedarians. The institute was reopened nearly a century later, in 1862.

In the school church, with its facade from 1651 (a copy of the original one of 1610) and mainly baroque interior, there is an image of the Virgin, which is held to be miraculous. According to tradition, on May 9, 1636, trickles of water began to flow from the picture, and some pieces of cotton that had been steeped in that water led to the miraculous cure of many sick people.

On May 9, 1936, Pius XI granted the Coronation to the picture of Our Lady, which was transferred to the wall over the high altar. Our Lady of Miracles was named the patron saint of the Argentine branch of the Society of Jesus.

Bergoglio arrives at the iconic institution of Santa Fe—symbol of a complete education—after finishing his degree in philosophy at the Colegio Máximo San José, of San Miguel, Chile, where he studied for three years after his novitiate.

In the past, the institute had a military formation, like St. Ignatius himself. In fairly recent times it had prefects, brigadiers, and armories, and according to Jesuit tradition, competition was encouraged: the students were divided into two big groups, Rome and Carthage, headed, in turn, by their respective "consuls."

The school population, entirely male, goes to Mass every day. On certain occasions students wear a uniform consisting of a suit, blue tie, and white shirt, while on other days they wear ankle-length khaki-colored overalls with a narrow leather belt. The students play many sports, and with a Jesuit spirit, to inculcate love of one's neighbor. At least once a week the students take on socially useful work, taking meals and other assistance to the poor quarters of Santa Fe—such as Alto Verde on the banks of the Paraná River—and teach the catechism.

"There was a rather strict atmosphere, orders reechoed from the old walls, but in contrast to them there were the silent steps, in his rubber-soled shoes, of Bergoglio, smiling and peaceful, who talked in a low voice," recalls Eduardo Pfirter, a former student.

When Bergoglio arrives at the school, he is twenty-eight. He is very thin and tall, wears a cassock and a black belt, and looks quite young. Hence his nickname *Carucha*, or "Baby Face." From his first day teaching literature and psychology to the fourth- and fifth-year students, he wins them over with his refined intelligence, his sense of irony, and his gift for always reaching people's hearts.

With just one question, certainly a great one, he can put an audience of adolescents from high society into his pocket. He arrives in class clean-shaven, although his cassock is somewhat wrinkled, and he greets everyone in an educated way and presents himself by launching a challenge with a word play in Spanish: "Qué es el arte?" or "What is art?"

His voice is soft, his face serious. The students begin to offer all kinds of definitions. They are intent on showing this young Jesuit professor, with an Italian surname, that they have the best answers, or so they think. The minutes pass, the professor shakes his head: "No, you are all wrong," he announces, with a disappointed look on his face. "If you stand on the patio in your shirt in full winter you will know." The students are aghast. No one understands. *Helarte*, pronounced just like *el arte* (art) in Spanish—"is to stand in your shirt on the patio in the height of winter and freeze to death," he reveals, making everyone laugh.

"With this joke, he won us all over," Germán de Carolis, a former student of the future pope, tells me.

In contrast to the other teachers, Bergoglio is neither traditional nor solemn. "He was serious as far as personality went but youthful and with a sense of humor. He had authority, earned respect, and was popular with the students. His knowledge of the subjects he taught was immense, and his literature lessons captivated us. You could tell that he liked teaching and that he was totally convinced of his priestly vocation. It was impossible to doubt it. He was very serious and you could feel he was a priest even if he wasn't one yet," explains de Carolis.

The Scholastic of Italian origin from Flores charms them mainly with his sense of humor. One day he asks a lazy student to tell him who wrote *Cantar de Mio Cid*. When the student doesn't answer, the teacher proposes two alternatives:

"Did Cervantes or Anonymous write *El Cid*?"

"Anonymous."

"Good! Carlos or Juan Anonymous?"

"Juan," the student replies, making the whole class burst out laughing.

Besides being a teacher of literature and psychology, in 1964 Jorge becomes vice director of the Santa Teresa de Jesús Academy of Literature and joins the college Academy of Oratory. In 1965 he becomes director of the Academy of Literature.

"What he taught attracted me not only because he made me discover infinite pleasures and possibilities in writing and reading, but also because he stimulated me to think. He insisted that we explore everything with our minds, even in the religious field—a teaching that was not his main responsibility but was obviously very much present in everything he did. In this field he conveyed certainty and joy," recalls Rogelio Pfirter, an active member of the academy and later the diplomat who distinguished himself as the Argentine Ambassador in London during the period of British-Argentine reconciliation after the Malvinas-Falklands war (1982).

"He spoke clearly and wrote on the blackboard with the same speed and precision as when he wrote on paper. The blackboard was always full of arrows linking facts and ideas inside circles. He encouraged any type of question, and his answers were always fast and accurate. I never saw him hesitating," adds Pfirter.

Bergoglio was popular, but not inclined to sentimentality. "When we got our diplomas," Pfirter recalls, "one of us dared to shed a few tears because he was leaving school and had fears for the future. Jorge immediately stopped the incipient weeping and encouraged him not to stay anchored to the past but to go forward, strong in what he had learned, with joy and total dedication toward the future."

Over the course of 1964, Bergoglio the Scholastic teaches Spanish literature and covers a vast field: the troubadours, Cervantes, Fray Luis de León, (apart from de León's writings, Bergoglio stops for some time to explain the trial by Inquisition that led him to prison and culminated in his famous *Dicebamus externa die*), the baroque poets, the dispute between Góngora and Quevedo, Sor Juana Inés de la Cruz, modernism, and the Machados. The same year, as Holy Week approaches, he dedicates a lecture to reading a study of the terrible physical pain suffered by Christ on the cross, from the first nail to his death, from a medical point of view. He dedicates the 1965 course to Argentine literature, mainly *Martí Fierro* and to *gauchesco* literature in general, a subject that interests him a great deal.

High-school policy encourages university-type experiences, so Bergoglio adds an innovation to stimulate his students even more. He starts inviting a number of writers to take brief two- or three-day courses, open to the public, on various authors and literary themes. So, as invited teachers, María Esther Vázquez (who talks about Borges, Eduardo Mallea, and Manuel Mujica Láinez), María Esther de Miguel (who lectures on Argentine narrative), and even Jorge Luis Borges himself (who talks about *gauchesco* literature) pass through the institute. Brief courses on socioeconomic subjects by well-known Argentinians José Luis de Imaz and a very young Mariano Grondona are also added.

"Borges arrived in Santa Fe with a bad cold and was by now nearly blind. At Jorge's command we students shared tasks, doing our very best to assist him; I still remember well his great accessibility and his unique, quiet voice," Pfirter recalls.

Pfirter's brother Eduardo remembers a dinner with Borges and the future pope at the Ritz Hotel in Santa Fe. "I was a friend of the hotel proprietor's son, and a semipermanent guest. Thanks to this condition I managed to share a meal with Bergoglio, Borges, and the hotel proprietor. I remember Borges explaining that rice, which was an essential part of his diet, had to be cooked to the point where 'every grain could keep its personality.' On that occasion Bergoglio behaved with great simplicity, keeping a low profile and not taking part in the discussion, an attitude not very common among Jesuits at that time."

From that visit by Borges, whose works Bergoglio makes his students study in depth, came the publication of a book called *Original Tales*, an experiment of Bergoglio's to compile fourteen stories written by seven students, all of them members of the Santa Teresa Academy of Literature. He himself conceives and carries on the project, recruiting even Borges to help him select the authors and write the preface.

The book sold out, and a second edition was published; today it owes part of its success to a banner bigger than the title that reads in all capital letters, "Prologue by Jorge Luis Borges." The book is short and includes, among others, two stories each by Rogelio Pfirter; Sereno O. Grassi (a student from Paraná gifted in drama and literature); and Jorge Milia, a very creative fellow from Santa Fe who would become a writer and a close friend of Bergoglio's.

"The 1965 class of the Immacolata—'the 65s'—is now mainly scattered throughout Argentina, Germany, the United States, and Venezuela, but it has stayed united in time thanks to Bergoglio. Many of us, over the years, have declared ourselves 'produced by Bergoglio' . . . On August 28, 2010, we joined him and remembered all kinds of stories, told him about some private events, and discussed for a long time issues of everyday life, both political and spiritual," recalls Rogelio Pfirter. "We all left with the wonderful feeling that time, which had passed in decades, had actually not passed at all."

The year 1965 marks the end of the golden age of the Institute of the Immaculate Conception. It is then that the Second Vatican Council reaches its climax and Father Pedro Arrupe is elected Superior General of the Society of Jesus. Arrupe visits the institute that same year and there meets the young Bergoglio. Besides his well-known commitment to teaching the truth, his total immersion in national reality, and his passion for Argentine literature, Bergoglio dreams of being a missionary in distant lands.

Indeed, he writes to Arrupe, requesting to be sent to Japan (in that country Arrupe witnessed one of the great dramas of humanity: the dropping of the atomic bomb on Hiroshima on August 6, 1945). But because of Bergoglio's health problems, permission is denied. This is a hard blow.

"I wanted to become a missionary and wrote to the Superior General, who was Father Arrupe, asking to be sent to Japan or somewhere else. But he thought about it and told me, with great kindness, 'You have had a problem of the lungs; you are not fit for such a demanding job', and so I stayed in Buenos Aires," says Bergoglio, now Pope Francis, during a meeting with some students of Jesuit schools.

"Father Arrupe was very kind because he said to me: 'You are not saintly enough to be a missionary.' And what had given me the strength to become a Jesuit had been the prospect of the missions: going far away and proclaiming Jesus Christ, and not staying shut up in our often antiquated structures. That was what had inspired me," he reveals.

Arrupe's policy and the gradual rise of liberation theology make a deep impact on the Jesuit community and have repercussions on the institute, which little by little changes its position. At the same time many priests who have taught there abandon the Order. Some students who had graduated between 1963 and 1964 end up after 1966 occupying high posts in the hierarchy of the Montoneros—the left-wing urban guerrilla movement of the Peronist party in Argentina.

Bergoglio's two years at the institute turn out to be key to his future. There he meets many Jesuit priests, such as Ricardo O'Farrell, who will become Provincial of the Jesuits before him, and Víctor Zorzín, who will succeed him. He also meets older priests, such as Father Peralta Ramos, much loved by his students, from whom he learns a great deal.

"We all competed to go to confession with Father Ramos, who knew young people well and forgave us everything … You could tell him about any atrocious behavior and he would forgive every sin," Germán De Carolis recalls. Germán is convinced that in some way the institute, and above all, the miraculous Virgin in its church, had a great deal to do with the destiny of the Scholastic who ended up becoming pope.

"In 2000 I asked a fine painter to make a copy of the picture of the Miraculous Virgin to give to Bergoglio. Every morning for two years, when he was teacher at the Institute, we used to go into the church to venerate the Virgin before our lessons. I went to the archbishopric—I had the picture wrapped in paper—and said to Jorge, 'I have a surprise for you, which will follow you and protect your destiny.' When he saw the picture of the Virgin, he was deeply moved. He said, 'It's beautiful, wonderful, thank you.' And I said, 'Jorge, you're not the one who guides your destiny; it is Divine Providence that guides you.'"

# 6

# A Jesuit under Fire

On the evening of the *Habemus papam* announcement, March 13, 2013, the bells of Rome's churches ring out and Catholics everywhere celebrate the election of Pope Francis. But in the *casa generalizia*—headquarters—of the Society of Jesus, at Borgo Santo Spirito No. 4, an icy silence reigns.

Even though the first Jesuit pope in history has been elected, there is no celebration behind the massive walls of the ancient palace, only a few meters from St. Peter's Square. It is the same in many of the Society's houses throughout the world.

"You must be joking!" exclaims Father Andrés Swinnen when they wake him from his nap in the Jesuit House at 1639 Buchardo Street, in Córdoba, to tell him that his old friend, Jorge Bergoglio, is the new pope. "All over Latin America—after the first positive reactions—Jesuits murmured when they heard who had been elected," says Jesuit priest Jeffrey Klaiber [who died a year later, March 4, 2014].

Among many of the twenty thousand Jesuits in the world, there is amazement and bewilderment. Bergoglio's past as Provincial of Argentina in troubled times means that many Jesuits don't appreciate him. When he comes to Rome as Bishop, he is not invited to lodge in the *casa generalizia* at Borgo Santo Spirito. Perhaps he is not welcome there.

Gossip by some Jesuits has created an image of Bergoglio—who in 1973, at age thirty-six, became the youngest Provincial in recent Jesuit history—as a hidebound, conservative enemy of innovation and liberation theology. This negative picture goes back to the 1970s. These were difficult, turbulent times, full of expectation and serious conflict, not only in the Catholic Church, swept by winds of revolutionary change inspired by the Second Vatican Council (1962–1965), but also in Argentina, which was sinking into its Dirty War.

Those were stormy years. Bergoglio, though very young, faced his first great challenge of government with determination and strong nerves, but undoubtedly he made some mistakes. "My government as a Jesuit had, at the beginning, many defects. I was thirty-six: it was a crazy state of affairs. I had to tackle difficult situations, and I made my decisions in a sharp, individualistic style. My brisk and authoritarian way of making decisions led to serious problems and accusations of being ultraconservative. I certainly wasn't a saint, but I have never been right-wing. It was my authoritarian way of decision making that created problems," Francis admits, in a historic interview with the journal *La Civiltà Cattolica*.

His critics at the time accused him of "supporting pre-Vatican II manners and values" among the Jesuits, which meant, according to Klaiber, that the Argentine province was not up to date with the rest of the Society in Latin America. In addition, he was accused of having sold several properties of the Society at a time of huge financial problems. Another of his initiatives that was not well received was his decision to entrust the direction of the Universidad del Salvador to secular authorities, many of whom belonged to Guardia de Hierro, right-wing Catholic supporters of Perón, who were close to Bergoglio and opposed to the left-wing Montoneros.

However, the most serious accusation against him was of having collaborated with the dictatorship by handing over two Jesuit priests, Orlando Yorio and Francisco Jalics, persecuted for their social work in the shantytowns, who had disappeared on May 23, 1976. This accusation was fomented by his enemies, in particular by the journalist Horacio Verbitsky, a former Montonero and president of the Centro de Estudios Legales y Sociales (CELS), who declined my invitation to be interviewed for this book.

The true story is a very different one. In silence, Bergoglio did everything he could to get the military to release Yorio and Jalics, who were tortured during their five-month detention and then released on October 23, 1976. Always acting discreetly, he helped many other people, victims of state terrorism, hide or flee from that demented Argentina.

Shortly before he died, Eugenio Guasta, a man of culture and a priest, a friend of mine and of my family and an admirer of Francis, told me this story to confirm that Bergoglio was not much loved among the Jesuits:

"Once an old Jesuit asked me, 'Well? How are things going with Archbishop Bergoglio?' 'Very well, he has given us his private phone number, we have a good rapport, he is concerned about each one of us,' I said. 'Fine,' he replied. 'Perhaps a bad Jesuit can become a good Bishop.'"

Just as he has become pope at a time when the Catholic Church is sailing through stormy waters, so Bergoglio became the youngest Provincial of the Society of Jesus when the Order was in crisis, in Argentina and in the rest of the world. The issues: the dearth of vocations, the departure of priests, and grim financial problems. In addition, there were lacerating internal divisions, the result of a complex ecclesiastical and political situation.

The winds of renewal of the Second Vatican Council coincided with the election of the Basque priest Pedro Arrupe, in 1965, as head of the Society of Jesus. Arrupe led the Order in a socially progressive direction. While Paul VI's encyclical *Populorum progressio* (May 1967), which concentrates on social questions, made a strong impression, particularly in the Third World, liberation theology also had begun to have a big impact throughout Latin America.

Arrupe was living on a volcano. Not everyone among the Jesuits interpreted the demand for reforms promoted by the Second Vatican Council in a balanced way: some, fearing change, thought only of applying the brakes; others, too enthusiastic about the new elements, wanted to dispense with all caution. In 1968, the Latin American Episcopal Conference meeting at Medellín, in Colombia, discussed "the Church at the present time of transformation in the light of the council" and declared a preferential option for the poor. It called for the formation of "grassroots communities" in which the poor could be taught to read the Bible, with the aim of freeing the people from the "institutionalized violence" of poverty and letting them know that poverty and hunger could be avoided, that they are not the will of God.

All of this and what happened later made an explosive cocktail for Provincial Bergoglio. In the middle of the Cold War, with de facto military governments in Latin America and guerrilla movements inspired by Marxism, waving the banner of class warfare, many priests were leaving the ministry. Some committed themselves to the cause of the poorest, and some were motivated politically by extremist ideologies that called for taking up arms. But Bergoglio could not accept this.

During his second year as Provincial he went to Rome to take part in the Thirty-Second General Congregation of the Society of Jesus (the supreme organ of the Order) from December 2, 1974, to March 7, 1975. Its fourth decree, "Our mission today: serving the faith and promoting justice," became a milestone for the Jesuits of the whole world and marked an important change. It provoked discussions and different reactions, some of them very radical.

In December 1975, Paul VI's apostolic exhortation *Evangelii nuntiandi*, on the evangelization of the modern world, declared, "We must say and repeat that violence is not evangelical, it is not Christian; and that sharp or violent changes of structures would be deceptive, inefficient on their own, and certainly not consistent with people's dignity." For Bergoglio, a young Provincial in the midst of a storm, *Evangelii nuntiandi* was a beacon.

Though concerned about world poverty, Paul VI, during the last years of his pontificate, didn't hide his anxiety about the Marxist interpretation of the Christian message adopted by some priests committed to social justice, many of whom were Jesuits in Latin America. His successor, John Paul II (1978–2005) expressed himself more directly in this sense, striking hard—with the aid of Cardinal Joseph Ratzinger, at the time custodian of Catholic orthodoxy—at liberation theology.

"The Society was divided between people more to the left and people more to the right. In Spain, for example, there was a group of ultraconservative Jesuits who wanted to break away and form an authentic Society of Jesus," says Father Humberto Miguel Yáñez, a Jesuit and professor of moral theology at the Pontifical Gregorian University in Rome.

"We Jesuits were scattered, everyone doing what he felt like. And then Bergoglio arrived to put order in the flock and move things ahead. Understandably, this created controversy within the Order," declares Father Swinnen, Master of Novices when Bergoglio was Provincial, and later Provincial when Bergoglio ended his term in 1979.

Just as he became pope after the unexpected resignation from Peter's throne of Benedict XVI, so Bergoglio was appointed Provincial of Argentina at a surprisingly young age after an unexpected incident.

"Father Luis Escribano, who should have become the next Provincial, died in a car accident on his way back from Córdoba. At that time, I was ill with pneumonia and was in hospital. Bergoglio often came to visit me, and once I said to him, 'You will be the next Provincial.' And I was right. After the death of Escribano, everyone supported Bergoglio, who was then Master of Novices," says eighty-two-year-old Juan Carlos Scannone, famous Jesuit theologian, advocate of the so-called "theology of the people." This is a kind of Argentine interpretation of liberation theology, further defined by Father Lucio Gera, which was to influence the future pope.

It is believed by some, however, that even without that unexpected death, Bergoglio's fate was settled. He had already achieved a high degree of credibility in the Order, where he held a number of important posts: he was a Province Consultor (the council at that time was led by Father Ricardo O'Farrell) and vice director and Master of Novices, in addition to being professor of theology. And the Superior General of the Jesuits, Pedro Arrupe, at the time of appointing a new Provincial from a short list of candidates, had no doubts. He chose the young Scholastic he had met in 1965 during his memorable visit to the Institute of the Immaculate Conception. "Without doubt the Father General chose such a young man because of his charisma, his talent for leadership," says Father Ernesto Giobando, a fifty-three-year-old Jesuit, Superior of the Casa Regina Martyrum of Buenos Aires and Prefect of the eponymous Church. "Bergoglio has a charisma which concentrates the will, and that is a gift."

But let's go back in time. In 1966, after the period of teaching at the Institute of the Immaculate Conception, Bergoglio continues his training by teaching the same subjects—literature and psychology—at the Jesuit Instituto del Salvador. So he goes back to his beloved Buenos Aires. A year later, in 1967, he begins studying theology at the Colegio Máximo, in the province of Buenos Aires, where he will live as student, teacher, and rector for eighteen years. On December 13, 1969, a few days short of his thirty-third birthday, he is ordained a priest by Ramón José Castellano, Archbishop Emeritus of Córdoba, in the Colegio Máximo.

The whole of his family attends the ceremony: his mother, his brothers and sisters, and his beloved grandmother Rosa. His mother, Regina, so reluctant at the idea of her firstborn becoming a priest, at the end of the ceremony kneels before him and asks for his blessing.

Grandmother Rosa—who has taught him to believe, not to mention having taught him the Piedmontese dialect that the pope now uses with every Italian from that part of Italy—writes him a letter for the occasion. Half in Spanish, half in Italian, this letter, which the pope keeps in his breviary with loving care, had been written in case Grandma Rosa died and was unable to attend such a fundamental moment in the life of her beloved Jorge:

> May these grandchildren of mine, to whom I have entrusted the best part of my heart, have a long and happy life. But if one day sorrow, illness, or the loss of a loved one fills them with despair, may they remember that a sigh before the tabernacle, where the greatest and most august martyr lives, and a glance at Mary at the foot of the cross, can make a drop of healing balm fall on the deepest and most painful wounds.

And speaking of wounds, the most important person absent on that day of ordination is Mario, Grandmother Rosa's son and Jorge's father. He has died prematurely, and Jorge and Rosa miss him greatly.

A year after his ordination, Bergoglio makes his first trip to Europe. He goes to Spain for his Tertianship, a period that concludes the Jesuit training, in the Institute of Saint Ignatius of Loyola at Alcalá de Henares. This period consists of thirty days of silent spiritual retreat, following St. Ignatius's *Spiritual Exercises*, and pastoral activity among the poor.

On his return to Argentina, Bergoglio graduates in theology and begins to take on a position of responsibility in the emblematic Colegio Máximo de San Miguel, which is housed in an imposing red-brick building, established in 1931, in the middle of a large park. In 1971 he becomes Vice Rector and Master of Novices of the house of Villa Barilari. The following year he is nominated professor of theology, and in the year after that he becomes a Province Consultor.

On April 22, 1973, Bergoglio completes his long period of religious formation by taking his "last vows": he renews his vows of poverty, chastity, and obedience and makes a fourth, only for the most qualified Jesuits, of obedience to the Holy Father. April 22 is an emblematic date for all Jesuits: it is the day in 1542 when Ignatius Loyola and his first companions pronounced their solemn profession in Rome after their new Order had been approved by Pope Paul III. This took place in the Basilica of St. Paul Outside the Walls, before the same image of the Virgin where Francis was to stop to pray on Sunday, April 14, 2013, after the Mass in which he took possession of this Roman pontifical Church.

On July 31, 1973—the same day as the return of Juan Domingo Perón to government in Argentina—Bergoglio is appointed Provincial of the Jesuits of Argentina (a province that includes the country of Uruguay). Two months later, he travels to Rome for a meeting of the new Provincials with Father Arrupe. Afterward, at the beginning of October, he travels to the Holy Land. But he can't see much of the land of Jesus; two days after his arrival, the Yom Kippur War between Arab states and Israel breaks out, and he is confined to his hotel.

When Bergoglio takes over as Provincial, the Society of Jesus is going through a critical, difficult time. When he first joined the Order, there were about 400 members and vocations; now, in 1973, only 166 priests, 32 brothers, and 20 novices are left.

"There were contrasts, different points of view. Some Jesuits became extremists. Others went into hiding or attempted to support the revolution, represented at the time by the Montoneros. In spite of the accusations, it is more than evident that Bergoglio did not collaborate with the dictatorship. At that time the situation in Argentina was very difficult . . . I was sixteen and already aware that there was a call to join the revolution. In fact, I was actually asked to join," Father Giobando of Santa Fe recalls.

When he was fifteen, Giobando asked Bergoglio, then Provincial, to let him enter the Society. "Boy, you are still very young; come back next year," the Provincial replied, but the following year, in spite of the dearth of vocations, he refuses him again. "Go on praying, come next year," he said. In 1977 Bergoglio admitted him but put off his entry to the following year.

From the beginning, Bergoglio applies the principles of Ignatian spirituality, which encourages reflection, prayer, and discernment in the midst of the constant daily struggle between good and evil.

At a time when everything is being questioned, Bergoglio remains faithful to Rome. "It was a turbulent time for the Society of Jesus, where there were people who criticized the pope. But Bergoglio always held a very clear position of support of the Holy See, which he always backed," recalls Father Yáñez.

"There was a great deal of confusion in the country, and one of the favorite targets were the Jesuits, because of the great weight they represented in the Argentine Church," says Carlos Velasco Suárez, founder of the Movimento Humanista, inspired by social Christianity, who died in 2013. He developed a deep friendship with Bergoglio through his academic work and because, as a psychiatrist, he helped priests Bergoglio referred to him.

"They [the Montoneros] would get at the Jesuit students and priests by two different techniques: indoctrinating them with liberation politics or distracting them with women. At the time Bergoglio was doing courageous, heroic deeds, using all his strength, skill, and intelligence to put an end to all this . . . Here was a man steeped in the philosophical, sociological, and political trends of his day. He was inclined to put himself in the place of others to understand what was happening. I have no doubt that Bergoglio saved the Society of Jesus. And he saved it by two characteristics he had and still has: firmness in guiding people and a profound spiritual nature, which he used to help 'the boys' escape from those traps. He was very active, which made him hated by all the people who believed in that crazy idea of liberation and who at a certain point had gained access to posts of leadership within the Church . . . I can testify that Bergoglio showed great determination for which he was punished by an unexpected move: transferring him to Córdoba," says Velasco.

"In that context of ideological confusion and the sociological schemes that were creeping into the Church, he once said to me: 'You see, Doctor, the only pastoral charge I understand is face-to-face, I don't believe in those utopian depersonalizing and dehumanizing schemes.' His attention to his priests showed this. He was a real father who took care of them, following them one by one."

At such a turbulent time Bergoglio tried to consolidate a pastoral team inspired by vocation and promoted a return to Ignatian spirituality.

"During this time of confusion, he and others ventured into the heart of renewed Ignatian spirituality. This was happening throughout the Society at a universal level. Father Arrupe himself proposed going to the source of our spirituality, joining that spirituality to the most popular theology, that of popular piety. Such a synthesis between Ignatian spirituality and the theology of the people helped at that time to discern the mission we should be following," Giobando explains.

Bergoglio has a steady hand. When he sees one of his priests leaving the right path, he acts. For example, he objects to the activity of the Jesuit father Alberto Ibáñez Padilla, a member of the group Comunión Renovada de Evangélicos y Católicos en el Espíritu Santo (Renewed Communion in the Holy Spirit of Evangelicals and Catholics in the Holy Spirit, or CRECES).

"On September 24, 1977, I founded, with other collaborators, la Comunidad de Convivencia con Dios. These were weeklong spiritual retreats that followed Ignatian spirituality but were marked in a special way by the charismatic movement. Four months after its foundation, Bergoglio forbade me to take part in these meetings and asked me to devote myself to spiritual direction. With time, this turned out to be a great blessing because it meant that laypeople took over," Ibáñez Padilla recalls.

One of the first things Bergoglio did as Provincial was to transfer the provincialate—which has its seat on Calle Bogotá, in the capital Buenos Aires—to the Colegio Máximo, in the province of Buenos Aires, to follow the novices more closely. "He often used to come to Villa Barilari; he has always been very close to us, in the Jesuit style," says Father Yáñez.

This being close to people is not confined to Jesuits. "I got to know him through a letter. I had become a seminarian in 1976 in Rosario. At a certain point I had a crisis of vocation, I didn't know if I should or shouldn't become a Jesuit, and the best thing I thought of doing was to write directly to the Provincial, who in 1978 was Bergoglio. He replied with a wonderful letter, and I was very surprised that someone so important had put himself at my disposal to discuss my vocational problems. I didn't become a Jesuit, I remained a diocesan priest, but I shall always remember the moment when someone paid attention to me, when he helped me, listened to me," Sergio Alfredo Fenoy, Bishop of San Miguel, remembers today.

Because there are few vocations and many Jesuits have left the Order, Bergoglio, the Provincial, decides to renew Jesuit training. Study courses must be reorganized, and he replaces the juniorate stage (which follows the novitiate) with preuniversity studies, giving them a focus that insists mainly on national culture and popular religiosity.

"We studied Argentine literature and history, that is to say *our* culture, concentrating on the critical study of history," Yáñez says. "It was a new trend, which sought to overcome the 'official' history, which despised our Argentine culture as 'barbarous' while presenting European culture as 'civilized.' Bergoglio belonged to an Argentine cultural movement that supported the so-called revisionist school of history of José Maria Rosa and Vicente Sierra. This movement aimed at going beyond a vision of history inspired by liberalism and the Enlightenment, which left in the shade the contribution of the Spanish conquest and the Catholic Church, allied to Spanish colonialism. For example, the work of the Jesuits, particularly in the Jesuit Reductions in Paraguay, was not studied at school. And revisionist history rediscovered works of prime importance for the understanding of the culture of large parts of Argentina, Uruguay, southern Brazil, and Paraguay."

Bergoglio, like many other Jesuits, is convinced that it is useless to talk about liberation if you don't know the culture of the people. Thus, from the start he encourages his students to get to know the shantytowns that are growing around the Colegio Máximo and to go on mission throughout the rest of the country.

A good Jesuit, he sees the world as the place where Christ walked, talked, and embraced people. He believes that no apostolic action exhausts the good it is possible to do, which is why Jesuits are involved in every type of work. The goal is to find God where God can be served best and where the people can be served best.

In accordance with the Thirty-Second General Congregation of the Society of Jesus, Bergoglio believes the crucial challenge of our time to be "the struggle for faith and the struggle for justice, which faith itself demands" and that "the promotion of justice is an absolute requirement, as it is part of the reconciliation between men required by their reconciliation with God."

As Provincial, he sets up a missionary team, which lives in the most remote parts of the country, places rich in culture and popular piety. "Actually, during my novitiate I spent two months among native tribes in two different places. The first time was in a desert area of Santiago del Estero, where we went from one village to another, among the huts, eating what our host families gave us and working with them, and another time in Salta," recalls Father Yáñez.

The year in which Bergoglio is appointed Provincial, Father Arrupe visits Argentina, Chile, and Brazil, South American countries that are politically on the precipice and need relief. In Argentina the military coup has not yet taken place—it will come in March 1976—but there is a climate of disorder and violence. So much so that, as Bergoglio himself recalls in 2010 when giving evidence in the case of the Escuela Superior de Mecánica de la Armada (known as ESMA, a secret detention center during the Dirty War), Arrupe's arrival in Argentina sparks unpleasantness in many sectors because the Jesuits are working with the poorest. Bergoglio remembers that at the time it was "taken for granted" that the priests who worked with the poor were considered "on the left."

"It was a very fruitful visit," recalls Father Giobando. "[Arrupe] gave all his support to Bergoglio, in the first place because he had appointed him at such a young age. I happened to read Arrupe's letters, which revealed great support for the Provincial. Those were very difficult times; we had come out of a big purge, with a great loss of Jesuits. He came to visit us, to encourage us, to console us and support the Provincial."

At that same time the financial situation of the Society's province is disastrous. Bergoglio decides to sell a number of properties. "Inflation was very high at the time, and the university was a million dollars in debt. It was an astronomical sum, and if something hadn't been done, the Society would have lost all its assets. It's true that he sold some properties . . . I remember for example that at Mendoza the Society of Jesus owned a whole block in which there was a school, the seat of the community . . . one of those very old houses with a park, a well, and spaces for meetings, reception halls . . . Bergoglio sold a quarter of the block, which did not represent any loss for the community . . . He sold the old novitiate of Córdoba, and we didn't need even that because it was a very old building, it was much more sensible to live in the small house where I served my novitiate at Villa Barilari rather than in an old barracks like the one in Córdoba. He sold the old home of the novitiate, the school, the church—the whole block—and the church was rebuilt, it's modern today," Yáñez recalls.

These decisions don't go down well with many people. "I always found everything very reasonable . . . But certainly these are questions that touch the emotions, and someone who served his novitiate in a certain place might feel resentment . . . Bergoglio has always been a character with a clear-cut personality, and this has brought him great support and also great rejection. He is a man of great personality and originality, and it's also difficult to place him because some claim that he is a conservative and then say, but how can that be, if he talks about the poor? He's outside the categories," Yáñez adds.

Bergoglio—whom some Jesuits nickname "La Gioconda" or "Mona Lisa," because he seems inscrutable—also hands over, by order of Father General Arrupe, the running of the Universidad del Salvador to a group of laypeople, some of them belonging to the group Guardia de Hierro. The Jesuits go on teaching there, working as pastors, but no longer have institutional responsibilities. They still have another university, the Catholic University of Córdoba.

"When Bergoglio became involved with the Universidad del Salvador, it was up to its neck in debt. To pay it off, he sold many properties owned by the Jesuits, and this inevitably created friction, as did his decision to allow laypeople to take over the University," says Father Swinnen.

"Bergoglio decided that the Jesuits should leave the university in the hands of laymen so that they could go and work with ordinary people, returning to the poor districts. The Jesuits stayed in the pastoral field and still had a role in the theology school," recalls Francisco José "Cacho" Piñón, one of the first lay rectors of the university and a director of the Guardia de Hierro. "Bergoglio would meet us, but he wasn't a leader or a militant. The Guardia de Hierro was not right wing at the time; it was just a group that believed in liberation, before the coming of the Montoneros, who sided with the left," says Julio Bárbaro, historian and former leader of the Peronist movement.

When the Universidad del Salvador passed into the hands of laypeople, the administrative team was kept in place. "In March 1976, after the coup, the challenge was to leave the university in peace, by working. Many people wanted to work in a difficult context. The university was a space that stayed pluralistic, open to dialogue even in the midst of a dictatorship, and here the Jesuits had a key role. During the years when I was rector, till 1980, Bergoglio was always by my side, but he had no part in academic decisions, which were my responsibility. I always remember him as an attentive father," says Piñón, now Rector of the Universidad de Congreso in Mendoza.

During his term of office, on November 25, 1977, the Universidad del Salvador conferred a degree *honoris causa* to Admiral Emilio Massera, then head of the navy and member of the military junta that governed Argentina. Massera, who died in 2010, was tried and sentenced for human rights violations in 1985.

"Massera was invited to give a lecture according to an agreement for the protection of human lives," Piñón adds. "Bergoglio was not present. The lecture was an important decision made to save lives. Lives of people from the university, from Peronism, many people."

In those violent years of political and social turmoil, Bergoglio is not living in a bubble. He knows perfectly well that the situation in the country is horrific, and he does what is in his power to help those in need. On May 11, 1974, Father Carlos Mugica, pioneer of the priests of the shantytowns, is murdered. The slaughter increases after the military coup of 1976. On Sunday, July 4, 1976, five religious members of the Pallottine Order serving at the Church of San Patricio in the Belgrano R. neighborhood of Buenos Aires are killed. On July 18, 1976, alleged members of the Federal Police abduct and murder the priests Gabriel Longueville and Carlos de Dios Murias at Chamical, in the province of La Rioja, in the north of Argentina.

The following morning, several hooded men go to look for the parish priest of Sanogasta, but on the advice of the Archbishop of La Rioja, Enrique Angelelli, he has left. When the layperson who opens the door to them tells them that the parish priest is not there, he is riddled with bullets. A few months before, Angelelli had asked Bergoglio to protect three seminarians of his diocese who were in danger: Enrique Martínez Ossola, Miguel La Civita, and Carlos González. They are saved by hiding in the Colegio Máximo.

On August 4 of the same year, Angelelli himself dies in an alleged car accident. "I have not come to be served, but to serve. To serve everyone, without distinction of social class, way of thinking or faith; like Jesus, I want to be the servant of our brothers the poor," Angelelli had said when he became Bishop of La Rioja in 1968. Words very similar to the ones Pope Francis was to say many years later.

"We were very worried; our novitiate at Villa Barilari was searched twice. Several of my companions were frightened one night when soldiers came and took them into the garden in their underwear . . . At the time no one knew what could happen," Father Yáñez recalls.

In the midst of so much horror, Bergoglio tries to act like a protective father. He warns the Jesuit novices and priests working in the shantytowns with the poor that they are in danger because they will be listed as subversives.

He tries to help the former head of his chemical laboratory, Esther Ballestrino de Careaga, after the disappearance of her daughter Ana María and her son-in-law. He does not hesitate to hide some Marxist books from her library because she fears that the military could use them against her. In her struggle to find her daughter, Esther becomes one of the founders of the Mothers of Plaza de Mayo. She is one of the twelve people seized in the Church of Santa Cruz, on the corner of Urquiza and Estados Unidos streets, together with other mothers and relatives of *desaparecidos* (the disappeared) and the French nuns Léonie Duquet and Alice Domon. They all disappeared on December 8, 1977, in an ESMA raid led by the former navy captain Alfredo Astíz.

"What is going to happen will be very bloody, terrible; come and live with me," Bergoglio said in February 1976 to Alicia Oliveira, an old friend and an ex-magistrate removed from her position by the military junta, former defender of the city's people and a fighter for human rights. "I'd rather be taken by the military than live with priests," replies Oliveira, whose youngest son, Alejandro Jorge, is a godchild of the future pope.

During the dictatorship, Oliveira hides in the apartments of several friends. "At the time one of my sons went to Universidad del Salvador, run by the Jesuits, and I was very scared that he could leave and not find me here, that he wouldn't be able to see me. So Jorge would take me from where I was hiding to the college, by a secret way. He would come by car and leave me in the courtyard, so that I could see my son," Alicia Oliveira recalled in an interview for *La Nación*.

She is one of the people who has raised her voice most often in defense of the present pope, who has been accused of having done nothing during the bloody military regime in Argentina. "He helped many people during the dictatorship, which he had a terrible opinion of, just as I did. I remember a case of a man he saved. He could not leave the country. He looked like Jorge, who gave him his papers and his priest's vestments, so that he was able to get away. Such actions could not have been done by just anyone . . . But there are other cases. Every Sunday we gathered at Villa San Ignacio, a house for spiritual exercises which is opposite Campo de Mayo. We would eat and say good-bye to the people who were leaving the country because they were persecuted," she recalled in an interview.

Alice Oliveira remembers also the emblematic case of the kidnapping of Yorio and Jalics on May 23, 1976.

Bergoglio has warned them twice that they are marked men, in danger, because of their social work in the Rivadavia area in Bajo Flores, near Villa 1-11-14. The regime is convinced that their pastoral work in the shantytowns is a facade used to conceal guerrilla activity. To protect them, and under orders from Pedro Arrupe, Bergoglio disbands their communities.

"When they were there, he was very worried; I remember, he used to tell them, 'You must go away,' but they insisted on staying," she said.

Bergoglio has known Yorio and Jalics very well, since 1961 at the Colegio Máximo. One has been his spiritual guide, the other one of his teachers. Yorio is accused of being a guerrilla and of not having kept his vows (which Bergoglio denies), and his license to celebrate Mass is taken away a few days before his kidnapping.

As is now common knowledge, Bergoglio immediately informed the nunciature (papal diplomatic mission) and the archbishopric of the disappearances, and he interceded twice in 1976 with Admiral Massera, at the beginning of the dictatorship, over the kidnapping of Yorio and Jalics.

"I met the commander of the navy twice at that time," Bergoglio declares in 2010 before the tribunal at Buenos Aires judging the crimes committed by Emilio Massera at ESMA, the dictatorship's main clandestine center of detention, torture, and execution.

"Listen, Massera, I want them to turn up," Bergoglio tells him, according to the video of his testimony in that trial for crimes against humanity when, as Cardinal Primate he is interrogated in the archbishopric of Buenos Aires. "It was a very hard exchange, and lasted less than ten minutes," he declares. That meeting took place two months after the first, when "I was already pretty sure that they [the navy] had them."

Bergoglio also twice meets General Jorge Rafael Videla, president and dictator of Argentina and member of the military junta between 1976 and 1981. Thanks to these interventions, on the night of October 23, 1976, Jalics and Yorio, drugged and transported by helicopter to a field in Cañuelas, in the province of Buenos Aires, are freed. Shortly after, under the protection of the nunciature, Bergoglio provides them with documents and helps them leave the country. He pays for a trip to Rome for Yorio, intervenes for him to be accepted at the Pontifical Pío Latino Americano College, and helps him enter Pontifical Gregorian University. Yorio died in 2009. As for Jalics, he went to Hungary, his homeland, and then on to Germany.

"Bergoglio put himself on the line for people; he helped many to escape. I categorically deny the tale according to which Bergoglio handed somebody over. It's true that he went to talk to Massera, but that was only to try to get Yorio and Jalics released. Jorge kept up good relations with the military government to find out when priests were in danger. He went twice to warn Yorio and Jalics that they were in danger. This subject was discussed in the council; I was a witness to it because I was a member," says Father Andrés Swinnen, Bergoglio's successor as Provincial, who mentions as an example Juan Luis Moyano, a priest who was helped to escape and continue his studies in Germany.

"Relations with the government of the time were very complicated, but he never handed over anyone—that is a legend invented by someone who doesn't know him. It's just a speck of resentment in the universe of joy he brings with him. There were adults who didn't allow him to help them, and I don't only mean Yorio and Jalics, but others too, but that doesn't mean that Bergoglio handed them over. I lived at the Colegio Máximo with four or five of Angelelli's seminarians whom he was protecting, and those were only the cases that I know about; there were many others," Father Ángel Rossi agrees. He was a student of Bergoglio's and now Superior of the Residencia Jesuita community in Córdoba.

"I really don't know, but the fact that he was concerned to save these people and that later they accused him of handing them over must have been very hard for him to bear," comments Father Yáñez.

"I was a great friend of Yorio's. We taught philosophy and theology together. I went to the Rivadavia area with him many times. When he and Jalics disappeared, Bergoglio told me of all the efforts he was making to save them. He did everything he could to find out where they were and then make it possible for them to leave the country. I always used to go to a neighborhood of San Miguel, Manuelita, and he would make sure that I wasn't taken away. He advised me on how and at what time it was better to come back. He would read my papers to check that there was nothing suspicious in them, to avoid my being censored," Father Scannone recalls. He then adds, "He was happy not to have lost a single Jesuit during the dictatorship."

The election of Pope Francis brings back the old, baseless accusations. They had already emerged on the eve of the 2005 conclave. On March 15, 2013, the Vatican attempts to dispel belief in the suspected links of the pope to the Argentine dictatorship with an unconvincing press release. Father Federico Lombardi, Vatican spokesman and a Jesuit like Bergoglio, claimed that it was a question of declarations launched by "an anti-clerical Left to attack the Church, which must be rejected with determination."

On the same day, Francisco Jalics breaks his silence. "Bergoglio did not denounce me and Yorio. It's wrong to affirm that our capture took place on Father Bergoglio's initiative. I have become reconciled with those events and for me, the episode is closed," writes the Jesuit, eighty-five, resident of the German town of Wilhelmsthal. "After our release, I left Argentina," he is reported as saying in a communiqué published on the website Jesuiten.org. "Only many years later did we have the chance to speak about these events with Father Bergoglio, who in the meantime had been nominated Archbishop of Buenos Aires. After that meeting, we celebrated a public Mass together and solemnly embraced each other. I wish Pope Francis the abundant benediction of God for his task," says Jalics. In a significant reunion, Bergoglio embraces him again at his residence at the Casa Santa Marta in October 2013.

In the days that follow his election, more voices chime in to defend the new pope. Among these is the Nobel Peace Prize winner of 1980, Adolfo Pérez Esquivel. After meeting Francis, he affirms that in Argentina "there were bishops who collaborated with the dictatorship, but not Bergoglio."

The writer and Peronist leader Julio Bárbaro has no doubts. "I believe that the dark past is Mr. Horacio Verbitsky's!" he exclaims, referring to the former member of the Montoneros guerrilla movement, now an investigative journalist and the main attacker of Francis. Bárbaro reveals that he had two handwritten letters from Jorge Bergoglio. "He wrote me long letters after the publication of an article of mine in *La Nación* and another in [the newspaper] *Clarín*, the first in 2007 and the second in 2012. He agreed with me on the fact that in Argentina we have never been able to discuss and criticize the guerrillas . . . And if you don't debate the guerillas, we continue in our foolishness."

A letter of gratitude written to Pope Francis by Gonzalo Mosca, a Uruguayan whom Bergoglio helped during those turbulent times, needs no comment:

Montevideo, April 15, 2013

Dear Jorge Bergoglio, today Pope Francis,

My name is Gonzalo Mosca, I'm the brother of Juan José Mosca, a Uruguayan Jesuit priest. I don't know if you remember me, but I suppose that you remember an experience we shared about thirty-six years ago.

I had fled from Uruguay, persecuted by the dictatorship and had arrived in Buenos Aires, but very soon the military began to look for me in Argentina. That was when my brother Juan José came to Buenos Aires to help me escape from the country. He had been your student of theology and got in touch with you at the Universidad del Salvador. You asked him to bring me to you, saying that you would try to help me. That was where I met you. I hadn't been sleeping for days and was stressed out. You drove us to San Miguel, you asked me to keep down and not to look at the road we were about to take, I remember that at that moment I thought, *Does this little priest know what risks he's running?* (At the time I didn't know that you were the Provincial of the Jesuits.)

The road seemed endless, and at every corner I was aware of the military and the police; in those days in Buenos Aires a great number of Uruguayans had disappeared, many of them my comrades.

At San Miguel you told me to take my wedding ring off my finger and pretend I was taking part in a spiritual retreat, as if I was about to enter the Society. I remember that in the evening you knocked on my door to have a chat with me, we talked about life . . . You brought me some novels to distract me and a portable radio so that I could listen to some music.

I don't know how many days I spent there, but there weren't many. One morning you called me to your study and my brother was there, too, and you explained to us the plan we were to follow. We would take a plane for an internal flight from Argentina to the area of the Iguazu

River, and from there we would cross the triple border into Brazil. I have a vague memory of nameless landscapes, because it was an internal flight, but I can't be more exact. You gave us a lot of instructions and details on what we should do or avoid doing. That day you drove us to the airport and accompanied us till the last moment, and by then I had already understood that you were very much aware of what you were risking. The airport was one of the key points controlled by the military and the police; we were all very tense and nervous. We passed through the controls and nothing happened. There we said good-bye and I never saw you again, though I had your news from my brother. We flew to the Iguazu River and walked up to the border, not taking a taxi or a bus, as you had suggested. There we waited for the last boat, which belonged to smugglers, and where the military controls were a bit looser, yet I can't begin to tell you how long those minutes seemed to last when we stood before the soldiers who were checking my identity card.

We entered Brazil and took the coach to Río de Janeiro, where I lived for a few months in a Jesuit community. There I said good-bye to my brother Juan who had been with me during all those difficult times.

Later I took refuge in the United Nations and flew to Germany, where they granted me political asylum, but that is another story.

A few days ago, I was with some friends when my mobile rang. It was my brother Juan, who was shouting: "Gonzalo, have you seen? They've elected Bergoglio pope!" We couldn't believe it, because it didn't seem possible that your name could come out, our joy was immense.

But nearly at the same time news began to appear in the newspapers and on the radio, where they began to accuse you of having collaborated with the dictatorship, of having betrayed two Jesuits, and so on. Everything that you already know.

So I called my brothers to come to supper with me, and I told them that I intended to go to the press and recount everything that you had done for me. They agreed. So I chose a very important Uruguayan journalist, known for his impartiality, to tell him the whole story we had lived through. After a few days many other newspapers and television channels transmitted that interview and called me up. I was interviewed by *La Nación*, *Clarín*, the University of Buenos Aires, and also CNN, French Radio-Télévision, etc.

In the interviews I always laid stress on your courage and clearness of mind, not only as a person but also in an institutional sense, because you were the Provincial of the Jesuits, running risks for me, a stranger.

I took the liberty of doing it not only because I owed it to you, but because it was a kind of contribution to the truth, always so relative during the periods of history we are called on to live through. Very difficult, confused historical times, times of extremism, with partial and biased information, during which all of us made many mistakes.

On the day of your election, you asked us to pray for you. I asked God to grant you, in the life which is beginning now, the same clearness of mind, the same courage and commitment which you showed thirty-six years ago in such difficult circumstances.

I still feel the need to embrace you and thank you.

Gonzalo Mosca

P.S. I never thought I would be writing a letter to the pope.

# 7

# Toward the Exile

"I joined the Society to study, not to look after pigs!" the seminarian Ernesto Giobando protests one day to Jorge Bergoglio, then Rector of the Colegio Máximo. "First go and feed the pigs, that's what the Society is asking of you now, then go and study," the future pope, then forty-two, wisely replies.

After the hard years as Provincial, Bergoglio occupies the post of Rector of the Colegio Máximo from 1979 to 1985. He teaches theology but doesn't stop at what is in the books. Neither does he shut himself up in his office. He preaches by example.

Bergoglio is an unconventional rector. He does the washing, cooks for everyone, works in the fields, and even takes care of the pigs. And he keeps the doors of the Colegio Máximo open to welcome the people of the poor areas that surround it. He gives away land and builds five churches, most with Jesuit names: the parish Church of St. Joseph the Patriarch—a saint he is devoted to—of which he will become parish priest; then St. Francis Xavier, in the Manuelita neighborhood; St. Alonso Rodríguez, in Don Alfonso; St. Peter Claver, in Parque; and the Holy Martyrs.

"We used to get up at six and go to pray at six thirty. During that time, Bergoglio would wash and hang out the washing. On Sundays he sometimes waited for us with food. These things came naturally to him, not that he was supposed to do them. I worked for several years in the pig sty, and the thing that was most beautiful, that gave us more strength, was that he stood next to us, rolled up his sleeves, and wielded the spade. He wasn't the kind to stay behind a desk. For a young seminarian these are very important things. You remember them," said Father Giobando.

"He was a man of God but also a man who is able to govern—a rare, indeed unique, combination. He didn't lose the spiritual dimension, but neither did he lose the human one. . . . He enjoyed cooking but also eating . . . he used to cook us paella—that was spectacular! He also appreciated music and literature," recalls Father Ángel Rossi, a Jesuit.

These are the 1980s, the dictatorship is about to end, and democracy is about to blossom. Even the Colegio Máximo is living its spring. At this time there is a boom in vocations; the seminaries are filling up, and the same holds for Colegio Máximo. The classrooms are full again, and not only with Jesuits. Franciscan and Scalabrinian seminarians are also studying there, as external students.

"He invited Father Jean-Yves Calvez, a Frenchman, one of the most expert Jesuits on Marxism and one of Arrupe's counselors, to teach at the Colegio Máximo. That's how we met to discuss the fourth decree of the Thirty-Second General Congregation of the Society of Jesus on faith and justice. But apart from this intellectual side, he insisted on going into the poor quarters and meeting people, to be a missionary among the people, always within a religious identity that aimed at the promotion of popular piety. This movement of study and popular practice led to the International Congress on the Evangelization of Culture and the Inculturation of the Gospel, held at San Miguel at the end of Bergoglio's rectorship, in 1985. It was immediately accompanied by a great popular mission to the poor areas to celebrate the 450 years of the Jesuits' presence in Argentina," Father Yáñez recounts.

When Bergoglio, a man of leadership with clear ideas, becomes rector, he organizes life inside the Colegio Máximo and revises the plan for studies at a general level. As he had done as Provincial, he starts up another phase of academic reorganization. After the Second Vatican Council, theology had begun to be studied together with philosophy. But Bergoglio takes a step back, convinced that it is better not to mix things in order to study them better.

The changes give rise to tensions. But what foments the negative image of the hard and repressive Jesuit is the fact that he imposes timetables and strict discipline in the Colegio Máximo. "We had to ask permission to go out. We weren't locked up, but perhaps before then we could go out more freely. We didn't have to ask Bergoglio for permission but a coordinator, and there had to be a reason and he had to know where we were going. That's how it was," Father Yáñez explains.

Father James Kelly, an Irish Jesuit who was teaching in Buenos Aires at the time and lived at Colegio Máximo for four years, doesn't hide his amazement at the "capacity for leadership" of Bergoglio, who, thanks to Kelly, would go to a Jesuit center in Dublin in January 1980 to learn English.

In what will be a constant trait in his life, Bergoglio always tries to help people who are suffering—the poorest, the excluded, the marginalized—in a practical way.

"Once I was right in the middle of eight days of spiritual exercises and, on the fourth day, Bergoglio called me and said, 'Don't come back to the seminary till you have found a home for that lady here, outside the door; she has four children and no roof over her head.' I had no peace until I had found a home for her, obviously with the economic help of the Society. Another time, Paulina, the secretary in the chapel St. Francis Xavier of the Manuelita neighborhood, was informed that her mother, who was living in Italy, was very ill. Paulina couldn't stop crying because she knew she didn't have enough money to go and see her. Bergoglio called me and gave me a round-trip ticket for her," Father Rossi recalls.

"There were always a lot of people who were given meals and other material assistance. They turned up at the Colegio Máximo and immediately Bergoglio would send one of us to visit one family or another, to find out what their needs were and how they could be helped. Bergoglio founded schools for children and a professional school to help young people find work. Besides catechism he would organize various leisure activities for children on the weekends. And Bergoglio involved us at every stage," Father Yáñez says.

"He was always a very simple character, ready to do anything. He would treat a cultured, high-class person like any humble worker, and occasionally he would take up cooking, which he adored doing. He even passed on to me a recipe I have used a lot and which I later called chicken *à la cardinala*," Father Swinnen recalls.

Bergoglio becomes a kind of super-hero for the hundreds of children from the working-class neighborhoods that surround the huge Colegio Máximo. "Padre Jorge was always concerned about what was happening in the area. So his home, the Colegio Máximo, was also our home. We studied catechism there, and I learned what a cinema was. It was the big Saturday program: we saw films like *Star Wars* or *Snow White and the Seven Dwarfs* and also a documentary on the World Cup in Argentina in 1978. How we cheered for the goals scored in a World Cup won four years before! He let us go to the cinema for free . . . [On] Children's Day (which in Argentina is celebrated on the second Sunday of August) we all went to the Colegio Máximo to enjoy hot chocolate and games, and to pray and bless the meal. And we left happily with the toys Father Jorge gave us, because sometimes our parents didn't have enough money to buy any and we knew that the Jesuits would not disappoint us," says Daniel López, now forty, with a degree in business administration and one of my most faithful followers on Twitter. I manage to contact him on the day of Bergoglio's election, when he tweets that the new pope had given him his first communion.

"Father Jorge even organized our summer vacations. I saw the sea for the first time, thanks to the camps at Chapadmalal, which he organized with his priests, even if he didn't come. I went every summer, from 1984 to 1987," says Daniel, and adds, "His Masses were sublime: he would come down from the pulpit and approach the whole parish personally. When he preached his sermon, he would make us shout: 'Long live the pope! Long live Jesus! Long live the Virgin Mary!' and then at the end, the icing on the cake, 'Long live the glorious patriarch Saint Joseph!'" During those Masses, always crowded, there weren't only acclamations. He talked about evil, too—and the devil, who is always waiting to ambush us, is booed. Once a boy actually shouted at Satan, "Son of a bitch!" (which in Argentina doesn't sound as bad as it does in other countries), identifying himself completely in the teaching of the inspiring and charismatic Father Jorge.

"He organized his seminarians in teams to pick up all the children, including me, and take them to Mass. And early on Sunday mornings it was quite usual to see those little priests looking for us through the streets of the quarter . . . When he wasn't at Sunday Mass he would ask us to pray for him. The times he wasn't there to say Mass we missed him. It wasn't the same thing," Daniel goes on.

Every now and then Padre Jorge makes a surprise visit to see the children in the soccer fields that he created next to the Church of St. Joseph the Patriarch. And he organizes championships between the five parishes in the area. "We were very happy because he brought little holy pictures, which the seminarians later handed round," says Daniel, who received his first communion from the future pope at the age of nine and today is devoted to St. Joseph, as the pope is.

"How did Father Jorge teach the catechism? He was a legend; we had him during our last year, because the regular catechism was taught by the seminarians . . . Then there was confirmation in 1983, and a Bishop authorized the parish priest to give confirmation, because Father Jorge was not yet a Bishop . . . What do I remember most about him? The Stations of the Cross of Holy Week. And if it was raining he didn't bother about mud on his shoes. He was a perfect Jesuit: he taught me to bless my meal, to thank whoever had made it, to be a faithful and loyal Christian, a decent person, to know how to give and to share—and to live by the values of St. Ignatius of Loyola," Daniel adds.

Mario Fabián Maidana, Daniel's former schoolmate and today a sports journalist, also clearly remembers Father Jorge and his time camping with the priests, thanks to which many children first saw the sea. "Before we boarded the coaches and left, Jorge would appear, always smiling at those happy little faces. And he gave us his blessing, asking St. Joseph and the Virgin Mary to enlighten us."

Nora Mabel Castro also meets Father Jorge in the parish of St. Joseph the Patriarch in 1980. She is living near the Colegio Máximo, she is young, and she likes helping others and dreams of becoming a missionary. The Jesuits carrying out pastoral duties in that parish call her to be a catechist. She, too, comes from a humble neighborhood family. She works and studies at the same time, and she waits eagerly for the weekend, when she gathers the children in a field and gives them catechism lessons.

Father Jorge, who is supervising the groups at the time, doesn't hesitate to help her when she loses her job. "I was living with my parents, who were ill, I talked a lot with him and managed to find work at the Colegio Máximo, in the printing works. Since that day I have always thought that God had put him on my path. I entrusted all of myself to him and adopted him as my father confessor, and told him that I would work with all my strength for the parish. I always wanted to do more," Nora recalls, adding, "I liked him when he walked down the corridors of the Colegio Máximo with his hands behind his back, chatting with some Jesuit brother and going back and forth. And I thought that I should like to confess in this way, walking up and down the corridors and looking at the floor. He listened to me and then gave rules, firmly, with decision. Once I told him that I should like to become a missionary, go to Chaco and live with the indios [the native people], and he said, 'No, you can be a missionary here, we need you. In fact, I name you the first woman Jesuit.' And he gave me a little cross, like the ones they used, and I was beside myself with joy, even though I knew that there couldn't be women Jesuits. But what he said was sacred for me, and so, as far as I'm concerned I'm still the first woman Jesuit."

According to Nora, Padre Jorge is different from the others. "What did he have that was different from the other Jesuits? First of all humility, kindness, the desire to help, in different and splendid ways—and I'm not the only one who says so. He didn't like pretending or showing off; he was simple in soul and in deed."

While working at the Colegio Máximo, Nora types *Meditaciones para religiosos*, one of the many books that Bergoglio has written. Even though she doesn't expect to get married, in June 1987 Nora meets Ricardo Nazario Kinen, whose nickname is "Gringo," and changes her mind. He also belongs to the parish and in September asks for her hand. Nora says that if they aren't married by Padre Jorge, she won't get married at all.

"One day I went to him and said, 'Father, I must tell you something. This is my boyfriend. We want you to marry us on March 19, St. Joseph's feast day; you can't refuse me.' He greeted my (future) husband in a very friendly way and said to me, 'Ah, you've finally got one!' and gave me his telephone number," she recalls with a smile that transforms her face.

Nora, the first woman Jesuit, gets married on March 19, 1988, St. Joseph's Day. Jorge Bergoglio celebrates the marriage in the parish of St. Joseph the Patriarch, together with three Jesuit priests: Ernesto López Rosas, Alejandro Gauffin, and Ernesto Giobando.

"I wondered, *why so many priests—are they afraid I'll run away?* It was a lovely ceremony and my husband loved Father Jorge at once, because before I reached the altar he had won him over by speaking to him in German." As always, after any ceremony followed by a social event, Father Jorge did not attend Nora's wedding party. But his gift is her honeymoon: train tickets to Mendoza and money for expenses.

Nora gives birth to her first daughter, Flavia, on May 29, 1989. She stops working to look after her. On January 12, 1991, her second daughter, Estefanía, is born, and on April 15, 1992, a son, José María. These are difficult times. There is never enough money; every now and then she rings up Father Jorge but doesn't dare ask him for help.

On December 17, 1993—the day Father Jorge, already Auxiliary Bishop of Buenos Aires, turns fifty-seven—Nora's husband dies in a tragic accident. Shortly after, Bergoglio invites her to meet him at the archbishopric. She tells him that she needs to work, because now she is a widow; her pension is not sufficient, and she must look after the house and feed her three children. "But do you really believe you can work? You'd be out of the house twelve hours a day. . . . There's no question about it! I'll help you as much as I can, so you won't need to go out to work," he told her.

From then on Nora goes to the archbishopric once a month to pick up an envelope containing the equivalent of a salary, to which Padre Jorge adds two holy pictures: one of Mary Untier of Knots and one of St. Joseph.

"Every month, for years, he never missed the commitment he had taken on. Five years ago, in 2008, since I was ashamed of still depending on him, I asked him again to admit me to the Universidad del Salvador, even if he always went on helping me. Every time I went to see him with my children he always told his secretary, Otilia, to go and get soft drinks and sweets for them. Once Father Jorge turned up with a puppet of a little clown playing a drum in a box and gave it to my little boy . . . During those years I wasn't well and had problems, and decided to talk to him. I wanted to ask him to bless me and pray for me, because he was a direct intermediary with the Lord . . . But he was always ahead of me: 'Pray for me, Nora,' he said. And I thought, *Damn! He has got there before me again!*"

In 1985, before leaving his position as rector, Jorge Bergoglio organizes the International Congress on the Evangelization of Culture and the Inculturation of the Gospel at the Colegio Máximo. In a speech he defines Pedro Arrupe as "a man who is a father for all Jesuits." "We have grasped the need to learn the logic of the people we live with and apply this same logic to evangelization," he goes on. But Arrupe is no longer Superior General, the head of the Society, owing to serious health problems. John Paul II takes advantage of this to intervene in the Order to oppose progressive positions. In September 1983 the Dutchman Peter-Hans Kolvenbach is elected head of the Jesuits.

Antonio Quarracino, the son of Italian immigrants like Bergoglio and at the time Archbishop of La Plata, attends the International Congress on the Evangelization of Culture and the Inculturation of the Gospel; he is to play a fundamental role in the destiny of the future pope.

The following year, while Bergoglio is at the Colegio Máximo, a sort of counterreformation begins; authorities introduce many changes, the opposite of those carried out by Bergoglio. Bergoglio asks for permission to go to Germany. He intends to write a thesis on the Italian (naturalized German) theologian Romano Guardini (1885–1968), whom he greatly admires (he is also admired by Benedict XVI). In March 1986 he arrives at the Jesuit Sankt Georgen Graduate School of Philosophy and Theology in Frankfurt, where, in the library, he finds a full bibliography on Guardini.

During his stay in Germany, Bergoglio travels around the country. It is in the Church of St. Peter am Perlach, in Augsburg, that he discovers for himself and falls in love with the picture of the Virgin Mary, untying knots in a ribbon that two angels are offering her. It is the by-now famous Mary Untier of Knots, whose cult he is to import to Argentina through holy pictures. He then promotes the building of a sanctuary with the replica of the picture enthroned in the Church of San José del Talar, in the Agronomía neighborhood of Buenos Aires.

At this time he spends two months of study at the Goethe Institute of Boppard, in Rhineland-Palatinate. He is the guest of Helma and Joseph Schmidt, a couple now in their nineties, whom he is still in touch with by post. "He was very humble, very simple, very normal," says Helma. "He would always pray as he walked in the garden and never stopped sending us news and good wishes for Christmas and Easter," she added, showing a pile of old envelopes that she never thought would acquire so much value over time.

While he is in Germany, Bergoglio, who defines himself as a homebody, not a great traveler, is homesick. "I remember that when I was in Frankfurt to write my thesis, in the evening I would walk to the cemetery. From there you could see the airport. Once I met a friend who asked me what I was doing there, and I answered, 'I'm waving to the airplanes—the airplanes going to Argentina,'" Francis reveals in *The Jesuit*.

Although some say that Bergoglio didn't finish his thesis because his superiors called him back to Argentina (at the time the Provincial was Father Víctor Zorzín) and sent him to Córdoba in exile, the true story is very different. It's Bergoglio who asks to return. Not so much because he is homesick, but because he thinks he must make an attempt to stop the effects of the counterreformation started in the Order, which he does not believe in.

"Many people would have been happy if Bergoglio had stayed in Germany for quite a few years, to finish his thesis. But he wanted to return to Argentina," one source declares.

With books and photocopies on Guardini under his arm, he goes to live in the Colegio del Salvador in Buenos Aires. His plan is to present his thesis (which he will never complete) at the Colegio Máximo, where he goes on giving lectures on pastoral theology.

The Society is facing internal difficulties and struggles. Bergoglio still enjoys great credibility in most of the Order and is elected Procurator for a congregation of the Society in Rome in 1987, after which he travels to Japan. In spite of his trips abroad and within Argentina to visit and inform various Jesuit communities about what is happening, the presence in Buenos Aires of Bergoglio, a man of great influence, is troublesome to those who don't like his style of ministry and leadership.

To neutralize him, or rather, "to remove him from the map," his superiors relieve him of his chair of pastoral theology at the Colegio Máximo, without warning, on June 25, 1990. They decide to send him as confessor to the main residence of Córdoba, a virtual exile that starts on June 16, 1990, and ends on May 20, 1992. "At that time he was my teacher of pastoral theology, and they took away his class. The rector said, 'Bergoglio won't be coming back to teach theology here.' There was a very painful reaction—we were all struck dumb. Bergoglio's exile was a traumatic event for the Jesuits," says Father Giobando.

Not many Jesuits want to speak about this period, when Bergoglio's telephone calls were censored and his correspondence controlled. Speaking with a Cardinal about those old and painful experiences, Francis draws a parallel with the family: "In a family there may be differences, but the family always stays united and strong."

"Córdoba was something humanly unjust, but he transformed it into a period of gestation. It was a time of loneliness, but for great men like him, exile strengthens the soul. Those who had decided to exile him did him a great favor in the end," Father Rossi affirms.

"In the Society you may first go very high and then find yourself at the bottom, sociologically speaking. There is no doubt that what happened was the consequence of his leadership. He was a charismatic personality; during his exercise of government he kept a very clear and well-defined profile, and he wasn't ready to negotiate. He doesn't like compromises—he goes to the bottom of what he sees and feels to be the will of God . . . Even if it's history—and I believe it's not a good thing to go into details about something that is now over and done with—neither the Society nor Bergoglio stopped there. All of us Jesuits are very much aware that it was a difficult time. We don't deny it, but we know that in this case no one has the absolute truth of the matter. We all had to go through a profound transformation. Many people stayed on track, others were hurt, and yet others did not succeed in overcoming that moment," declares Giobando.

The present Superior General, the Spaniard Adolfo Nicolás, who celebrated Mass with Pope Francis, the first Jesuit pope, at the beginning of his pontificate, is very clear in the letter addressed to the whole of the Society of Jesus on March 26, 2013: "Pope Francis deeply feels himself to be a Jesuit and has shown this on many occasions in the last few days." After making clear the wish of the Society to be near to the Holy Father, he promises the unconditional support of all the brothers of the Order: "every resource of ours and our help, both in the theological field and in the scientific, administrative and spiritual ones, in view of the complex questions and problems he will have to face." And he warns, "This is the moment to make our own the words of mercy and kindness that Pope Francis repeats in such a convincing way and not allow ourselves to be moved by the distractions of the past, which could paralyze our hearts and lead us to interpret reality according to values that are not inspired by the Gospel."

# 8

# The Return to Buenos Aires

Jorge Bergoglio lives the twenty-two months of his exile in the main residence of Córdoba, from July 1990 to May 1992, with resignation. He prays a great deal, and in his prayers he includes those who have condemned him to such an unjust exile. He is the confessor and spiritual director of the principal Jesuit church in Argentina; he helps people, organizes spiritual retreats, and offers aid.

"He took advantage of his stay in Córdoba to read and write. There was no need for a special authorization for that. During that period he may have tried to continue the doctoral thesis in theology he had started in Germany. Because he had occupied many roles within the Order—as Provincial for six and a half years, Rector of the Colegio Máximo for six more in addition to other long periods dedicated to teaching—he was in touch with an enormous number of people. I imagine that answering the letters he received must have taken him quite some time," says Father Ignacio Pérez del Viso, a Jesuit and professor at the Philosophical and Theological Faculty of San Miguel.

Bergoglio has played a key role in the internal Jesuit struggles of the preceding years. He is convinced that if God now wants him to stay in the main residence of Córdoba, he must accept this, like a good Jesuit. In fact, he accepts it to the point of imagining that his life will go on there for many years, in exile.

But the divine plan is different. Antonio Quarracino, Archbishop of Buenos Aires and Cardinal Primate, appears in Bergoglio's life and releases him from exile. Born in 1922 in Pollica, a village in the province of Salerno, Italy, Quarracino immigrated to Argentina when he was very young. President of the Argentine Episcopal Conference and the Latin American Episcopal Conference, Quarracino concentrates his attention on Bergoglio soon after Bergoglio becomes Provincial in 1973.

Quarracino attends the International Congress on the Evangelization of Culture and the Inculturation of the Gospel organized by Bergoglio in the Colegio Máximo in 1985. Years later, he will take part in a spiritual retreat that Bergoglio organizes in Córdoba, at his request, for about thirty priests from Buenos Aires.

Determined to make this brilliant Jesuit, son of Piedmontese immigrants, his right-hand man in Buenos Aires, Quarracino moves heaven and earth. Thanks to his influence in the Vatican and the support of the nuncio to Argentina at that time, Monsignor Ubaldo Calabresi, who also looks favorably on this brilliant and charismatic Jesuit whom he often consults on various matters, Quarracino works hard to reach his goal.

"Quarracino had been president of the Latin American Episcopal Conference and knew the reality of Latin America very well. He was perfectly aware of who was who in Argentina and knew that Bergoglio was a trustworthy man for the Holy See," said Carlos Velasco Suárez.

Bergoglio's career is well known in the Vatican. They know that he became Provincial at a dramatic time and that he acted prudently and firmly to stay on the right path. According to the files the nunciature prepared on him, starting from the beginning of the 1980s, the Holy See considers Bergoglio to have all the qualities required to become Bishop.

Quarracino has a very clear vision of what is happening inside the Church at that time. It's during the first term of Carlos Menem and his neoliberal government. And Quarracino brings to Rome the name of this Jesuit—who is not greatly loved by a certain sector of the Jesuits—because he possesses two important qualities: he is a true man of God (Quarracino calls him *el santito*, "the little saint"), and he has a practical intelligence. On May 20, 1992, Quarracino achieves his aim, when John Paul II designates Jorge Bergoglio titular Bishop of Auca and Auxiliary Bishop of Buenos Aires.

Bergoglio receives the news from the nuncio Monsignor Calabresi that the destiny that had confined him to exile almost 450 miles from Buenos Aires now has a surprise in store for him.

"Calabresi called me to consult with him about some priests who were candidates to be bishops. One day he called me up and told me that the consultation had to be confidential. Since the airline company ran the Buenos Aires—Córdoba—Mendoza flights, he asked me to meet him at the [Córdoba] airport while the airplane flew to Mendoza and back. We started talking—it was May 13, 1992—and he asked me for advice on several serious issues. And when the airplane, which had already returned from Mendoza, was ready to go back to Buenos Aires and the passengers were being called to get ready for boarding, he said, 'Ah—just one more thing . . . You have been appointed Auxiliary Bishop of Buenos Aires, and the news will be made public on the twentieth.' He told me just like that, as if it were not important," recounts Bergoglio in *The Jesuit.*

How can a Jesuit become a Bishop if, apart from his solemn vows, he has made another vow that during his life he will not seek to obtain any position outside the Society of Jesus? "The vow of obedience to the Roman pontiff prevails," explains Father Gianfranco Ghirlanda, Jesuit and expert in canon law at the Pontifical Gregorian University.

"In the case of his episcopal nomination, it is obvious that it could be ordered only by the Superior General of the Society of Jesus (at the time Peter-Hans Kolvenbach), on the instruction of John Paul II in person and now, in the case of the papal election, only Jesus," he adds.

On June 27, 1992, Bergoglio is ordained Bishop in the cathedral of Buenos Aires by Antonio Quarracino; the apostolic nuncio Calabresi; and the Archbishop of Mercedes-Luján, Monsignor Emilio Ogñénovich.

As Auxiliary Bishop of Buenos Aires, Bergoglio is not alone. There are five other auxiliaries: Monsignor Héctor Aguer, since 1998 Archbishop of

La Plata; the Monsignor Raúl Rossi; Rubén Frassia, Bishop of Avellaneda-Lanús; the Monsignor Mario José Serra; and Monsignor Eduardo Mirás, Archbishop Emeritus of Rosario.

Bergoglio is immediately nominated Episcopal Vicar of Flores, the district where he was born. He knows the area by heart. He moves into a hundred-year-old two-story building at 581 Calle Condarco, with its high ceilings and big windows. The building occupies half the block and is within a few meters of the bustling Dr. T. Álvarez Hospital and the Avenida Avellaneda, where the Hogar Sacerdotal (a home for retired priests) stands today.

After his exile in Córdoba, Bergoglio feels he is a man reborn. This is the neighborhood of his childhood and youth, with its trees, its quiet paved lanes, and its people. A few blocks from the seat of the vicariate stands the Church of San José de Flores, "his" church. Here, when he was seventeen, God chose him after he had made a confession. It was September 21, 1953, the first day of spring, Students' Day, but also the feast day of the apostle Matthew. This is the saint who inspired him when he chose his episcopal motto: *Miserando atque eligendo*, which translates roughly as "He [Jesus] looked at him with mercy and chose him." It is a passage from a homily by St. Bede, a Benedictine monk, who was commenting on the Gospel account of the calling of Matthew, a tax collector who gave up everything to follow Jesus. When he is elected pope, Bergoglio will keep this motto, together with his episcopal coat of arms, characterized by simplicity and the presence of the letters *IHS*, symbol of the Society of Jesus.

Bergoglio is fifty-five when he begins his new life as Auxiliary Bishop, and he is not well-known among the Buenos Aires clergy. Owing to the negative reputation and rumors that have been woven around him, some of them don't even trust him.

"When I met him, a little more than twenty years ago, he didn't have good references. It was a question of his career in the Society of Jesus and the different situations he had lived through," admits Carlos Accaputo, president of the social pastoral ministry of the archbishopric of Buenos Aires, who would become one of the key advisors of Bergoglio. "When they made him Auxiliary of Buenos Aires, I said to myself, 'Oh Lord! The same old soup...' I had two religious friends, Alba and María Agustina, who knew him intimately and spoke very well of him. Alba said to me, 'Let's eat an *asado* [barbecue] together, so you can get to know him.' 'First I want to meet him, then we can have an *asado*,' I answered. On the day of his episcopal ordination, I go to Mass and begin to see that people go to greet him. And I discover that there are very poor people there, people from the district of San Miguel where he had worked as a pastor. I realized something didn't fit... what was happening? One day I was giving a lecture on the social doctrine of the Church in a church of Flores and the parish priest said to me, 'Carlos, Monsignor Bergoglio called and wants to come and talk to you after your lecture.' At twelve o'clock he was there. We went to talk in the priest's room. I was sitting on the bed, he was on a chair, or vice versa, I don't remember, and we drank some *mate* [typical Argentine herbal drink]. And he says to me, 'Listen, I've come to see you because I want you to work with me at the Flores Caritas.' And I answer, 'No problem, but first you must know what I'm like and what I think, then you can tell me what you want to do. I'm an orthodox thinker, neither a conservative nor a progressive. Conservatives create a model into which they insert people and say, if you live your faith in this way, you are a Catholic. Otherwise, no. And the progressives make so many speeches that at times they end up emptying the faith of any meaning. Faith is much more than that. I believe that faith is for living, so that everyone can receive it.' And I tell him my points of disagreement with Monsignor Quarracino, who was the Archbishop and whose great friend I later became... And Bergoglio says to me, 'Very good, fine.' And so we began to build a relationship," recalls Accaputo.

"When Bergoglio arrived in Buenos Aires as Auxiliary Bishop and we started to understand the way he was, it seemed as if the Holy Spirit had breathed into us. The television production company covered the episcopal ordination, and he radiated fatherhood," says Julio Rimoldi, who at the time worked in a company that produced social and journalistic documentaries in the television center of the Archdiocese and who, years later, would become director of the Archdiocese's Channel 21.

The Episcopal Vicar of Flores, a man of action, walks along the streets and visits the parishes, where he arrives without notice. He drinks *mate* with the priests, talks with them, and tries to understand their situations. Buenos Aires is a very lively metropolis, full of corruption and contradictions. But as a good *porteño* (native of the city of Buenos Aires), he recognizes when there's something fishy going on. Bergoglio relates this story in connection to bribery among the clergy in *On Heaven and Earth*:

> Once, at the time of "one to one" [when Carlos Menem was president in the 1980s, and one Argentine peso equaled one US dollar], two officials came to see me at the seat of the Flores vicariate, saying that they had some money for the districts that were in emergency conditions. They introduced themselves as very Catholic and after a while offered me four hundred thousand pesos as aid for the shantytowns. It seemed odd to me. I began to ask them what their plans were. And finally they told me that though I was to sign a receipt for the four hundred thousand pesos, they would give me only half. I got out of the situation gracefully because the offices of the vicariates didn't have bank accounts, and neither did I. So I told them that they would have to deposit the money directly to the curia, which accepted donations only in the form of checks or when shown the receipt of a bank deposit. The characters disappeared. If those people came with such a proposal without any problem, I imagine it was because in the past some clergyman or religious had accepted such an operation.

Bergoglio is Episcopal Vicar of Flores, but as further proof that Quarracino has great plans for him, the Cardinal promotes the future pope to be his Vicar General on December 21, 1993. As he is now second only to the Archbishop, his responsibilities increase. He takes on administrative and organizational functions and intensifies relations with the priests of the Archdiocese of Buenos Aires, to whom he begins communicating his chief concerns: poverty, education, and dialogue between religions. None of this stops him from keeping a low profile. Bergoglio never forgets the wise advice that his father used to repeat to him: "Greet people while you go up, because you will meet them again when you come down. Don't think you are somebody special (in Spanish, *no te la creas*)." This is to be one of the keys to his success.

As Vicar General, Bergoglio starts to show strong support for the team of priests in the shantytowns.

"He used to visit the poor districts, be with the priests, and it was there that he began to forge that link and got to know life in the shantytowns better," says Father "Pepe" Di Paola, leader of the priests working in the shantytowns, who has known Bergoglio since 1994. "In 1997 Cardinal Quarracino nominated me parish priest of Caacupé [in the Villa 21 area of the Barracas neighborhood of Buenos Aires] . . . on Bergoglio's request. There was a great Paraguayan immigration, so we brought the statue of the Virgin of Caacupé there on August 23, 1997, with the idea of celebrating the tenth anniversary of the parish, but also to take advantage of the holiday to mobilize people. A group went to Paraguay to fetch the image of the Virgin, and the whole community went on pilgrimage to the cathedral to take it back to the Villa 21. That day I said good-bye to Bergoglio in the cathedral and walked on with the people, carrying the image of the Virgin toward our church. We stopped in a number of churches on the way, and when we reached the Church of Santa Lucía, between Montes de Oca and Martín García streets, already in Barracas, a lady said to me, 'Have you seen that man in a poncho? But isn't it the Bishop?' And indeed so he was, with a rosary in his hand. I was surprised, because as Bishop he could have made it evident that he was accompanying us, but he hadn't said anything and had mingled with the people. Someone called me, saying, 'Hey, they're looking for Bergoglio because he has to sign some papers. Hasn't he come with you?' And I answered, 'No, I said good-bye to him in the cathedral.'"

In *The Jesuit*, Bergoglio recalls his resistance to further promotion: "Since I was the Vicar General, when Quarracino asked Rome for a coadjutor [a Bishop with the right of succession in the Archdiocese], I asked him not to send me to any diocese but to let me come back to being an Auxiliary

Bishop in a district of Buenos Aires. 'I come from Buenos Aires, and outside that city I'm incapable of doing anything,' I explained to him."

Once more it is the apostolic nuncio Ubaldo Calabresi who informs him about the new challenge. "On May 27, 1997, around midmorning, Calabresi called me and invited me to lunch. After coffee, when I was about to thank him for his invitation and say good-bye, I saw that they'd brought in a cake and a bottle of sparkling wine. I thought it was his birthday and was going to congratulate him. But when I asked him if it was, there was a surprise. 'No, it's not my birthday,' he answered with a big smile. 'The fact is that you're the new Coadjutor Bishop of Buenos Aires,'" recalls Bergoglio, who admits that he is once more struck dumb with surprise.

Logically, this designation means that he will be the next Archbishop of Buenos Aires, the first from the Jesuit Order. The news is a bombshell in the ecclesiastical world of Argentina. In the past, to become the Archbishop of the Argentine capital (an important see that brings with it the cardinal's red hat), one first had to be a Bishop in another city. But in this case the procedure is not respected.

On June 3, 1997, just as Calabresi had announced, the designation is made public.

Becoming Bishop Coadjutor with the right of succession represents another promotion in record time. Shortly after, on February 28, 1998, Quarracino's unexpected death catapults Bergoglio to the head of the Archdiocese of Buenos Aires, which could become a springboard to the papacy.

"Quarracino pulled him out of a place where nobody knew him and brought him to the episcopate without any of the Buenos Aires clergy knowing him. And he prepared him to become Archbishop. I believe Bergoglio was always very grateful to Quarracino for all this, he has always been very loyal to him," says Monsignor Óscar Ojea, the present Bishop of San Isidro.

"Quarracino didn't have a happy end—he was ill, he had to deal with certain bankers from the city of La Plata, he was considered too close to President Menem. But the Quarracino of earlier days, before he went to

La Plata and to Buenos Aires, was a man of great kindness and brotherly feeling," says José María Poirier, director of the journal *Criterio*. "Quarracino was greatly esteemed in Rome because he was very loyal to the pope. Later he was discredited by the Latin American Episcopal Conference because he was unable to get the contrasting positions to agree, and though he had always been very open, he ended his life, strangely, branded as a conservative. Although he made many political mistakes, he was able to spot Bergoglio," comments Poirier.

It is not without significance that, when John Paul II ordains him as Cardinal on February 21, 2001, Bergoglio decides to celebrate his first Mass on February 28, the anniversary of Quarracino's death. At this service, all the priests recite an Eternal Rest over his tomb in the cathedral of the capital. "It was a clear message: 'Everything I am, in the last resort, I owe to Quarracino,'" claimed a monsignor who witnessed that moving ceremony.

Just as he pays homage to Quarracino, so years later, when Calabresi, another man of providence, dies, Bergoglio does not hide his grief. "The death of a man I love strikes me to the heart," he confesses at a Mass in Calabresi's memory on June 17, 2004.

It makes sense. Calabresi was a true visionary, according to Carlos Cecchi, a dentist and friend of Bergoglio's for seventeen years and, before that, of the nuncio who discovered him. Cecchi recalls that one day Calabresi contacted him and said, "Carlitos, I want you to come to the nunciature because there is a priest of Flores who has dental problems . . . I believe that this man will do great things for the Church and for Argentina.'"

# 9

# A Different Sort of Archbishop

Years earlier, Jorge Bergoglio had to sail through stormy weather as the Provincial of the Jesuits. Now when Quarracino dies on February 28, 1998, and Bergoglio becomes the new Archbishop of Buenos Aires automatically, without an installation ceremony, destiny again puts him to the test. A time bomb explodes in his hands: the scandal of the bankruptcy of the Banco de Crédito Provincial (BCP, August 1997), which affects thousands of investors and involves the Archdiocese of Buenos Aires through the shady financial management of Monsignor Roberto Toledo, one of Quarracino's close collaborators.

The BCP is a bank with headquarters in La Plata, which during the 1990s starts to expand and collect investors. It is run by the sons of Francisco Trusso, a former Ambassador to the Vatican who had been appointed by Carlos Menem and is very friendly with Quarracino. In mid-1997, when a rumor spreads that the bank was in free fall, its customers begin withdrawing their savings, and the BCP begins to falter. At that point, Quarracino becomes involved in a suspicious operation. Trusso, who is in urgent need of cash, exploits his acquaintance with the Archbishop and manages to obtain a loan of ten million dollars from the Sociedad Militar Seguro de Vida, or SMSV (military life insurance). Trusso withdraws the money and escapes, leaving the Archbishop overwhelmed by the scandal. Quarracino falls seriously ill (doubtless with grief) and dies soon after.

Shortly after Bergoglio becomes Archbishop, the storm breaks when in a television program, the well-known journalist Jorge Lanata reveals the network of criminal offenses that involves the Catholic Church in a fraud engineered by the BCP—"God's bankers"—against a military company. So much so that on December 16, 1998—one day before Bergoglio's sixty-second birthday—the police search the archbishopbric in an unprecedented operation related to the fraudulent bankruptcy.

"The first thing Bergoglio did was to engage an international consultancy firm, Arthur Andersen, to audit all the accounts in order to see if the money was, or was not, there. Secondly, he presented all the accounts to the judge to prove that the money had not entered the Archdiocese. In addition there was an expert's report on handwriting analysis, which proved that the signature on the document according to which the Archdiocese received a loan from the SMSV [Sociedad Militar Seguro de Vida] was not Quarracino's. Subsequently, he [Bergoglio] made an agreement with the SMSV to act together against the bank, because in point of fact they had both been cheated," says Father Guillermo Marcó in an interview, who in the middle of this hurricane was nominated spokesman of the archbishopric.

Trusso is arrested in August 1999 in São Paulo after more than two years in hiding. As soon as his extradition to Argentina is confirmed, the banker flees again and is arrested on August 9, 2001, in Miramar, Argentina. Sentenced to eight years in jail for criminal association, repeated embezzlement, and administrative fraud, Trusso is released at the end of 2003 after the Archbishop of La Plata, Héctor Aguer, posts the million-peso bail to get him out of prison.

Another front against the Archbishop comes from within the Church: a conservative and orthodox wing, resentful of Bergoglio's nomination by Quarracino, seeks to discredit him. Some Argentine prelates go to Rome to attempt to denigrate him before a number of Vatican congregations.

After the death of Quarracino, Bergoglio's personal austerity and evangelical simplicity do not change. You don't need to live in a grand palace or
have a chauffeur or wear expensive clothes to announce the gospel. He
decides not to use the residence reserved for the Archbishop at Olivos, in
the province of Buenos Aires, and transforms it into a venue for spiritual
retreats. He prefers a small, simple apartment of the curia in Buenos Aires.
He doesn't even use the Cardinal's official study, with its antique furniture,
pictures, and elegant carpets, which is large enough for a whole family to
live in. He uses it to store books, sacks of flour, pasta, and other things
people give him—things that he, in turn, will give to those who need
them—and settles in a smaller and more modest office nearby.

When in February 2001 he is named Cardinal, Bergoglio follows the
same policy of austerity and asks anyone who wants to accompany him to
Rome to celebrate the event not to go and to give to the poor any money
they would have spent on the journey; this is advice he is to repeat when
he becomes pope. He doesn't buy a new scarlet vestment but adapts that
of his predecessor, Quarracino. "Even now that he is pope, he still uses the
same miter, which he has had since his ordination. And his chasuble is still
the same," says Father Silvio Rivera, director of the Hogar Sacredotal, the
home for elderly priests at 581 Condarco, in Flores.

On the day of the solemn ceremony of the imposition of the cardinal's
ring and biretta, he comes to the Vatican on foot. He hides his scarlet
vestment under a black coat. He likes to keep a low profile; he hates
ostentation.

He loves, though, public transport, which allows him to be in touch with
people's everyday lives (a shepherd must always be near his flock); he gives
away his official car, and he finds another job for the chauffeur. And when
he becomes Cardinal, he refuses the bodyguards that come with the new
position.

"Everyone knows that he's always been like that. Austere to the point
of sacrifice. Because you must admit that when you have weighty responsibilities, you must use the means that will allow you to make the best
use of time. But Bergoglio is consistent with his deeply felt choice of a life

of poverty. He has never felt that he deserves to be served, and his way of serving in a simple way, avoiding a show of superiority, is well known," says Father Víctor Manuel Fernández, Rector of the Universidad Católica Argentina (UCA) and designated Archbishop by Pope Francis.

Santiago de Estrada, former Ambassador of Argentina to the Holy See, recalls: "One day a nephew of mine, a priest, when leaving his seminary to take a taxi to visit his family, met Bergoglio, who asked him where he was going. On hearing the answer, the Cardinal said to him in a tactful way, 'Three blocks away bus number X passes. Why don't you come with me and we can take it together?' This was the way he exercised his authority."

Bergoglio is tireless. He has an enormous capacity for work. He listens to anyone who knocks at his door and establishes a personal, fatherly relationship with each one of the priests entrusted to him. Even if he will never have a mobile phone, everyone knows he can be reached. If you ring him early in the morning—he wakes at 4:15 to pray and do his spiritual exercises—he answers. Otherwise, later in the day, his personal secretaries, Otilia and Elisa, will make a note of the name of whoever calls and then he himself, without intermediaries, will call back. It's the same with the letters he receives; he answers them punctually.

"He has always accompanied every priest. He has always had the inclination to take care of his priests; you could go to him at any time. You could even say that you didn't agree with how he managed this or that . . . But to this day I have never seen a priest who asked him for help and didn't receive it. He is a man who practices mercy. Any man of government always has his strong points and weaknesses, because when you make decisions you always end up hurting or disappointing someone," says Father Accaputo.

The phrase Bergoglio believes in even after his election to the Throne of St. Peter is that priests should "smell of sheep." They should go to the existential peripheries, to help the lowest, the marginalized, and those who an "anesthetized" society calls "trash."

Above all he supports the so-called *curas villeros* (shantytown priests) and their work with the poorest in the slums of Buenos Aires, which is where he recovers and reaffirms the manifestation of popular religion.

"What interested him about our work was that we should be there, in the flesh. And that we pray," says Father Juan Isasmendi, a *villero* priest, since 2007 in the parish of Our Lady of Caacupé. "The first thing he asked you when you met him was, 'Have you prayed? Are you praying?' He always asked the same question. You sat down to talk to him and he said, 'Do you pray?' and the whole conversation turned on that," says the thirty-two-year-old priest from Salta.

Bergoglio gathers crowds in the Church of San Cayetano every August 7, to ask for bread and work; on the day of San Ramón Nonato, the protector of the unborn and the patron of pregnant women, on August 31; for the annual pilgrimage to the sanctuary of Our Lady of Luján, patron saint of Argentina; and on the feast of San Pantaleón, patron of the sick, in the Mataderos neighborhood.

He believes that power means service and wants a Church that is not self-referential, that isn't concerned with only its own interests, that isn't locked in on itself. And he repeats this as pope, always speaking in a frank, colloquial way, without beating about the bush. He prefers this to a Church that is sick and paralyzed; instead, a Church may stumble so long as it is going outward.

He is annoyed when he finds that there are priests who think "from the belt down," obsessed by sexual morality, or who refuse to impart a sacrament like baptism to the children of single mothers. He tells priests who take confession to be neither severe nor permissive but merciful.

"He always told priests not only to be merciful but to know how to adapt themselves to people, not to support morals or ecclesiastical practices that are rigid, and not to complicate people's lives with rules arbitrarily imposed from above. 'We are here to give the people what the people need' is a conviction he has always insisted on," says Archbishop Fernández.

"Every December 23 there was a queue of people in the archbishopric who were bringing him presents or simply wanted to greet him. He received them all, one by one. When someone regretted that he had gone to see him empty-handed, he would reply, 'You haven't brought me a gift, but now I shall give you one,'" recalls Father Silvio Rivera.

The Cardinal had planned to live there when he retired. He would have occupied room 13; it is on the ground floor, comfortable and simple, with a bed, a big wardrobe, a wooden bedside table, and a window that looks out onto one of the sunny courtyards. There is also a bathroom, and another room with a desk and a bookcase, intended for the reception of visitors.

Father Rivera, who calls himself Bergoglio's spiritual son and who sometimes accompanied him by car, will never forget his example. "Once I had prepared an envelope with some money that I had to return to him. While I was waiting for him in the car in front of the cathedral, I saw him stopping to talk to two people. When he finally boarded the car, I gave him the envelope and he held it in his hand, without looking at the money or counting it. It seemed odd to me, but I didn't ask him anything. After we had gone a few feet, he asked me to turn back. I obeyed without asking questions. Then he got out and went back to the people he had been talking to, and gave them my envelope. I found out later that they were father and son, and that someone had stolen the computer they were working with. They had been left with nothing. The money in the envelope was exactly what was necessary to buy a new computer . . . He was always like that; when he helped somebody he didn't hesitate even for a second. He often said to me, 'You must always have something for the poor when they need it, without thinking about how much it is.' Every time someone approached him to ask him for help, he would take everything he had in his pocket and give it to them, without looking."

As Archbishop, Bergoglio doesn't confine himself to inviting his priests to go to the peripheries. Consistent with his words, he himself goes out to meet people. Inaugurating a new missionary style, he celebrates the traditional washing of feet on Maundy (Holy) Thursday not in the cathedral of the capital but in hospitals, prisons, and maternity wards, where he approaches patients with HIV/AIDS, prisoners, and single mothers.

Doctor Alberto J. Benítez, former consultant of Unit 7 of the Ricardo Gutiérrez Children's Hospital, is impressed when, in April 2006, Bergoglio kneels in front of twelve sick children, whose feet he washes and kisses, repeating Jesus' act of "love to the very end" during the Last Supper. "One Thursday afternoon I went to the chapel of our hospital for the celebration of Maundy Thursday. Thanks to our chaplain, Father Juan de Aguirre, we knew that Cardinal Bergoglio was to preside over the ceremony. It was beginning to get dark when unexpectedly I saw the Cardinal coming toward me in the corridor, wearing his usual trousers and black jacket. He stopped to greet me. He told me that he had come early in case we needed anything. Luckily, Father Juan came to my aid and took him to visit the patients in intensive therapy. Because the Cardinal was to wash the feet of twelve child patients, we had to choose them. Many children wanted to be chosen. One of them suffered from hereditary epidermolysis and was in Unit 7 with serious lesions, especially in the lower limbs. I asked Father Juan if that could result in the Cardinal's refusal. He assured me that it couldn't. The Mass was full of emotion, affection, and religious feeling. He washed the feet of all the children who were there, including the patient with epidermolysis."

Benítez continues, "At the end we invited him for a coffee in the director's office. There were many people—the director, the nurses, the interns, the doctors, the cleaning staff, the maids, with the Cardinal sitting in the middle, chatting with us and enjoying the coffee. When he had to go, several of us offered to drive him. He said no, because there was a bus that would leave him exactly in front of the cathedral. He asked us only if we could open the gate on Gallo Street, to shorten his journey. He left on foot, as he had come. I shall never forget his humble, quiet, confident figure, his precious words full of love."

As Archbishop, Bergoglio shows a great capacity for leadership. He listens a great deal—he has an exceptional memory, typical of great states-men—reflects, selects, and compares information, and when he is alone, he makes a decision and then sticks to it. From my years of knowing him and my conversations with many others about him, I have learned that what he appreciates most in the person he is talking to is frankness, honesty, a direct way of expression. On these grounds, he respects everyone. He hates unclear speeches, ambiguity, and hypocrisy.

"Besides being a pastor, he is technically a very capable leader, a political animal. The two strongest features of his character are, on the one hand, being close to and interested in other people, and on the other, being a man who knows how to exercise authority. This is also evident in his relations with the clergy. The priests of Buenos Aires appreciate him greatly, and this is odd because it isn't usual for an Archbishop to be loved, because he represents authority. Bergoglio was very close to them, almost like a father, but at the same time it was always clear who was giving the orders," José María Poirier, director of the journal *Criterio*, affirms.

"He had a personality that won you over. With a few words, at times with just a gesture, his charisma as a leader came through. He charmed you with that very intelligent look, and an intimacy, a trust he knew how to create in any relationship. At those times he was completely there with you and for you, and was looking for points of agreement. There was even a certain complicity, some comment about another person who might not be liked by either of you. I remember that once I said to a Jesuit who often clashed with him, 'But he's a very interesting person.' 'Ah, no doubt about it,' he replied. Even those who didn't agree with him admitted that he had a capacity to attract and captivate people. And all this in a personality that had nothing exaggerated or excessive about it. In fact, he was a man of great sobriety," recalls the editor of *Criterio*, also stressing Bergoglio's amazing memory. "Great political leaders have always displayed a prodigious memory, and Bergoglio has one too. If he sees you once, he remembers you, a fact that makes a strong impression on the person he's speaking to. He has a phenomenal photographic memory of people."

The Archbishop also has great intuition. This is illustrated by a story he told a young priest who was a friend of his, when talking about the difficulties of priests and of religious orders. "Some time ago I was in a meeting and suddenly a woman came in and, God forgive me, I thought, *She's come looking for a husband.* Then they introduced her to me as a mother superior . . . But I wasn't mistaken, because shortly after, she found a husband and left the convent."

"Time prevails over space," "unity prevails over conflict," "reality prevails over ideas," and "the whole prevails over the parts"—these are Bergoglio's four coordinates of action. He goes on accumulating positions: in 2002 he refuses the nomination as president of the Argentine Episcopal Conference, but three years later, after emerging as the second-most-voted-for candidate at the 2005 conclave, he is elected president of the conference and then, in 2008, is reconfirmed for another three years.

He is convinced that power means serving others, and he creates bridges with other faiths. He also immerses himself fully in the political realities of his time: first the excesses of untamed capitalism and the corruption in the wake of President Menem (1989–1999), then the collapse of the government of Fernando de la Rúa, who fled in a helicopter from the roof of the Casa Rosada presidential residence in December 2001, while the Plaza de Mayo was in flames and the smoke of tear gas seeped into Bergoglio's room together with the clamor of the demonstration. Then, as Argentina fell into another deep economic crisis there were the soup kitchens, disruptions of all sorts, the presidency of Eduardo Duhalde (2002–2003), and finally the political arrival of Néstor and Cristina Kirchner and their presidencies.

He is not a silent witness. He denounces what is wrong and becomes a troublesome figure for the government.

"He was concerned for his country, as his sermons at the Te Deum every May 25 [Argentina's May Revolution Day] confirm, during the governments of Menem, De la Rúa, Duhalde, Kirchner. . . . They are impressive for their contents and depth. Bergoglio thinks and acts like any inhabitant of Buenos Aires, a true citizen. A man you can sit down to talk with about anything in complete freedom, a man who understands. Once he said to me, 'First life and then organization, this must be the ground and the expression of life,'" says Accaputo. "Bergoglio's attitude toward political life, the trade unions, entrepreneurs, and social organizations has always been one of respect, dialogue, and collaboration from the Church's point of view. In the Archdiocese, we created with him the social pastoral ministry, which deals with dialogue with these sectors, to establish and propagate the social doctrine of the Church and act in reference to various social problems. That is why he enjoys great prestige in these sectors, which have found him close to them and ready to help every time it was necessary. Bergoglio, as Archbishop of Buenos Aires, has kept up a dialogue with all sectors, beyond ideologies. For him this, too, is an area of evangelizing."

In 2001, in harmony with this attitude, he promotes the formation of the Argentine Dialogue Board (Mesa del Diálogo Argentino); representatives of a number of faiths take part in this initiative, working for the country in a context of grave social disintegration. Says Eduardo Duhalde, president of the country at that time: "While the government I was responsible for survived, Diálogo Argentino began to incorporate new members, broadening its aims and transforming itself into a factory of programs. They established clear grounds for indispensable agreements and tackled transitory or long-term solutions for varied problems concerning health, political reform, social and labor problems, and the functioning of the three powers of the state."

In 2002 Bergoglio creates the Institute of Interreligious Dialogue, together with Omar Abboud, to represent Islam; Rabbi Daniel Goldman; Bergoglio's Jewish friend Luis Liberman; Father Guillermo Marcó; and José Maria Corral, an education official in the Buenos Aires city government.

In March 2003, on the eve of the United States' invasion of Iraq, Bergoglio supports setting up a prayer tent for the representatives of different religions. The idea came from Sheik Mohsen Ali, director of Casa para la Difusion del Islam (the House for the Propagation of Islam), to be set up in the central Plaza de Mayo.

In June 2004 Bergoglio becomes the first Cardinal Primate of Argentina to enter the building of the Argentine Israelite Mutual Association (AMIA), a Jewish center and headquarters of the Federation of Jewish Argentine Committees, on Pasteur Street, reconstructed after the terrorist attack of 1994. He offers a wreath of flowers and prays before a picture that recalls the eighty-five victims of the attack. In the association's book of illustrious visitors, he writes: "Count the sands of the sea, so numerous shall be thy descendants, I thank the Lord because this day He has allowed me to share part of the way with our elder brothers who are greater than the little grain of sand that I am."

In 2007 he inaugurates the course Formation of Leaders in and for Interreligious Dialogue in the headquarters of the Archdiocese University Pastoral Ministry, that also runs the website Valores Religiosos (Religious Values) as well as the Institute of Interreligious Dialogue. Apart from institutional contacts, Bergoglio makes friends with representatives of different faiths, including rabbis and Protestant pastors, all of which results in practical action.

"The Waldensian pastor Norberto Bertón, Rector of the Instituto Universitario Evangélico de Educación Teológica, had been seriously ill for some years and was a patient in a geriatric hospital. Seeing him in this condition, Bergoglio decided to move him from there to the elderly priests' home [Hogar Sacerdotal], even though he was not a Catholic. He paid all his expenses," says Father Rivera. "We also took in Father Sergio, a priest who suffered from lateral multiple sclerosis and could communicate only by blinking. When we told Bergoglio how much his treatment would cost, he replied, 'If we have to sell chalices, we'll sell them.' We took care of the father for four years, till he died," he added.

"An Anglican pastor, too, Carlos Halperín, lived in the home for elderly priests at Bergoglio's invitation. Halperín died after residing there for two or three years with other priests, and he was able to celebrate his own worship services there," says Father Francisco Giannetti, in charge of the

Archdiocesan Commission for Ecumenism and Interreligious Dialogue and a member of the charismatic movement, or CRECES.

"Bergoglio has left his mark both on ecumenism and on interreligious dialogue: he visited the Orthodox bishops in their cathedrals and attended Jewish ceremonies. For example, when the patriarch of the Armenian Apostolic Church, Karekin II, came, he lent him the cathedral to celebrate a ceremony. In 2009 he attended a service of homage to Rabbi León Klenicki in the capital's cathedral. In addition, every year we commemorated Kristallnacht [the Night of Broken Glass] in different churches in the center of Buenos Aires. Last year it was held in the metropolitan cathedral," Father Giannetti recalls.

"Bergoglio supported and endorsed the creation of CRECES and took part in its annual meetings. We organized a retreat for priests and pastors, and he took part. At the first CRECES meeting, held in Luna Park, he was out among the people. I found him, and he told me that he would speak later. When the time came he mounted the platform without notes and spoke of how good it was to be together, of the Father's embrace, the wounds of the Son, and the breath of the Holy Spirit. He spoke for a few minutes, but he remained at the meeting for the whole afternoon."

Father Alberto Ibañez Padilla, a Jesuit and a member of CRECES who had been stopped from taking part in some charismatic meetings by Bergoglio when he was Provincial, stresses the Archbishop's willingness to change his mind. "As he gradually came to understand that charismatic renewal was something that came from God, he began to open up. He was a person capable of changing his opinion and accepting something he had not understood before. Once he told me, 'I've been converted; first I was against, now I'm a supporter and have become a point of reference for the charismatic renewal in the Argentinian Bishops Conference.'"

At the CRECES meeting in 2007, Bergoglio asks not to privatize the gospel. "Let's not privatize the name of Jesus. If we don't share him with others, it's because we don't understand him."

Bergoglio, who has been a teacher, is also concerned with education, the great unsettled problem in Argentina. As Archbishop he founds the Vicaría Episcopal de Educación in the Archdiocese of Buenos Aires and intends it to become "a bridge for culture and a fundamental aspect of the mission of the Church."

"Bergoglio knows well that developing education is a job that must be done by everybody for everybody. Before then there was the schools department of the archbishopric, which dealt with forty-four parish schools altogether; now there are sixty-five," says Santiago Fraga, executive secretary of the vicariate since its creation.

"The number of enrolled pupils has increased by 80 percent. It's very important that they should be good schools, apart from being religious schools. They are chosen for their quality and offer faith as an invitation, not an imposition. This has to do with the way Bergoglio understands education. During a chat with a group of catechists, he insisted that things imposed by force end by blowing up, which is why he spoke about educating in freedom, respecting the conscience and also the identity of the other person, who she or he is and where he or she comes from," he adds.

Every year Bergoglio also presides over the Mass for education organized by the Vicaría Episcopal de Educación, together with seven hundred Buenos Aires schools. It is attended by primary and secondary school students, directors of the schools, and various government authorities of the city and the nation.

"With those Masses—which began inside the cathedral and were then moved into the square because there were too many of us—Bergoglio promoted a meeting space that went beyond the range of Catholic education. He saw the need to give vitality to education and he meant *vitality* as building together. That is why networking greatly interested him," says Fraga.

As president of the Argentine Episcopal Conference, Bergoglio plays an active part in the Superior Council of Catholic Education (Consejo Superior de Educación Católica, or CONSUDEC), the official national-level educational secretariat of the Church, which represents Argentine Catholic education and is organized by diocesan councils.

After the economic collapse of 2001, on the occasion of celebrating Mass for the beginning of the school year, Bergoglio sends a message to the educational community, asking them to concentrate on education at this dramatic time: "The children of the *gauchos*, the migrants arriving in the towns from the country and also the foreigners landing on our shores, found in basic education the elements they needed to transcend their particular origins and find a place in the common construction of a project. Even today, with such a rich plurality of educational offers, we must concentrate on this: education is everything."

"An unescapable mission for every Christian educator is to concentrate on inclusion, work for inclusion. Is it not an ancient tradition of the Church to take education to the most forgotten? Have not many congregations and educational institutions been created with this aim? Have we always been consistent with this vocation of service and inclusion? What winds of change have made us lose this evangelical direction?" Cardinal Bergoglio wonders aloud in April 2003, in his message from the cathedral to the educational community.

That same year, Bergoglio publishes *To Educate: Diligence and Passion—Challenges for Christian Educators*, one of the many books he has written on the subject, addressed to Christian teachers. He invites them to take on their profession as "a summons, a challenge, a vocation."

As a result of his educational crusade, Bergoglio gets to know many government officials. One of these is Manuel García Solá, Minister of Education in 1999 after the resignation of Susana Decibe, at a very difficult time when universities were protesting budget cuts. "He [Bergoglio] became my spiritual guide. He taught me to pray again, and I was forty years old. The day I took up my post, I went to the archbishopric to ask him for spiritual help for the challenge of taking on the Ministry in the very midst of that conflict. 'Preserve plurality,' he said. He had a very simple desk, and at the end of our talk he asked his secretary for an envelope with one hundred holy pictures of St. Joseph the Patriarch. He blessed them and gave them to me. 'The condition for putting yourself under the protection of St. Joseph and the Virgin Mary is becoming devoted to them.' And I obeyed," says García Solá.

"When I had to make another very hard decision, that of leaving politics in 2003, I went to talk to him and said, 'Cardinal, I don't know what to do, I feel a great emptiness.' And he answered, 'Manuel, live your exile. I lived mine. And you will come back. When you come back you will be more merciful, kinder, and you will want to serve your people better.' He granted me such peace. . . . I came to him with my soul in pieces and left smiling. That's Bergoglio, a man who knows souls."

On the evening of December 30, 2004, a firework thrown during a concert given by the rock group Callejeros starts a fire in the Cromañón disco in Buenos Aires. One-hundred ninety-four people die, and seven hundred are injured. It turns out that the disco was unsafe and, that evening, overcrowded. The national and city authorities are late showing up to give an explanation.

Bergoglio is on the spot early in the morning. He prays at the morgue with the families of the victims and visits several hospitals. He entrusts his Auxiliary Bishop, Jorge Lozano, with the task of giving spiritual assistance to the family members, relatives, and survivors. He also charges him to celebrate Mass on the thirtieth of every month and to stay close to the relatives of the victims.

Many relatives bear witness to the presence of the Cardinal, saying that he is the only one from whom they received words of comfort. This presence continues. Bergoglio, who backs their demand for justice, celebrates Masses and baptisms in the sanctuary spontaneously created by friends and relatives of the victims within a few feet of where the tragedy took place. "We don't make experiments with boys and girls, we don't play Russian roulette with our young people!" he denounces during the Corpus Christi procession, five months after the tragedy.

"I should like to tell this city, which is so concerned about so many things, to look with a mother's heart—because a city, too, is a mother—at these children who are no more[,] and to weep . . . Buenos Aires works, searches, does business, worries about tourism, but has not mourned enough this hard blow. Buenos Aires needs to be purified by tears for this and so many other tragedies!" he affirms in 2005. He says to the young people who the same year march from the sanctuary at Cromañón with candles and a banner with the names of the victims: "Don't lose your enthusiasm, don't let them steal your hope!"

He gives the same absolute, total presence—listening, consoling, giving serenity, embracing his flock—when the terrible railway tragedy of Once happens on February 22, 2012. On that day, at 8:32 in the morning, a passenger train of the Sarmiento line coming from Moreno, with more than 1,200 passengers on board, enters the Once station in Buenos Aires but cannot brake and crashes into a buffer.

Fifty-two people are killed, and more than seven hundred are injured.

The same afternoon, Monsignor Eduardo García, Auxiliary Bishop of Buenos Aires, presides over the Ash Wednesday Mass, asking for prayers for "the eternal rest of the victims, the consolation of their relatives, and the speedy recovery of the injured."

After a month, in response to the families' wishes, Bergoglio celebrates a Mass in the capital's cathedral. In the homily he is clear and direct: "We want justice to be done! We know that behind all this there are authorities who were irresponsible, people who didn't do their duty; we don't want punishment for its own sake but to correct their hearts because their irresponsibility has cost us dearly, there is no price that can repay a life! Nearly all those people came here to earn their living! With dignity! Father, let it not become a normal thing that to earn a living people must travel like cattle. Let it not become a normal thing, Father, that in this city no one is mourned, everything is passed over. Let it not become a normal thing, Father, to wash one's hands saying, 'Thank God it didn't happen to me' and immediately think about something else."

The life of the first Jesuit Archbishop of Buenos Aires is very disciplined. He gets up at 4:15 a.m. After showering and shaving—he always appears clean shaven—he meditates and prays in his room on the third floor of the curia in Calle Rivadavia or in a little chapel nearby, where there is an image of the Virgin of Luján and a little statue of the patient Christ, who sits with his head in his hands.

After breakfast—a couple of drinks of *mate*, which he prepares himself, and sweet cookies—he reads the daily *La Nación*, which his personal news deliverer brings him every day from the Plaza de Mayo. Sometimes he switches on the radio, not to hear the news but to listen to classical music. At 6 a.m. he starts receiving calls from priests, people asking to see him, old friends seeking a word of comfort or advice. In his diminutive handwriting he jots down his future appointments in his little black diary.

At 8 a.m., when his secretaries—Otilia and Elisa—arrive, he has already answered a number of letters and checked documents. He doesn't use a computer, and it is the two women who answer all the e-mails he receives, following his indications. If there are no pastoral or institutional engagements on his agenda, he gives audience the whole morning: he sees bishops, politicians, entrepreneurs, trade unionists, friends of friends, officials, people he has been helping since the time he was Rector of the Colegio Máximo.

At 1 p.m. he has lunch. If he has a guest, the nuns who run the kitchen cook, and he eats in the big dining room of the curia, with its high ceilings and antique boiserie (carved wooden panels) that matches the table and chairs. He never sits at the head of the table—that is the place for his guest—and doesn't want to be served. The nuns know this by now and leave the tray with the day's dish, wine, and a carafe of water on the table. The Cardinal and his guests help themselves. After the arrival of the second course or the dessert (he loves sweets but controls himself), the Cardinal gets up and takes the tray back to the kitchen. After lunch, he gets up and takes away the dishes, and thanks and compliments the sisters on what they have cooked that day. He accompanies his guests to the main door of the curia and bids them good-bye with his usual "pray for me."

Half an hour's rest is enough for him to recuperate his energy and go on with the rest of the day, answering calls; dealing with administrative, pastoral, social, and educational questions; preparing sermons; writing and reading. In the evening he hardly ever goes out. He goes up to the little kitchen on the third floor, next to his room, and cooks himself a simple meal. He goes to bed early, at about 10 p.m. Accustomed as he is since childhood to a spartan way of life, he never goes on holiday.

The Cardinal avoids going to the suppers, social events and galas, cocktail parties, theatrical and cinematic shows to which he is invited. "Once they sent me an invitation to a supper in aid of Caritas. The cream of society—as they say—was to be at the tables. And I decided not to go. On that occasion the president of the time was invited. Various articles were auctioned and after the first course a Rolex gold watch was presented. A real outrage, a degradation, a mistaken use of charity," Bergoglio himself relates in *On Heaven and Earth*.

If he goes out, he does so on tiptoe, as it were, and always using public transport, to go to the hospital to visit a friend or a patient, or else to the prison to comfort an inmate, or to give relief to some forgotten inhabitant of a marginalized neighborhood.

"A mutual friend of ours had recently become a father. At midnight he informed Bergoglio that he had a son, and to his great surprise at one o'clock in the morning he turned up at the hospital," says Santiago de Estrada, former Ambassador to the Holy See. "At two o'clock Sunday morning, the burglar alarm rang in the offices of Channel 21, on the fifth floor of the Archdiocese. A bat had flown in, so I hurried in to solve the problem," says Julio Rimoldi, director of the archdiocesan TV Channel 21. "Once I had caught it, at three thirty in the morning, I met the Cardinal on my way down. I told him the story of the bat, but he interrupted me: 'What are you doing here? Have you been drinking and then come here to get over your hangover?' And I answered back: 'And what are you doing here?' He answered: 'I'm going to San Pantaleón. I'm taking the 126 bus. I want to be in the confessional when the first pilgrim arrives.'"

Bergoglio argues and gets annoyed, like anyone else. Then he raises his voice a bit, or glares, but he never loses his head.

"On November 1, 2012, All Saints' Day," recalls Father Alejandro Russo, rector of the cathedral, "I asked the police for help because the abortionists had turned up, and invading churches had become the fashion. I didn't pay attention, and the Federal Police blocked the cathedral with palings so that it looked like a kind of concentration camp, because they were the tall, blue kind. The Cardinal wasn't there, and when he arrived and looked out the window, I said to myself, *My God, he'll be furious!* Someone advised me, 'Don't go to him, he's so angry that he'll tell you off.' But I went and explained to him: 'Listen, I called the police but it was they who put up the palings; I can't start telling them how to do it.' Bergoglio laughed. 'Tell them to take them away at once and leave the cathedral open!' he said. And I told him, 'Not only will I open the cathedral, I'll also celebrate the six o'clock Mass.'"

When Bergoglio makes a mistake, he admits it, says Sister Geneviève Jeanningros of the Congregation of the Little Sisters of Jesus, niece of Léonie Duquet, one of the French nuns who disappeared during the Argentine dictatorship. Sister Geneviève tells me in an interview, "On September 25, 2005, after her body had been identified, my aunt Léonie Duquet was buried in the courtyard of the Church of the Holy Cross, in Buenos Aires, together with mothers of the Plaza de Mayo, among whom was Esther Ballestrino de Careaga, who had been Bergoglio's boss at the chemistry lab. The ceremony was attended by civil personalities, but there was no one from the bishopric. And I was sorry about this, because I love the Church. So I wrote to Bergoglio. I left him a letter in the Casa Internazionale on Via della Scrofa, where he usually stays, in October of the same year, when he came to Rome for the synod. I had written my telephone number on the letter, and to my great surprise he called me at once.

He asked me to forgive him and told me that he had authorized the burial of my aunt in the Church of the Holy Cross together with the mothers. I replied that it wasn't enough, that the Church should have been present. He asked me again to forgive him and said, 'Sister, you were right to tell me this, that's what we should do between brothers and sisters.'"

When Sister Geneviève greeted Pope Francis on Saturday, April 20, 2013, he remembered her letter and their telephone conversation perfectly. "I didn't expect it, my legs shook! My aunt died for a poor Church for the poor, and he is a person with a heart."

# 10

# Clerical and Political Adversaries

Unpredictable, inscrutable, and with clear ideas and strong nerves, Bergoglio goes on collecting enemies. When he was a young Provincial of the Jesuits, people opposed him because he was considered rigid and conservative. As Archbishop and Primate he is judged too meek by a right-wing sector of the Argentine church that maintains strong links with an influential part of the Roman Curia.

This group, which will soon start waging war against him, accusing him in Rome of not being orthodox enough, is reinforced in April 2003 by the arrival in Buenos Aires of the nuncio (Ambassador to the Holy See) Adriano Bernardini, a man working for Cardinal Angelo Sodano, the influential Secretary of State between 1991 and 2006—who does not like Bergoglio at all.

"Most of their differences concerned the method of nominating bishops. In Rome, candidates were added or the names on the short list sent from Buenos Aires were changed. It was a fact that there was bad blood between Nuncio Bernardini and the Cardinal. Most of the episcopate became aware of this. In his first public Mass in the Iglesia del Socorro (Church of Our Lady of Help), the nuncio preached a very stern homily: it was as if he were speaking to the Dutch episcopate at the period of the Dutch rebellion. He actually rebuked them. Afterward I said to a Bishop I know well, 'You're weak, why didn't you get up and leave?'" says José Ignacio López, editor of the religious journal *Vida Nueva*.

López goes on: "That was just the beginning. Then matters became more serious, and there were a number of episodes of crossed wires between the Episcopal Conference and certain sectors of the Roman Curia. Some became influential at the conference thanks to their contacts there. In Rome some of these sectors opened the way for a number of allegations. That's how allegations by a right-wing sector against the bishops began: accusations that certain things were happening in a certain diocese. At one point, for example, they criticized the priests of Neuquén or Río Negro for celebrating Mass without wearing vestments."

Monsignor Héctor Aguer, Archbishop of La Plata, several minor bishops, and members of priestly and lay institutions, including some professors at the Catholic University of Buenos Aires (UCA), belong to the group against Bergoglio. Working in the shadows is the former Ambassador to the Holy See from the time of Carlos Menem, Esteban "Cacho" Caselli, a very controversial person, and one who has easy access to the Vatican palaces because of his friendship with Cardinal Sodano, thanks to whom he is nominated a "gentleman of His Holiness" in 2003.

Bergoglio is accused of not defending doctrine, of making pastoral gestures that are too daring, and of not arguing publicly and with greater determination with the Argentine government of the time. In other words, they criticize his ways of being a pastor and of understanding the Church.

In Rome they accuse the Cardinal of baptizing children born out of wedlock and even for reproaching priests of his Archdiocese who refuse to administer the sacrament to such children, as he does in public in December 2012. "In our ecclesiastic region there are priests who do not baptize the children of single mothers because they have not been conceived in holy matrimony. Those are today's hypocrites. Those who have clericalized the Church, who deny salvation to the people of God. And that poor girl who faced the choice of getting rid of her child and has had the courage of giving it birth, goes on a pilgrimage from parish to parish to have it baptized!" says Bergoglio, in a declaration that surely made the hair of his right-wing adversaries in the Roman Curia stand on end.

"Bergoglio suffered many attacks against his person and his style of governing. The sectors that represent a very conservative Church hit him hard for fifteen years. Many belonged to the Roman Curia. Bernardini and Monsignor Aguer turned out accusations like a machine," an old prelate says to me in a low voice.

The maneuvers of part of the Roman Curia against Bergoglio, head of a moderate episcopate, gradually increase as he becomes a more important figure on the international level. The cardinals start becoming aware of the Archbishop of Buenos Aires at the end of 2001. After the terrorist attacks of September 11, 2001, in the United States, the Archbishop of New York, Cardinal Edward Egan, is forced to leave the October Synod of Bishops in the Vatican to return to his diocese. And it is Bergoglio (ordained Cardinal by John Paul II in February of that same year) who replaces him in the key post of general rapporteur. This public appearance, which leaves an excellent impression on other cardinals, is the starting point of Bergoglio's visibility on the international scene.

In the meantime he is appointed member of a number of Vatican departments: Congregations for Divine Service, Clergy, and Institutes of Consecrated Life; the Pontifical Council for the Family; and the Pontifical Commission for Latin America.

During the conclave in 2005 to elect the successor to John Paul II, Bergoglio is a step away from becoming the first Latin American pope. Before the election, he avoids joining any lobby or bloc. His enemies are busy circulating to the cardinal-electors by e-mail a "dossier" reviving the old and false accusation of journalist Horacio Verbitsky, that Bergoglio was an accomplice of the last Argentine dictatorship.

In spite of these attempts, the Archbishop of Buenos Aires becomes Joseph Ratzinger's chief challenger. According to information confirmed by a number of participants, the Argentine Archbishop, candidate of the most progressive wing, in opposition to the ultraconservative wing backing the Prefect for the Congregation of the Doctrine of the Faith, receives about forty votes during the third, penultimate vote of the conclave. But during the lunch break, before the fourth ballot, Bergoglio takes a step back, concerned that his candidature might block the most newsworthy conclave of all time, giving the world the image of a divided Catholic Church.

In spite of his detractors, Bergoglio goes on distinguishing himself. In October 2005, at the first Synod of Bishops celebrated after the conclave that elected Joseph Ratzinger, he receives the most votes from the 252 synodal fathers of the 118 countries that elect the twelve members of the Post-Synodal Council. The Jesuit Archbishop of Buenos Aires is elected representative of the Americas by eighty votes—another demonstration of great appreciation.

And it is in this context that, between the end of 2005 and the beginning of 2006, the attack against Bergoglio (which I followed closely as correspondent of the daily *La Nación*) reaches its culmination. Bernardini and his Roman Curia friends intervene directly in the nomination of a number of conservative bishops. Among these are the Archbishop of Rosario (Santa Fe), José Luis Mollaghan, and the Archbishop of Resistencia (Chaco), Fabriciano Sigampa. These nominations create great uneasiness in the Argentine episcopate.

Neither Mollaghan nor Sigampa had been proposed in the preliminary poll of the Argentine bishops: they were imposed following the indications of the Vatican's Secretariat of State in the short list presented by Bernardini to the pope. According to various sources, this intervention is linked to the old friendship between Sodano and Esteban "Cacho" Caselli. Caselli often plays tennis with the private secretary of the number-two man at the Holy See, Monsignor Timothy Broglio, nicknamed "Timbroglio" (which means roughly "I cheat you" in Italian). Broglio, later Archbishop for the U.S. Armed Forces, is awarded the Great Cross of the Order of San Martín Libertador and the Order of Mayo by the republic of Argentina. Even when he is no longer Ambassador, Caselli keeps up direct relations with Monsignor Maurizio Bravi, official of the second section of the Secretariat of State, which deals mainly with Argentina and is in close touch with Leonardo

Sandri, at the time the third-ranking person in the Vatican structure as Substitute of the Secretariat of State.

After the election of Benedict XVI, Bergoglio's adversaries conspire in attempts to move him away from Argentina, well aware of the Cardinal Primate's attachment to Buenos Aires and his rejection of that style of Church diametrically opposed to his own that reigns in the velvet-draped palaces of the Vatican. They know that sending him to the Roman Curia would be a mortal blow for him. "I shall die if I go to the curia," the Cardinal confides to Reuters Agency after the daily financial newspaper *Ambito Financiero* circulates a rumor in May 2005 according to which he might become the Vatican Secretary of State—that is, Benedict XVI's right-hand man—or else head of another department of the Roman Curia.

Such a rumor is a reflection of the then-current political campaign (which does not please Bergoglio at all) championed by an Argentine political and ecclesiastical sector and supported by the usual people in Rome.

At that critical time between the end of 2005 and the beginning of 2006, even though Benedict XVI—whom Bergoglio gets on with very well, as there is a feeling of mutual esteem between them—is already reigning, power is still in the hands of Secretary of State Angelo Sodano and his deputy Leonardo Sandri, whose mandate is soon to lapse. Pope Benedict XVI will replace the two of them with Cardinal Tarcisio Bertone and Archbishop Fernando Filoni.

After directing a spiritual retreat in Spain for the bishops of that country, Bergoglio arrives in Rome at the beginning of February 2006 to take part in the meetings of the Post-Synodal Council. In the meantime he also takes the opportunity to visit some Vatican offices.

But that visit causes a great commotion. False rumors begin to circulate, according to which the pope did not want to receive him, when the truth is that Bergoglio never asked to see him, and so the operation to tarnish his reputation is exposed.

On February 3, the same day Bergoglio is received by Sandri, still deputy at the Secretariat of State, to tell him of the uneasiness provoked by some of the recent nominations to the Argentine episcopate, the Vatican announces that the pope has chosen Monsignor Óscar Domingo Sarlinga as new Bishop of Zárate-Campana.

"Conservative or not, Sarlinga is close to Caselli and was nominated just at the time that Bergoglio was in Rome," a source explains, to give an idea of the slap in the face suffered that day by the Cardinal Primate. The nomination, a few months later, of Monsignor Marcelo Martorell as new Bishop of Puerto Iguazú, to replace the retiring Bishop Joaquín Piña, is a faithful reflection of this frustrating situation.

During these hectic days, a Bishop of the conservative anti-Bergoglio group gets in touch with me. He says that he wants to meet me and fixes an appointment at the Casa Santa Marta, where he is staying. He surely can't imagine that six years later Pope Francis will be living there. We talk for more than an hour in one of the little parlors on the ground floor, with the same green velvet armchairs that Pope Francis now uses when he gives a private audience. The conversation is cordial: we speak about the Church, the Vatican, my family, mutual acquaintances. At the end, still with a smile on his lips, the Bishop asks me to stop writing those "too fanciful" articles on the conflicts between Bergoglio and some persons at the Secretariat of State. And he warns me that it would really be a pity if my permanent accreditation to the Vatican Press Office were to be taken away.

Bergoglio shocks Rome on the pastoral level by his intolerance of the obsessive strictness of some clergy on the subject of sexual ethics. He is convinced that the worst thing is to insist on and seek direct confrontation on these subjects. In 2010, in the midst of the episcopate's battle to stop the passing of the law on same-sex marriage in Argentina, the idea for a prayer vigil is announced. Esteban Pittaro, who works for internal communications at Austral University (of Opus Dei) sends an e-mail to the archbishopric of Buenos Aires, informing them of this idea. The following day he sees a missed call on his phone and realizes that it is the number of the Archdiocese. Pittaro calls back, and Bergoglio answers.

"I think it's a fine thing that you are praying. But staying in the square all night—it'll be cold! Go home, pray at home, with your family! If you want, find another night to pray," the Cardinal tells him. Recalls Pittaro: "I supported the march, but he was right to advise against the vigil; that wasn't the best night because the next day there were demonstrations in favor of equal marriage rights. He wanted to avoid confrontation. At the end of our telephone conversation I was struck by a question of his. In the e-mail I had sent to the head office, I introduced myself as a married layman, so he asked me, 'And what's your wife's name? How long have you been married? And do you love her? And do you show her that you love her?' He began to ask me about my marriage and give me advice. It was a great lesson, because the debate about the nature of marriage was in the air. Our chat went on for about ten minutes, and toward the end I told him that we couldn't have children. In November of the following year I sent him my doctoral thesis and told him that my wife was pregnant. He answered my e-mail saying, 'I give you my word that I'll read the thesis you have sent me and I'll pray for your child, to be born in March.' He took it for granted that it would be born. My son was born two days before his election. When Bergoglio came out on the balcony of St. Peter's basilica dressed as pope, I had my son in my arms."

The conflict between Bergoglio and a sector of the Roman Curia intensifies during his last two years as Archbishop of Buenos Aires. Involved in this is Monsignor Víctor Manuel "Tucho" Fernández, one of Bergoglio's chief collaborators during the meeting of the Latin American Episcopal Conference in Brazil in May 2007. The Cardinal has to engage in a battle that lasts for two years to get the Vatican to give clearance for Fernández's nomination as Rector of the Universtidad Católica Argentina.

In a direct message to those who waged war against Bergoglio about that nomination, Fernández becomes the first Argentine Bishop to be nominated by Pope Francis on May 13, 2013. In an article published in June 2013 in *Vida Pastoral*, Fernández reveals the details of that time. And he stresses that opposition to Bergoglio lasted until the conclave that elected him the first Latin American pope. Fernández writes:

> Thinking that Bergoglio was now about to retire, and imagining him secluded in the home for retired priests, several churchmen were responsible for intrigues with the aim of consolidating the power they had accumulated during recent years, believing him to have left the scene. I personally took part in meetings where a number of Argentine bishops and some important representatives of the Holy See (I exclude the current nuncio Emil Paul Tscherrig, who is a gentleman) enjoyed themselves by criticizing him shamelessly. They reproached him for not being demanding enough with the faithful, for not showing clearly his identity as priest, for not preaching enough on questions of sexual morality.... Shortly before the election of Pope Francis, I attended a celebration where some of them—not imagining what would happen—believed in their own imminent victory. Theirs was another idea of the Church: powerful, triumphant, judge of the world.

"The concentration of power in certain sectors of the Church and the impossibility of solving all problems with Roman centralization has given rise to an arrogant attitude that many Argentine bishops tell of having suffered during visits to the Holy See (excluding the kind and respectful attitude of the then Cardinal Ratzinger)," adds the present Rector of UCA, recounting in the same article for *Vida Pastoral* his "sad personal experience":

> When, after a period—a "test period" which we decided on together—Cardinal Bergoglio sent the request to Rome to allow me to take the oath formally as Rector of the Universidad Católica Argentina, we discovered that someone had sent some of my articles from Argentina, considering them to be unorthodox. To prove how absurd the whole thing was, I can point out that one of these writings was a very short newspaper article published years ago, on the request of my Bishop, in a daily of Río Cuarto ... Even prior to this experience, I always asked myself, *Can somebody be contested by anonymous persons and have no chance to defend himself?* As if that wasn't enough, it appeared to be impossible to have a different opinion even on freely discussed theological subjects, because all the subjects acquired the weight of

dogmas of faith, within a doctrinal corpus where every detail appeared absolutely untouchable.

That time I was planning a trip to Rome. I was afraid they wouldn't give me a hearing, but the Cardinal sent a letter to a Vatican Congregation asking them to listen to me. I got an e-mail confirming the date and time when they would receive me. I traveled with a copy of Bergoglio's letter. But after I arrived, I was informed on the day before the appointment that they would not receive me. I called the Cardinal, who was extremely upset by the incident (I'd better not repeat the words he used!) and asked me in a fatherly way to be patient and not get depressed. He told me that if I gave up now I should be confirming that those anti-evangelical methods could be successful. Since those accusations could not be objectively justified, Bergoglio held out, applying one of the principles of Juan Manuel de Rosas, which he always quotes: "Time prevails over space."

Last year, 2012, I asked the same Congregation for a hearing again, and they agreed. When I arrived there, they told me that I had not been registered. I insisted and they finally devoted a few minutes to me. Last November I asked in advance for a hearing in April 2013. They didn't even answer. In December I tried again, so that I could organize my time. Once more I didn't get a reply. On February 4, I asked the nuncio (the Swiss Archbishop Emil Paul Tscherrig) to forward my request, but they didn't answer him either. Last week, after Pope Francis's election, the nuncio made a fresh attempt and immediately obtained the requested hearing. I must explain that this Congregation always receives any priest, even some who turn up without asking for a hearing.

Anyone who knows me is aware that I'm neither a saint nor a martyr. But I feel that even the dregs of society deserve a little more respect. I don't judge the intentions that may have inspired such treatment, but they are certainly proof of a style that is not Bergoglio's: he always answers telephone calls or writes an affectionate greeting to the humblest little old woman who shares her worries with him.

To what extent did Bergoglio suffer from that arrogance that, according to Fernández's article, many Argentine prelates suffer when they visit the Holy See?

"He knew how to suffer in silence," the UCA Rector tells me. "Others complained bitterly. During the visits to the Vatican, some officials behaved rudely and even with a certain contempt toward the 'poor Latin Americans.' Bergoglio kept quiet and bided his time. But that didn't happen with the then Cardinal Ratzinger, who was a man of exquisite courtesy and respectful in an exemplary way."

Bergoglio is vindicated at the fifth General Conference of the Latin American Episcopal Conference at Aparecida, in Brazil, in May 2007. During this meeting he is elected president of the committee editing the final document. With this text he calls for a permanent continental mission and ratifies the choice to give precedence to the poor, which will, a few years later, represent the program of action of Pope Francis's pontificate.

But let us go back. The first meeting of the Latin American Episcopal Conference is held in Rio de Janeiro in 1955; the second in Medellín, Colombia, in 1968; the third in Puebla, Mexico, in 1979; and the fourth in Santo Domingo, Dominican Republic, in 1992. On this last occasion "the interference of the Vatican Curia is so excessive that Latin American enthusiasm is stifled," Fernández exclaims.

During the Jubilee Year of 2000, when John Paul II is already ill, some Latin American cardinals start insisting on the possibility of having a fifth conference of the Latin American bishops. Perhaps foreseeing that from this different episcopate—close to the people, from the south of the world, there might come a revolution that would change everything, the Vatican resists, and instead of a conference, the celebration of a synod in Rome is proposed.

"There was a lot of resistance on the part of some members of the Holy See, in particular by Cardinal Sodano, and also on the part of some Latin American bishops who were in Rome. In the 1990s there were stronger pressures by certain sectors of the Roman Curia to control the Church in Latin America. Not so much because Latin America was undisciplined, but because centralization had increased and they were not in favor of personalized or specific expressions of the churches in this area," explains

Father Carlos Galli, a theologian nominated by Benedict XVI as an expert at the Aparecida conference.

Finally, on the insistence of cardinals such as the Chilean Francisco Javier Errázuriz, Bergoglio, and the Honduran Óscar Andrés Rodríguez Maradiaga, John Paul II decides that the conference can take place. And his successor, Benedict XVI, chooses as the venue the Sanctuary of Aparecida.

In May 2007 I was five months pregnant with Carolina, my second child—and my husband Gerry was obsessed with mosquitos, because an epidemic of dengue fever had just broken out—when we, too, went to Aparecida to follow Benedict XVI's first journey to Latin America. It is hard to forget the day when we were with Bergoglio in a hotel, having coffee. He tells us that they are proposing that he join the commission editing the final document of the meeting. And he confesses that he is doubtful about accepting, that it is a hard job, that he is tired. "You can't say no. You must accept!" Gerry tells him.

The story that follows is well-known. At the meeting, a list of the thirty-one bishops nominated by the bishops is presented and a vote is taken. The eight bishops who receive the most votes will make up the commission, and the Bishop most voted for will be president of the commission. As always, Bergoglio doesn't campaign. With an overwhelming majority of 112 votes out of 130, he is elected president of the editing committee, partnered with two other important cardinals, the Brazilian Cláudio Hummes—who will tell him "not to forget the poor" when he is elected pope on March 13—and Rodríguez Maradiaga, whom Pope Francis will nominate coordinator of a group of eight cardinals from all the continents to advise him on the reform of the curia and in the government of the universal Church.

"Bergoglio did a fine job of organizing the editorial work. In three weeks we got a document covering over 550 points that respected and harmonized the opinions of twenty-two episcopates. Editing such a document in three weeks is a miracle. I'd say it's the work of the Holy Spirit, of the dialogue between bishops, of the work of the editors, of the prayers of all God's people—there were many prayers, we worked in the crypt of a Marian sanctuary—and there was a big dose of Latin American magic realism . . . In no other part of the world could one produce such a precious document in three weeks!" says Father Galli.

"Even if it's a collective work, the document has a Bergoglian imprint. Many of the main ideas are typical of Bergoglio's spiritual and apostolic vision. In particular it puts the accent on the meeting with Jesus as the basis of discipleship and, starting from the union with Christ, it highlights the tasks of being missionary. Disciples and missionaries of Christ. The document continually insists on the mission to those who are far away, to those who have left the Church, who have joined the sects, who have never been Christian or have forgotten that they have been. Starting from this point, it insists that the pastoral structure must be rethought in order to reach everyone. This idea is typical of Bergoglio and it's clear that it's what he did in Buenos Aires with the problem of the shantytowns," says Father Mariano Fazio, regional vicar of Opus Dei in Argentina, Paraguay, and Bolivia, and an expert at Aparecida.

It is a race against time to finish the document, a gigantic task. "On May 30 at two thirty in the morning, only our Cardinal Bergoglio with three other people was still working, and he was the most clear-headed," recalls Fernández. The Cardinal Primate again stands out for his kindness and sense of humor.

"He introduced me to his brothers in the episcopate and invited me to spend those days with them. It was an act of courtesy, because I wasn't a member of the Argentine delegation, I was an expert nominated by Benedict XVI, I hadn't lived in Argentina for twenty-six years and had little contact with the bishops of my country. I shared meals, walks, and work with them. One day when it was hot, while we were walking toward the sanctuary, I asked him why he had so many clothes on and he spoke to me about his lung problem. We also talked about some mutual friends, and his tone was very affectionate," recalls Fazio, author of many books. "A gesture that shows his humanity took place on May 25. Since this was Argentina's national holiday, he wanted to celebrate it with an Argentine wine. The hotel we were staying in was the best in Aparecida, but they were not prepared to give lodging to travelers for more than one night, and we stayed for twenty-one days. In the evening the diocese of Aparecida gave us wine, which was not the best, which was why he wanted to show us this courtesy. Bergoglio is a mystic with his feet on the ground. Once, when we were in a self-service restaurant with our plates in our hands, he said to me, 'Well, then, are you going to stop writing books?' It's typical of the *porteños*, the inhabitants of Buenos Aires, to use irony to build bridges, for friendship's sake. I know that he has recommended my books to the Argentine Episcopal Conference, and in this he showed an open mind, since he was a Jesuit Cardinal while I was an Opus Dei priest."

If relations with part of the Roman Curia are tormented, those of the Archbishop of Buenos Aires with the then-current government of Argentina are hardly less so. His relationship with Néstor Kirchner—President of Argentina from 2003 to 2007—and with Kirchner's wife, Cristina, who succeeds him, is particularly turbulent. It's a relationship marked by distance and missed opportunities.

President Néstor Kirchner (who died in October 2010) actually defines Bergoglio as "the head of the political opposition." The repeated calls of the Cardinal Primate to combat poverty, corruption, lack of security, and social inequality generate hurt feelings at the Casa Rosada. On the one hand, the president protests because he feels the Cardinal does not recognize the merit he believes he deserves for his struggle against poverty. On the other hand, the episcopate claims that its criticism is not directed at the government and that Bergoglio and the bishops are talking to the whole of society and denouncing poverty as they have always done.

"Things that [Bergoglio] would have said to anyone were read as attacks against Kirchner. At the time I believe the government needed to create an enemy, and the Church was an easy enemy," says Father Jorge Oesterheld, spokesman of the episcopate presided over by Bergoglio.

Besides his biting homilies, during his six years as president of the Argentine episcopate (2005–2011), Bergoglio exchanges very stern messages with the government about the proposed law on marriage between persons of the same sex. Among Kirchner's supporters Bergoglio's contacts with leaders of the opposition are also seen as annoying. "He never closed the door in anyone's face, and he conversed with many parties," says Father Carlos Accaputo, who chairs the social pastoral ministry in Buenos Aires and is held to be the "political operative" of the former Cardinal.

On August 6, 2003, shortly after becoming president, Néstor Kirchner has a cordial meeting with Bergoglio, when he receives the Episcopal Commission chaired then by Monsignor Eduardo Mirás, Archbishop of Rosario. But at the traditional Te Deum of May 25, celebrated the following year in the cathedral of Buenos Aires, the differences begin. A cryptic homily by Bergoglio speaks of "exhibitionism and ostentatious announcements." It does not refer directly to the president, but it does not need to.

The government's response is to have the religious services for May 25 celebrated far from Buenos Aires, in "friendlier" dioceses. The following year, Santiago del Estero is chosen. In 2006, however, the celebration comes back to the Buenos Aires cathedral. "If Néstor Kirchner had taken less seriously the reproaches heard at the Te Deum, he would have limited Bergoglio's power. Instead Néstor transformed him into an enemy, and I think he was wrong," says Poirier, director of journal *Criterio*.

In February 2005, the case of Antonio Baseotto, Bishop for the military service, and a biblical quotation misleadingly applied to the health minister Ginés González García, who supported the decriminalization of abortion, is the coup de grâce of the relationship. Baseotto sends the minister a letter of criticism with a Gospel quotation from Jesus: "If any of you put a stumbling block before one of these little ones who believe in me, it would be better for you if a great millstone were fastened around your neck and you were drowned in the depth of the sea" (Matthew 18:6). Kirchner thinks that Baseotto is referring to the "death flights" of the military dictatorship in Argentina, when prisoners were thrown into the waters of the Río de la Plata, and he has the Bishop removed from his position.

Both sides admit that there were unsuccessful attempts at a mutual approach. "It was my great political failure. I tried to bring them together. I was a friend to both Néstor and Bergoglio. But Néstor was not interested in religion; he was pragmatic," says the historian and Peronist leader Julio Bárbaro.

In April 2006 there is an informal meeting between Kirchner and Bergoglio during the ceremony in memory of the five members of the Pallottine Order murdered in 1976 during the military dictatorship. "I've come to attend a religious ceremony; I've never had bad relations with the Church," says Kirchner. "The important thing is to pray together," says the Cardinal. At that time many believe that there has been a reconciliation. But one of the facts that most disturbs Kirchner is Bergoglio's alleged intervention in the elections in the province of Misiones, in October 2006, when the Emeritus Bishop Joaquín Piña (a Jesuit like Bergoglio) decides to run for governor against the incumbent Carlos Rovira.

The debate over the government of Misiones is distorted and starts to be seen as a battle between the Church and the president. With the Piña victory, Bergoglio becomes, in Kirchner's mind, the hidden architect of the president's first election defeat.

"There has always been a tug of war for power. Besides being an austere man with a spiritual life, the Cardinal is a man of power who knows how to move the pieces on the chessboard," says José Ignacio López, director of the journal *Vida Nueva*.

In the middle of the battle for the Misiones election, and after a number of exchanges between officials and bishops, Father Guillermo Marcó, spokesman of the archbishopric at the time, provokes the government by declaring, "A president who foments division ends up a danger to all." Kirchner does not stay silent and during a conference answers him, "Our God belongs to everyone, but be aware that the devil, too, reaches everyone, whether they wear trousers or cassocks."

On the fringes of the battle, another thorny subject comes up: the role of the Church during the military dictatorship and in defense of human rights, propelled by a series of articles and books by Bergoglio's chief detractor, Horacio Verbitsky.

The conflict starts in 2004, when the episcopate publishes the document *Necesitamos ser nación* ("We must be a nation"), which calls for healing the wounds of the past. This is in open contradiction to the official policy of condemning the violations of human rights during the 1970s. Kirchner then says in a public address, "In the name of reconciliation in Argentina anything can be forgiven."

During the following years the government continues its criticisms of the Church, and in particular against Bergoglio, for his actions during the dictatorship. Faced with all this, the Cardinal always chooses silence.

"They were very personal attacks, and he felt there was no need to rebut them. He wasn't the kind of man to leap up and react to an attack. History would answer and so, in fact, it did," declares Oesterheld, spokesman of the episcopate presided over by Bergoglio. Tensions go on until 2006, when the episcopate publishes a harsh document on the social and political reality of the country, denouncing poverty, drug consumption, and inequality.

With the coming to power of Cristina Kirchner *née* Fernández in December 2007, relations seem to get better. They are certainly more fluid than in Néstor's time. "Cristina was more inclined to dialogue; at least she asked people on the secondary level to try to bring the positions closer together. She did this with Óscar Parrilli (general secretary of the presidency) and Guillermo Oliveri (secretary for religious affairs) and ministers who were supposed to deal with certain subjects," says a source close to Bergoglio.

The *presidenta* tones down the strategy of conflict and receives the Church commission headed by Bergoglio three times: in December 2007, November 2008, and March 2010. But hostilities continue. Bergoglio's closeness to the agricultural and livestock sector during the crisis of 2008 aggravates relations. In March of that year the government announces that state taxes for agricultural and livestock exports will rise from 34 percent to 44 percent, and the main producers' organizations call a strike.

In the middle of the conflict, Bergoglio calls for "a gesture of greatness" on the part of the president to unblock the situation. His communiqué is presented in an historic press conference of the episcopate, one of the few attended by Bergoglio.

But the conflict does not end there. After the communiqué, Bergoglio meets Vice President Julio Cobos, who voted against the proposed tax in the Senate, thereby blocking the law. The meeting infuriates the president.

This time of tension is followed by a brief period of calm, during which the president attends Mass at Luján, invited by Bergoglio, in December 2008. The following year they clash again. In September 2009, during the twelfth gathering of the social pastoral ministry, Bergoglio stresses that "the greatest risk is to standardize thinking." And he warns of the presence of "mindsets that paralyze and lead to discord" without specifying who favors them. Besides, he more than once in that year uses the phrase "social tension" (*crispación social*) to describe the political climate in Argentina; these words are adopted as a slogan by the opponents of the politics of the Kirchner presidents. In reply, the supporters of Cristina Kirchner speak ironically of social *Cris-pasión* (passion for Cristina).

The Cardinal goes on denouncing poverty in Argentina. "For years this country has not cared for the people," he declares during the celebration of San Cayetano in Liniers in August 2009. After this declaration there is a meeting between the president and the Cardinal in an attempt to bring back peace. The break becomes irreversible, however, after July 2010, when the proposed law on same-sex marriage, to which Bergoglio is sharply opposed, is discussed in Congress.

During the debate on the bill, which will become law in October 2010, Bergoglio makes public a letter he wrote to the four monasteries of Buenos Aires: "We are not naive: this is not simply a political battle; it is a claim to destroy the plans of God," he denounces in the letter.

"I am disturbed by the tone this question has assumed, it's presented like a problem of religious morality which is attacking the natural order, whereas in point of fact what is being done is recognizing a reality that already exists," responds the president. The debate on abortion does not intensify the clash, because President Cristina Kirchner puts a break on the polemical proposal relating to the interruption of pregnancy. This is interpreted as a concession to the Church.

Relations with Cristina Kirchener become more relaxed upon her husband's death on October 27, 2010. Bergoglio reacts quickly and within a few hours decides to celebrate a Mass for Kirchner's eternal rest in the cathedral of Buenos Aires. "The people must abandon any antagonism at the death of a man anointed by the people to lead it, and the whole country must pray for him," says Bergoglio.

The election of the Archbishop of Buenos Aires to the See of Peter on March 13, 2013 is bad news for President Kirchner. Even in her worst nightmares she could not have imagined that the chief political enemy of her and her husband (considering the lack of serious opposition in Argentina) could become the most famous Argentine in history. However, the *presidenta* does not hesitate to jump on Pope Francis's bandwagon.

Pope Francis, leaving behind old misunderstandings—though he knows well that some true supporters of the Kirchners booed at his election—stretches out his hand to his country and receives the president even before officially assuming the Petrine Ministry on March 19. The meeting, which takes place over lunch at the Casa Santa Marta, is warm and informal. Cristina is grateful and moved and gives him *mate*.

For his part, Francis gives her the Document of Aparecida, which stresses that preference must be given to the poor and challenges the instrumental use of poverty, opposes authoritarianism, and rails against corruption. "That's how you will understand what the bishops think," says the new pope, opening the door to reconciliation.

# 11

# The Slums of Christ

Shantytown Villa 1-11-14 of Bajo Flores is one of many often visited by the Primate Archbishop of Buenos Aires, a place where drugs, violence, protests, and dire poverty, but also hope, all live together. Never-ending lines of people wait for a meal, clothes, admission to social projects, or help dealing with all kinds of bureaucratic formalities. Mothers feed their children, laughing children play on swings, and others shriek to come out and play on the field. It is a little field built by the priests, where there is a mural representing Father Rodolfo Ricciardelli (parish priest of Santa María Madre del Pueblo and *villero* priest, who died in July 2008) and on the opposite side another mural, still being painted, where you can already recognize Pope Francis, the *villero* pope.

"The same children who painted the mural of Father Ricciardelli came to tell me that they wanted to paint one of the pope," says Father Gustavo Carrara, parish priest of Santa María Madre del Pueblo and head of the Episcopal Vicariate for the Pastoral Ministry in the Shantytowns, which Bergoglio set up in 2009. Father Carrara walks fast but conveys tranquility. He keeps his hands in his pockets and looks like a theologian—a muddy theologian who takes off his spectacles to smile.

"Bergoglio did what a Bishop should do, and with great dedication. He recognized the faith of the people of these districts. He believes that the poor resemble the suffering Christ, Christ on the cross. He saw a sacrament in the poor," says Father Carrara, age thirty-nine. "I stress the fact that he gave new value to people's faith. Here the people believe that God has to do with life and that life has to do with God. Religious expression is not something separate from life but is practically present in it. He included all this in the Aparecida Document."

Delicia Juárez, Ana Meza, and Gladys Rueda, fifty-something Bolivian women who have been taking part in parish activities for many years, are cooking a stew. "Bergoglio, who used to come here for the patronal festivals, came one July 9 for the feast of the Virgin of Itatí [patron saint of the province of Corrientes]," they say. "We were cooking the typical *locro* [stew] in the chapel kitchen when he came in, accompanied by the parish priest who introduced him to us. First he blessed the saucepan and then our hands, saying: 'I bless the hands that have cooked this *locro* which we are about to share,'" they add eagerly. "During these holidays the Bolivian community traditionally presents its folk dances. He has seen us dance the *cullaguada*. He was among us like anybody else. Now we miss him."

Celia Dalila Díaz is thirty-five and lives in Villa 1-11-14. On April 5, 2012, Holy Thursday, Bergoglio turns up at the Casa de Cristo built by the priest of the parish and dedicated to the rehabilitation of drug addicts. Celia has stopped taking drugs for a year and a half and is now a volunteer at the Casa de Santa María, also founded by the priests. She says, "I was told that a Cardinal was to come, but I didn't know anything about it. I didn't know who he was. He came with the priests and looked quite ordinary. I offered him a *mate* and we started talking. I realized that he was very humble in the way he talked. He shared the *mate* with the drug addicts—not everybody does that. In the half hour that we chatted by ourselves he asked me how long I had been there, what my name was, how I felt. I told him that the priests had saved me from the streets—that pleased him a lot. Suddenly he said, 'Would you like me to wash your feet?' I didn't understand a thing, I didn't understand what he was talking about and I said, 'Sorry, but I can wash them myself.' He answered, 'No, no, I want to bless your feet.' I told him, 'Oh, all right'... I didn't know that he would put me in front of everybody, that he would take off my shoes... I felt very ashamed. It's very rare for someone to arrive unexpectedly, wash your feet, and give you a kiss... But later I felt relieved... That day he also baptized my son."

The presence of priests in the Buenos Aires shantytowns goes back to the 1960s, when these settlements began to arise. Imitating the experience of French worker-priests, some priests go to live in the shantytowns in solidarity with the poor. In 1969, a year marked by militancy and political violence, Cardinal Juan Carlos Aramburu (1976–2004) created the Equipo de Sacerdotes para las Villas de Emergencia, to train priests to deal with issues specific to the shantytowns. Among these was the emblematic figure of Father Carlos Mugica, a priest from an upper-middle-class family, who died in 1974, shot dead by the Argentine Anti-Communist Alliance (Triple A), an organized parapolitical group of the extreme right.

When Bergoglio becomes Archbishop of Buenos Aires in 1998, social reality in Argentina is different, as are the challenges faced by the *villeros* priests. The Cardinal devotes affection and attention to them. Because he believes that the shantytowns hide a treasure that can do good for the whole Church—the deep faith and simple piety of the people—the work of the *villero* priests begins to occupy a privileged place in his agenda. In fact, it is one of his priorities.

The pastoral work dedicated to marginal areas grows at the same rate as the spread of the shantytowns. The number of priests committed to working there doubles. When Bergoglio becomes Archbishop, the team numbers ten priests; at the time he is elected pope, there are twenty-two priests working in the various shantytowns.

Apart from visiting and helping when necessary, he meets his team of priests and listens to them every month. He supports them in their attempt to solve two main problems: how to integrate the shantytowns in the life of the city and how to tackle the exclusion of their inhabitants. These problems are exacerbated by the scourge of drugs. The Archbishop's interest is also made evident by his actions to develop professional schools, kindergartens, rehabilitation communities, and the building of chapels, in addition to his own constant physical presence.

With regard to his own commitments, Bergoglio gives precedence to a saint's day celebration in Villa 21 over a commemorative Mass in the cathedral. He often visits the shantytowns and frequently arrives without notice. He takes part in patronal feast days, processions, services for Holy Week, and the administering of sacraments. He stops to talk with the families, remembers many of them, and helps them regularly. Today many people proudly show off their photos of first communion, confirmation, or baptism that include Padre Jorge, now Pope Francis.

"The people of the shantytowns feel that he belongs to them. They have taken possession of the pope. He is their Bishop, he has visited all the shantytowns, he doesn't know things just because he's heard about them but knows their griefs, their struggles, their joys. When he was elected pope there was a party, and these were the comments: 'The Pope has eaten the *chipá* I made.' 'The pope has drunk my *mate*.' 'The pope confirmed me, baptized me . . .' He left his mark on the shantytowns of Buenos Aires," says Father Nicolás Angeletti, age twenty-eight, who works in Villa 1-11-14 with Father Carrara and Hernán Morelli.

"When he came here, he would go down all the lanes—people would put little altars in front of their doors, and he would bless them. He would greet everybody, some in wheelchairs, others dirty or on drugs . . . He talked to everyone," recalls María Álvarez, a forty-five-year-old from Paraguay who lives in Villa 21. María will never forget the pilgrimage to the cathedral when they went to fetch the image of the Virgin of Caacupé. She still keeps and shows—as if it's a relic—the little blue plastic chair she had brought so that her daughter, four at the time, could sit when they stopped to rest. "'I can't go on,' my daughter said to me, and I said to her, 'Cheer up, let's go on, the Virgin will protect you, let's make this sacrifice.' Bergoglio's example impressed me, because he walked among us without fear or shame; we were all equal."

The clearest evidence of Bergoglio's support of the work of the *villeros* priests comes at the end of April 2009, after the threats received by Father José María "Pepe" Di Paola, at the time parish priest of Our Lady of Caacupé, in Villa 21. In March of that year, there is a debate in Congress on the decriminalization of drug use, and the team of shantytown priests signs a document declaring, "Here, where we are, drugs have been decriminalized in actual fact."

The same document also affirms that "the problem isn't the shantytowns but the drug trafficking," declaring, "Most of those who get rich on drug traffic don't live in the shantytowns." On the night of Monday, April 20, Father Pepe, who fights against drug use and trafficking in Villa 21, is threatened: a man he doesn't recognize shouts in the dark, "Disappear or you're a dead man!" and then runs away, saying, "When this drugs story ends up on television you'll be a dead man. Mark my words."

The next day Di Paola talks to Bergoglio. "The evening I was threatened, the priests held a meeting. I went to the meeting but preferred not to make any comments. Later I went on getting threatening messages on my mobile. On Tuesday I called Bergoglio and went to see him. I told him they had threatened to kill me. I remember that he took his head in his hands and was silent for a moment. Then he said, 'First of all we must be calm because we are acting in harmony with the Gospel.' I think he was asking himself if he had been prudent with that document, and I remember as if it was yesterday that he said, 'I shall ask God that, if there must be a dead man, it should be me. I shall ask God to take me and not you.' The following day he had a Mass with the Catholic schools and he said it in public. This was an intelligent idea, because he found the best way to protect me. He thought of the best thing for me. I informed the police, went to a press conference, and all this changed my life," recalls Father Pepe.

On April 22, during the traditional Mass in favor of education, which is celebrated on the steps of the cathedral, Bergoglio calls drug dealers "powerful merchants of darkness." "These forces of darkness are so powerful that yesterday one of my priests was threatened and we know that these threats must not be underestimated, we don't know how they can end ... It's a matter that doesn't just concern those priests but all of us[;] it concerns me and all the Auxiliary Bishops who support this declaration. Because we must defend our 'brood'—excuse the word—sometimes this world of darkness makes us forget our instinct to defend our cubs," he says.

But the Jesuit Archbishop doesn't confine himself to words. The following Saturday, when no one is expecting it, he turns up at Villa 21, walks through its dusty streets, makes himself visible, and spends the afternoon chatting and praying in the most distant building of the Caacupé parish with Father Pepe and the other *villeros* priests. Five months later, on August 7, he creates the Episcopal Vicariate for the Pastoral Ministry in the Shantytowns and nominates Father Pepe as vicar. With this decision he grants the team a hierarchy, recognizes the value of their work, and conveys a clear message: "This team is the arm of the Bishop in the shantytowns," Father Pepe affirms today.

In 2009, I meet Father Pepe—a priest whose beard and green eyes make him look like a Jesus figure—and a number of other *villeros* priests, during a visit organized by Father Jorge for my husband Gerry, who intends to write an article. It's the middle of winter, and in Buenos Aires everyone is fearful of swine flu—hand sanitizers are disappearing like hotcakes, and friends I meet in the streets greet me at a distance. But in Villa 21 this problem doesn't exist. During the visit we kiss and embrace every young drug addict, rehabilitated or under treatment, introduced to us by Father Charly—Carlos Olivero, our guide on an unforgettable journey through the workshops where people learn to bake bread, sculpt marble, and do other crafts so that they can find a job. There is poverty, but we breathe the cheerfulness of the people thanks to the extraordinary work of the *villeros* priests.

Villa 21 in Barracas is very noisy. There is music, construction work, greetings, shouts. The parish church of Our Lady of Caacupé is on a street where two bus routes pass. Their stops are right in front of the church, and that's why many passengers, when they get off, make the sign of the cross or kneel down on the pavement. The doors of the church are always open, and the interior attracts our attention. The pictures on the walls have been painted in bright colors. They reflect the devotion of the people of this shantytown: Paraguayans, Bolivians, Peruvians, and people from the Argentine coast. Obviously there are photos of Pope Francis, some candles burning and many already spent.

Father "Toto" Lorenzo de Vedia, forty-seven, laughs loudly while he answers a landline phone and two mobiles at the same time. "One for calling and the other for texting," he says, justifying himself. Toto has the difficult job of finding out what happened to the grill. He's worried because next day the parish of Our Lady of Caacupé is to offer a *polleada* (a grilled chicken barbecue) in aid of the parish mission to take place in 2014 in Paraguay. "Juan, have you got it? Where did you put it?"

Juan Isasmendi, thirty-two, is a priest from Salta. He has walked more miles in the shantytowns than in the streets of the city and has been working in this parish since 2007. He met Bergoglio in 2010, when he joined the seminary.

"Once, in the seminary, we asked him about the theme of our mission, about the life of the Church. We told him that at times we felt we were being prepared for a world that expected something quite different from us. We gave him the example of a seminarian who went up and down visiting ordinary homes, and I remember that he laughed a lot and used an expression that has stayed with me: 'It's always better to ask for forgiveness rather than permission, so cheer up, you must go ahead, if it's for Jesus and the Church, do it. You'll make thousands of mistakes and on the way you'll have to change your heart, your intentions, adjust your aim,'" says Juan.

Some blocks away, outside the shantytown, there is the parish of the Nativity of St. Mary of Barracas. The church is in perfect condition; it has just been repainted in blue and white, the colors of the soccer team Racing and of the Virgin, explains the parish priest, Father Juan Gabriel Arias, who belongs to the organizing committee of the soccer team. He's the only priest to whom Bergoglio has given permission to go and watch soccer matches every Sunday. Also, he lived in Mozambique for three years and now goes there once a year for three months. "From there I always spoke to him by phone; he sent me e-mails, or if anyone went there he'd send me a letter. Bergoglio has always supported all my pastoral work, like, for instance, the underwater Via Crucis [Stations of the Cross], which I organize every year at Puerto Madryn. He has also authorized me to work for

Racing; I am on the organizing committee of the club. He has always liked the idea of a priest close to people," he says.

Father Juan Gabriel, now a member of the team of *villeros* priests, admits that he was ordained thanks to Bergoglio. "When I was a deacon, three months before becoming a priest, the Racing team played a match for the Copa Libertadores tournament in Peru. There were some very cheap flights—Bergoglio authorized me to go. A month later, it was discovered that Menem was smuggling arms into Ecuador when it was at war with Peru. The Peruvians didn't want us, and there were clashes. They wrote a nasty article about me and put all kinds of things into it: 'The hooligan priest of Racing gets into a fight in Peru,' and they even published a photo in [the newspaper] *Crónica* where I appear circled in red. From that moment my ordination was contested, and I know that he interceded personally on my behalf."

Father Pedro Velasco Suárez, of Opus Dei, works in the same very poor neighborhood. Fifty-three years old and wearing an old cassock with some buttons missing, informal and passionate, he is the chaplain of the Colegio Buen Consejo of Barracas. This school is intended for the population of Villa 21 and has two hundred kindergarten students and six hundred primary and secondary school students. He, too, doesn't forget the Masses with a procession that Bergoglio used to celebrate every December 8 in Caacupé, the last one in 2012. "They were very powerful Masses. There were three thousand people, representing the whole population of Villa 21: Paraguayans, Bolivians, Peruvians, and people from the hinterland. Every year three hundred to four hundred confirmations were celebrated. Everyone came with their godparents. There were also baptisms and first communions. When he finished, he was exhausted, his hands stained with oil, but he seemed very absorbed. One must have a great interior life to succeed; he was never distracted, never impatient—he was at God's service."

From 1999 on, all the teachers of private and public schools working in Villa 21 meet every year in the chapel of Caacupé. "Bergoglio always came. He missed only one year. We read the Gospel, and he talked. There were forty of us teachers. The heart of each meeting was Bergoglio's ten- to fifteen-minute talk to us. We waited for those words because every one of them contained a world. He gave great importance to education and held us teachers in enormous consideration. Concerning the population we were working with, he told us not to give up, to elevate people. In 2011 he spoke to us about his hope of renewing the task of education. He wasn't a superficial speaker; you could see that he believed in what he was saying. When we left the meeting, we were all crying, moved, men and women alike," recalls Aída Vescovo, principal of the Colegio Buen Consejo.

"A few years ago, during one of these meetings, he referred to the subject of violence at school. He spoke about tenderness, of the need to show affection for these children physically. He told us to establish a physical contact. I remember that he conveyed this idea: 'Reach their hearts, so that the heart can reach the head and the head can move the hand'—that is how we were to combat violence at school."

"Once he came to the *colegio* to celebrate Mass and spoke to the girls with great affection. He came down with the microphone to be near them. Seeing the effect it provoked, from then on I started doing the same thing. He said to me, 'When you speak to the little ones, both the little ones and the big ones understand you, that's why it's better to speak to the little ones,'" says Father Pedro Velasco Suárez, who knows Bergoglio well—he was a great friend of his father's. And he tells of a significant incident: "At supper with my family, Bergoglio told us that he had been to a retreat with Father Mugica a few days before they murdered him. On that occasion he asked him if he wasn't afraid, and Mugica replied: 'My only fear is to die outside the Church.'"

Well aware of the drama of exclusion, in 2008 the Cardinal Primate begins to collaborate actively with La Alameda, a nongovernmental organization combating slave labor, child labor, and human trafficking. That same year, the organization's president, Gustavo Vera, writes to Bergoglio asking for his help and protection.

"We told him that we were not a Catholic organization, that our main goal was to fight against slave labor and human trafficking, and that we needed the support of the church because the attacks against us were getting more and more dangerous. By now he knew about the subject of drugs and the kidnapping of women, and he was learning about the subject of slavery. Nothing surprised him. He understood everything at once, and he thought of celebrating a Mass, the first against the slave trade and in favor of its victims. He celebrated it on July 1 in the Inmigrantes parish, in the Boca neighborhood. Many dressmakers and *cartoneros* [waste pickers, cardboard collectors] came," Vera recalls.

From that time on, Bergoglio's homilies against human trafficking, also accompanied by processions, will become history. "At school they taught us that slavery was abolished, but do you know what that is? A fairy tale! Because in the city of Buenos Aires slavery has not been abolished; in this city slavery is practiced in many forms. In this city workers are exploited in secret sweatshops, and if they are immigrants, they have no chance of escaping. In this city there are children who live in the street for years! . . . In this city women and girls are raped, subjected to the use and abuse of their bodies; their dignity is destroyed. In this city there are men who make money and feed on the flesh of their brothers, the flesh of all these slaves—men and women—the flesh Jesus took on and for which he died is worth less than an animal's meat, that's what is happening in this city! We care more for a dog than for these slaves of ours! Who are downtrodden! Destroyed!" he denounces on September 23, 2011, during a homily in Plaza Constitución, on the International Day against the Sexual Exploitation and Trafficking of Women and Children.

Bergoglio publicly supports the victims and those who have had the courage to speak, such as Nancy Miño Velásquez, a policewoman who in 2010 dared to denounce members of the Federal Police division where she worked for their involvement in human trafficking, as they took bribes from brothels. Bergoglio also openly supports Lorena Martins, who in 2011 denounces her father, an ex-agent of the Secretariat of Intelligence, as an owner of brothels in Argentina and Mexico and supporter of the campaign of Mauricio Macri, mayor of Buenos Aires.

But Bergoglio's commitment to the struggle against modern slavery starts before 2008. In March 2006, a fire starts in a clandestine fabric workshop in the Caballito district of Buenos Aires. Six people die, four of them juveniles, living in conditions of slavery. Bergoglio doesn't hesitate to celebrate Mass in front of the workshop door.

"When we began to organize in a more formal way the work of the *cartoneros*, one day he took the metro and appeared unexpectedly at the Plaza Houssay stop, where the *cartoneros* live. He had gone to drink a *mate* with them and support them. Every time they arrested me or abused me I would call him and he would make himself available. He always received us. He faced everyone and outlined things as elements of a system, not as if there were good people and bad people, but a system in which some have too much and others too little," says Juan Grabois, lawyer and militant of the Movement of Excluded Workers (Movimiento de Trabajadores Excluidos, or MTE), which brings together *cartoneros* who are trying to organize their work recycling trash in Buenos Aires and also works alongside the organization La Alameda in the fight against slave labor.

"In Bergoglio we see a person who openly says the same things that we say. And even in a clearer way than we do. He has always held that this situation is the consequence of unjust economic policies that pay no account to human dignity. I started to discover who Bergoglio was and noted a certain consistency in what he was saying from the time of the success of the neoliberal policies (in Argentina). Some people thought he belonged to the right. Others, especially in the northern area, San Isidro for example, saw him as a communist, disqualifying him on the grounds of his concern about poverty and exploitation. His austerity contributed to this idea," says Grabois. Together with Vera, Grabois takes part in a first meeting with Bergoglio in the Archdiocese in 2008, and there begins a close collaboration on various fronts.

Pedro Nicola is sixty-three. He is a taxi driver and a permanent deacon—that is to say, he belongs to the secular clergy and can do almost everything a priest does except say Mass and take confession. A widower for a year now, he works in one of the shantytowns of Buenos Aires and dreams that Pope Francis will ordain him a priest.

He has always worked in the shantytowns with his wife, helping in the soup kitchens and teaching catechism. Ten years ago he decided to prepare himself to become a deacon. He went to see Monsignor Mario Aurelio Poli, at the time Auxiliary Bishop under Cardinal Bergoglio, who told him, "The Cardinal doesn't much like deacons." But he joined the seminary just the same and trained for nine years.

"One day at last something happened," he says. "They told us that Bergoglio would receive me and a few others. We went to the curia. The Cardinal was in front of me and started by saying: 'It's true that I don't like deacons. Buenos Aires doesn't need them. There are already 269 priests . . . and they must work.' Then he was introduced to each one of us. And he said again: 'I don't like them, but the Virgin came to visit me last night and asked me for three deacons for Buenos Aires. She told me: one for the poor, that's you, Pedro, you're the poor people's deacon.' On ordination day in the cathedral, on April 15, 2011, he said at the microphone: 'Pedro, don't lose your taxi driver's smile!'"

# 12

# Bergoglio and the Media

It doesn't often happen that somebody calls you up on the phone to thank you for an article. That's what Jorge Bergoglio does to me at the end of February 2001, when I meet him during an interview for *La Nación*. The Archbishop of Buenos Aires has come to Rome to be made a Cardinal by John Paul II at the consistory of February 21 of that year.

According to what they tell me at the paper, he is not well disposed toward the press and is famous for not giving interviews; but when he is about to receive the red hat, the Archbishop of Buenos Aires makes an exception. As usual he is staying at the Casa Internazionale at 70 Via della Scrofa. I call him to arrange our meeting. The Archbishop of Buenos Aires, age sixty-four—I must confess that I know absolutely nothing about him except that he's a Jesuit—asks me shyly if I could please let him know in advance the subjects we will discuss.

I immediately send him a few lines by fax, presenting the topics I would like to talk about: how he feels a few days before the consistory (ceremony in which the pope creates new cardinals); what it means for Argentina to again have two cardinal-electors at a future conclave (another Argentinian, Jorge Mejía, working in the Roman Curia, is also to be created Cardinal); how he sees the Catholic Church in general and Argentina's Church in particular; his vision for Argentina, which is experiencing difficult times and in fact would collapse and default on its debt a few months later, at the end of the same year.

The appointment is for Thursday, February 15, at 4:15 in the afternoon. Bergoglio receives me in an elegant room with a high ceiling and antique armchairs with damask upholstery, on the first floor of the Casa Internazionale. He seems nervous but is courteous. To break the ice, I tell him a little about myself, that I have recently become *La Nación*'s correspondent in Rome and the Vatican, that I'm not an expert on ecclesiastical matters but that I do a little bit of everything. I also cover other countries, the Middle East, Kosovo, wars and politics.

When I switch on my tape recorder and we start the interview, he gradually begins to relax. He pays careful attention to every word. He speaks in a direct and simple way; many of his sentences could serve as headlines. Bergoglio doesn't have that superior, somewhat misogynistic attitude that I have noticed in some high-ranking prelates.

In spite of the difficult situation in Argentina, Bergoglio doesn't lose hope. He says he foresees what he calls a "transversal generation": men and women capable of forgetting which party they belong to, realizing that the country must be defended, rather than the "game preserve" of one's own party and interests. "I invite young people to enter politics and become responsible: politics is one of the most important forms of charity. It means working for the common good, and it's necessary to deliver politics from the circumstances that have soiled it," he says. He doesn't hide the fact that he is a priest who prefers the street to the cloister. When I ask him what he'd say to a young person thinking of emigrating from Argentina because of the dramatic economic crisis, he says that a few months earlier he saw a poster that read: "Ezeiza [airport] is not the only way out." "I thought it was a fine slogan," he says. "The way out of the country lies in work, in community organizations that guide the people, that give up some more personal things for the common good. Being a politician involves many sacrifices. And to young people I would say: 'Work in your country, as you can.' Now the problem is to create jobs, develop education, health," he declares.

The famous Cardinal Carlo Maria Martini, a Jesuit like him and recognized as an intellectual of a progressive wing of the Society, has expressed the need for a new Council. "Do you agree?" I ask. Bergoglio gives a categorical no. "Vatican Council II has such great riches that we haven't yet finished exploiting it," he tells me. When I ask him if it is correct to say that he is a conservative prelate so far as doctrine is concerned but "Wojtylian," with regard to the Polish pope's criticism of the excesses of capitalism, he once more answers no. "Definitions are always limiting, and that is a definition. I try to be not conservative, but faithful to the Church, and always open to dialogue," he says.

Faithful to his reputation of keeping a low profile, when I ask him how he is assuming his new role as a Cardinal, if it's like arriving at the top for him, he answers: "I live it religiously—that is, I pray, talk to the Lord, ask him to protect my diocese, and I do not live it as if I had arrived at something. According to the standards of the Gospel, every ascent implies a descent: you must go down to serve better. And I want to live it with this spirit of service."

When I talk to him about a possible conclave to elect the successor of John Paul II, who is ill, and say that because of his age, he could be *papabile*, he laughs. "I hadn't thought about it," he assures me. And when I point out that the number of Latin American cardinals has increased and ask him if we can expect the next pope to be Latin American, he replies with the words that, twelve years later, will turn out to be prophetic: "I believe it's one possibility among many . . . It could be anyone, from any continent. Usually when guesses are made the result is unexpected. For example, nobody thought that John XXIII would be elected, and neither that Luciani would become John Paul I . . . and then a Pole. These things look different from the inside; there is a lot of praying, and the needs of the Church are considered."

A few days later, after the article is published, the Archbishop of Buenos Aires calls me at home to thank me. This call surprises me—not everyone would do it. And I still don't know that it is the starting point of something that will only grow with time.

Yes, it's true, Jorge Bergoglio doesn't feel comfortable giving interviews (at least before he became pope). He has always said so. He doesn't know why, but he isn't confident that his words won't be manipulated. "If I give four notes to the journalists—do, re, mi, fa—they might end up composing a wedding march or a funeral march," he often says.

Just as he is clear in the homilies he writes, so in interviews he knows how to explain perfectly well what he intends to say. In both cases he makes use of the Jesuit technique of explaining concepts using three main ideas.

He is also aware of the crucial importance of the media to the Catholic Church in today's world. "The technological revolution and the processes of globalization shape today's world through a great culture of the media. This implies the capacity of recognizing the new languages that can help achieve greater global humanization. These new languages articulate the changes in society. In our century, so deeply influenced by the mass means of communication, the first call to faith, the catechism, or its further study cannot ignore these means," read paragraphs 484 and 485 of the Aparecida Document, clearly inspired by Bergoglio, which dedicates a number of reflections to the media.

As soon as he is nominated Archbishop of Buenos Aires, Bergoglio sets up a structure that deals with the media. Even though he doesn't watch television—"He found that television news had reached such a low level that he decided to stop watching it," says Federico Wals, head of the press office of the Archdiocese—he pays constant attention to this structure by providing guidelines and following what it is doing.

For anyone who is a member of the archbishopric's media office, it's difficult to keep up with a person who is used to managing himself; who doesn't use a mobile phone; and unless there's a particular urgency, prefers not to inform anyone about his movements. "Since he has always preached that one must go outside, not be a 'church of the sacristy' and tried to show this with his example, our work has multiplied," says Eduardo Woites, who is the son of the founder and current administrator of the Argentine Catholic Information Agency, created fifty-seven years ago by the

Argentine Bishops Conference. "It wasn't easy to follow him because he went everywhere. If we add the fact that he didn't use a mobile, it was difficult to know where he was. Our work was even more complicated because, apart from everything else, he was very direct. He would look carefully at the communications, revise the transcriptions, and correct the mistakes. We didn't publish anything he said without his approval," adds Woites.

During ceremonies and public events, Bergoglio always came in through a side door. At the feast of a patron saint, he went to celebrate Mass in the Basilica of the Sacred Heart of Barracas. "The Cardinal was supposed to be coming, they prepared a red carpet for him, we were waiting for him . . . We thought he was late but no, someone had seen him. 'The Cardinal came a while ago,' and we found him praying alone in the chapel of the Blessed Sacrament. In this he reminded me of John Paul II, who would reserve for himself one or two minutes to talk to God before meeting people," Woites recalls.

According to Woites, Bergoglio avoids speaking directly to the press "not because he despises it" but because that's part of his low-profile style. "There weren't any photos of him even in the curia, let alone in the parish churches. It hadn't been like that with the other Archbishops. As soon as they were ordained, they distributed photos, even in the parishes. He didn't, and still today in our offices we have a photo of Quarracino."

When Bergoglio takes on the leadership of the Archdiocese in February 1998, after Antonio Quarracino's death, the financial scandal linked to the Banco de Crédito Provincial, inherited from his predecessor, explodes in his hands, and he realizes that he needs help.

"He had asked me to see what I could do with the press when suddenly, one day at three o'clock in the afternoon he rang me: he was very calm, not in the least upset, and said, 'Are you busy? If you can, come to the curia, but don't come through the main entrance, pass through the cathedral, because there are about fifty journalists at the door.' 'Why? What has

happened?' 'No, nothing, well ... a search. When you arrive I'll tell you,'"
Father Guillermo Marcó recalls.

It was the first time in the history of the Buenos Aires Archdiocese that
somebody took the trouble to provide the official version of what had happened. The next day all the dailies called Marcó "a spokesman of the archbishopric"—a post he was to keep for eight years.

"The first thing I did was to organize a press office, which didn't exist,
and we invented a communication strategy. Second, we made clear that
[Bergoglio] didn't give interviews. The reason was that at that time he
didn't feel qualified to do so. What happened generally when a Bishop gave
an interview was that they would start asking him about the Virgin Mary
and end up talking politics, and what came out in the end was what he
hadn't wanted to say. So we decided that his presence should be objective.
How? Through his homilies, which we would give to the journalists before
they were delivered," says Marcó.

If the world gradually got to know the personality of this Cardinal who
doesn't want to appear on television, it is thanks to Father Guillermo. "The
Cardinal never said that he got up before five o'clock in the morning to
pray or that he traveled by bus. Those are things that I told the press. And
I told them because my theory is the one you find in the Gospel: 'You don't
light a lamp to put it under a bushel, but so that it can give light to everyone.' He often didn't want me to talk about these things, but I convinced
him. 'Listen, it's not for you, it's not to say how good you are, but because
it's a good example,' I would explain. At the beginning he didn't want the
television cameras when he washed the feet of young people in prison on
Maundy Thursday. When he became Archbishop, he never wanted to celebrate Maundy Thursday in the cathedral. But he didn't say so. As there
were many Auxiliary Bishops, he let one of them wash feet in the cathedral
while he went off to do what nobody knew he was doing," says Marcó.

A few days before the 2005 conclave, when Bergoglio leaves for Rome,
Marcó refutes the rumors circulated by Bergoglio's enemies that accuse
him of complicity with the Argentine dictatorship; some are reviving the
attacks of the journalist Horacio Verbitsky.

"So when many cardinals were granting interviews and he wasn't, I would give interviews, in English and Italian, and it was an important experience for me to be working with the foreign press," says Marcó. "I was impressed by the *Corriere della Sera*, which always devoted a quarter page to every cardinal, and the day before the conclave devoted half a page to him [Bergoglio]. And the title was 'He Travels by Bus,' which attracted a lot of attention."

At the end of 2006, after eight complicated years, Marcó is forced to leave his post as spokesman, having naively fallen into a trap. After Benedict XVI's slip at Regensburg (when he offends the Muslim world in a *lectio magistralis* on faith and reason), Marcó makes a declaration that will be taken out of context and used against the Cardinal by his detractors. "*Newsweek* magazine contacted me as copresident of the Institute for Interreligious Dialogue, and I said that the words of the pope had struck me as 'unfortunate.' But this is what the magazine did: they took a photo from their files, pretended that I had given an interview and titled it: 'The archbishopric of Buenos Aires against Benedict XVI,' though I hadn't spoken as the Archbishop's spokesman … That article in a magazine that nobody in Buenos Aires reads was photocopied and sent to all the departments of the Vatican, in an operation against Bergoglio that finally turned against me," says Father Marcó with regret. Not long after, however, he makes another comment, one that offends President Néstor Kirchner, and that leads to his resignation as spokesman.

Marcó's successor as head of the archbishopric press office, Federico Wals, a layman, is unlikely to forget a gaffe: "The Bishop of Humahuaca, Monsignor Pedro Olmedo, had written a document critical of the social reality in his territory. He had sent it to some papers and to press offices. I found it a well-written document, and I forwarded it to the media, making it clear that it didn't come from the Buenos Aires archbishopric. Next day the daily *Ambito Financiero* featured on a full page: 'Bergoglio criticizes the government on poverty in the north.' I took my head in my hands, thinking I had lost my job. I went to see Bergoglio, who said to me, 'Federico, what has happened? Why are you up so early?' 'Nothing, Father, I've ended up on the front page.' 'And why, if I didn't say anything yesterday?' 'That's the problem,' I answered. And he asked me only, 'How do you explain it?' He listened to my explanation, and the only thing he said was, 'I understand. Once in a while it's good to realize that poverty exists. Don't worry.'"

"Once," he adds, "after the publication of an editorial, the Cardinal said to me, 'Federico, I don't understand, the people on the Catholic right see me as on the left, and the people on the left as someone on the right, but I'm a shepherd who wants to walk in the midst of his people.'"

Bergoglio's press conferences can be counted on the fingers of one hand. One took place at the end of a permanent council of the Argentine episcopate in 2008, amid the conflict with the leaders of the agrarian sector. "It was necessary that someone who was not a spokesman for the Church should talk to the press. I told Bergoglio that it had to be him, and he replied that all twenty bishops of the executive commission had to be there. So we received the journalists in the headquarters of the CEA (Conferencia Episcopal Argentina). He started talking, and then the other bishops answered questions," says Father Jorge Oesterheld, head of the press office of the Argentine Episcopal Conference (CEA).

Also at the Vatican, journalists remember a few press conferences with Bergoglio, in the press hall in Via della Conciliazione. A memorable one takes place on October 17, 2003. The Argentine Cardinal has been given the task of explaining the contents of the post-synodal exhortation *Pastores gregis*, after being assistant rapporteur at the Synod of Bishops in September and October 2001. Obviously, I am there, too, to report on the event. Bergoglio seems more at ease and relaxed than at the preceding press conference in October 2001. Though he speaks Italian perfectly, he begins by saying that he prefers Spanish, "to be more exact and spontaneous" (an expression that he will use again as pope during his first journey to Brazil).

This time, at the end of a very clear and precise speech, Bergoglio takes many questions, which he answers in a brief and articulate way. Referring to a paragraph in the document that denounces "the dramatic inequalities between rich and poor," the injustices, the wars, Bergoglio answers a question about why there is so much poverty in Latin America even though the Catholic Church is strong, and whether this is due to a spiritual crisis. He says, "At the bottom of any failure or the defeat of hope there is a spiritual problem. Now, for example, to use the words of John Paul II, we are living through a period of weak thought, in a culture in which all the dramatic things mentioned in the text appear because the human spirit itself follows hopes that in the final analysis disappoint," he says. "But this happens all over the world, in one way or another: in some continents poverty is stronger, in others it is pride. In my opinion an attitude of pride is a failure, as much a defeat of hope as is a state of poverty: that's where you'll find man's failure." These words impress all present.

At the end of the press conference, surely a torture for him, I hear positive comments from fellow reporters. When, surrounded by television cameras, a CNN correspondent asks Bergoglio (with the aim of getting an interview) if he speaks English, he replies: "I forgot my English," in perfect English.

Although he doesn't watch television, Bergoglio understands its crucial importance and supports the creation of the archbishopric's Channel 21, a channel that he never intended to be parochial, but also above the level of so much popular programming, a channel with *sin mistas, ni trastes*, "no masses and no asses."

It's a story well told by Julio Rimoldi, an engineer who started working at the archbishopric more than thirty years ago as an electrician and is today director of Channel 21.

It all begins in 2000, when a channel is assigned to the Catholic Church of Buenos Aires, a channel that nobody is interested in and that eventually will be suspended for lack of use. In 2004 Julio Bárbaro, auditor of the government's Communications Authority talks to the nuncio Adriano Bernardini, to remind him that a television channel has been assigned to the church, and that the channel must be returned if not used. Bernardini calls Bergoglio and tells him to deal with the problem, a real hot potato.

Realizing that it is a challenge, the Cardinal, who is president of the episcopate at the time, presents the subject to the Episcopal Conference of Argentina and starts consultations. One day he calls Julio Rimoldi, whom he has known for some time because he works and has his office in the small television center of the archbishopric on the fifth floor of the curia building where he also lives. Rimoldi recounts their conversation.

"Julio, there's this story of a channel. What shall we do?"

"Look, if you ask me I say we should do it. But as you're not convinced I'll give you three reasons why we should do it: first, obviously, because the channel has been suspended. We're always talking about the fact that the sects have the upper hand, and have channels, media, and so on, and now we have the chance to answer back. Second, it's a question of moral authority: if we say that television has no real content, it's just trash, et cetera, we must offer an alternative. If we say no and go on criticizing, we lose our moral authority and must keep quiet. And then to tell the truth the third reason is that I never say no because I'm afraid—you know, nothing ventured, nothing gained."

"But it's a headache."

"Not just a headache, but a pain in your legs, your back, every part you can imagine . . ."

"That's fine, Julio, you have convinced me. Let's begin. But can you do it?"

"No."

"My God, are you crazy?"

"You know what it is, monsignor? We're proud enough to believe that because we are guided by the Holy Spirit, everything will be all right. And the media aren't a joke, they're important. It's the Church that commits itself. It's a very difficult job, but we must do it. There'll be a lot of people who'll join the project, they'll teach us."

"Draw up a project to present to the Italian Bishops Committee for Charitable Aid to the Third World. How long do you think it will take?"

"A couple of months."

"You've got two weeks. I'm not really convinced, so, everything depends on the message St. Joseph gives us: if the project is approved, it means I must do it."

Rimoldi goes on: "Bergoglio was very clever; against all the forecasts, although the deadline for the presentation of projects had already lapsed, we had sent it in too late, yet miraculously the project created in two weeks with a group of professionals was approved by Rome." And he recalls Bergoglio's instructions:

"Listen, Julio, I don't want a blessed channel. I want a channel people want to watch. I want a channel that is popular, humane, and interreligious. A channel with no masses, no asses, and no priests directing it."

From that time the director will be Rimoldi and the deputy director and manager will be a woman, Silvia Tuozzo. The test broadcasts begin in 2005, and the following year Channel 21 goes on the air. It will be a television station with general contents, based on pillars of service and solidarity. Rimoldi runs it against all obstacles and in the midst of a thousand difficulties, even internal ones, because many people don't approve of the fact that the priests' channel is run by a layman. But Bergoglio protects him.

"He said that we of Channel 21 had a basic mission: 'the image of the Church is in your hands.' Faithful to the idea that a Church must not be turned in on itself, but must go out into the streets, he thought that the television channel was an instrument to support this idea, to go out to meet people," Rimoldi stresses.

With his usual sense of humor, Bergoglio calls Rimoldi "my Tinelli," in reference to Marcelo Tinelli, a famous Argentine TV personality. "When he called the studio, he would say: 'Hello, Rimoldi's number? Is Tinelli there?' He didn't watch television, but he was given many DVDs, including *Life Is Beautiful*. One day he said to me, 'I want to see it.' I answered, 'I'll bring you a DVD player.' 'No, what are you doing on Saturday? Shall we watch it together?' Every now and then he would call me, he came up to the studio, we'd have some coffee and watch a film. 'Bring a couple of pastries,' he'd ask me, because he adored sweets. Actually, as he always gave away everything he was given, I started giving him boxes of sweets already opened," he recalls.

It's very difficult for Rimoldi to persuade the Cardinal to take part in the program *Biblia, diálogo vigente* ("The Bible, a Living Dialogue") with Rabbi Abraham Skorka and a Protestant friend of Bergoglio's, Marcelo Figueroa. "He didn't want to appear because he didn't want it to be said that he had opened a channel to publicize himself. But we managed to persuade him. We had already done thirty-two episodes, the only one left was on friendship, because every episode was like a chat over a cup of coffee. An issue of the day was broached—sexuality, fear, sadness, et cetera—and they began to talk," said Rimoldi, who visited the Vatican twice in 2013 when he was already director of Channel 21. The first time was to seal an agreement with the Centro Televisivo Vaticano, according to which he can start distributing in Italy Channel 21's immense archive on everything done by Cardinal Bergoglio before being elected to St. Peter's throne. The second visit was to deliver the Martín Fierro Award, the main Argentine television prize, awarded to Bergoglio for the program *Biblia, diálogo vigente*.

"I know that Channel 21 is one of the projects he's most fond of and which he carries in his heart. In fact I could say that Channel 21 is one of the new things he brought to the diocese. And I can quote words the Cardinal said, and not only to me: 'If I go down in history, it'll be because of the television channel.' I've always answered: 'I don't believe it!' And I haven't been wrong."

# 13

# A Man Called Francis

The revolution begins at the moment the Cardinal Archbishop of Buenos Aires, the first Jesuit to be elected to St. Peter's throne, chooses his own name: Francesco, Franciscus, Francisco, Francis. And not because of Francis Xavier, missionary Jesuit from Navarre, a saint who died in China in the sixteenth century. Nor because of another sixteenth-century saint, Francis de Sales, Bishop of Geneva and patron saint of the Salesian family, writers, and journalists.

He chooses it because of Francis of Assisi, patron saint of Italy, the saint of the poor; the name is, in itself, a program of government. No pope has ever dared use the name of Il Poverello of Assisi, who abandoned his riches to give himself to God, to God's creatures, and to the poor. How can all this be reconciled with the opulent world of the Vatican?

"Francis, go repair my house, which, as you can see, is all in ruins." These are the words that Francis, a rich merchant's son and a young man in deep spiritual crisis, heard repeated three times in 1205, while he was praying in tears before the crucifix of St. Damian's Church in Assisi.

Jorge Bergoglio, Pope Francis, takes up the reins of the Catholic Church, which is not in ruins but is experiencing a deep crisis. Consumerism and secularism reign throughout the world—a world that has forgotten the hereafter—and they reign most of all in the Europe with Christian roots, where vocations are dwindling and churches are empty.

Benedict XVI, refined theologian and acute observer of reality, did not succeed in stopping the "dictatorship of relativism," which he denounced time and time again after his election in 2005. The scandal of pedophile priests, which damaged the Catholic Church as no other scandal had before, blew up in his hands; with a new policy of "zero tolerance," the Church is now seeking to make up for this disgrace.

Joseph Ratzinger, an intellectual who has always admitted that he is not a man of government—"I had no talent for sports, or administration or organization," he said in his 1996 interview book with Peter Seewald, *Salt of the Earth*—did not even succeed, during his pontificate, in reforming the Roman Curia, a curia that seems more and more similar to its image in Dan Brown's thrillers, full of poison and intrigue of a very Italian style. Nepotism, corruption, and ambition are in full swing. "I'd kill the lot of them! The only thing that interests them is money and their business," a Roman taxi driver exclaims to me, summarizing the unedifying picture of the Roman Curia in the collective imagination: a kind of Vatican, Inc.

That is why the famous words "go repair my house" are on everyone's mind. And the choice of the name Francis, a very clear message, makes prelates all over the world tremble, those used to living—excuse the phrase—like popes. Pope Francis knows that everyone is waiting for him to roll up his sleeves and clean up the "filth" in the Church, already denounced by then Cardinal Ratzinger during the meditations of the Via Crucis (Way of the Cross) of 2005, the last of the pontificate of John Paul II, who was dying at the time. Pope Francis knows that he must repair the house.

The supporters of Benedict XVI try to find a continuity in Pope Francis. But the revolution is already evident in his first twenty-four hours as pope. Behind the ancient walls of the Vatican, decorated with priceless frescoes, pictures, and carpets, you can feel a fracture, a "before" Francis and "after" Francis.

After the *habemus papam* announcement on the evening of March 13, the 114 cardinals and the new pope go back to the Casa Santa Marta for supper. A black limousine with the license plate SCV (*Stato della Città del*

*Vaticano*, or Vatican City State) awaits the new Holy Father in the San Damaso Courtyard. The buses stand nearby. The Argentine pope, who has never had a car with a private chauffeur, is not going to change at age seventy-six just because he is now dressed in white. He explains with a smile that he won't take the limousine; he prefers going by coach with his "brother" cardinals.

The Vatican experts who believe in continuity will say that this is merely a cosmetic gesture. But that's not the case. And the same holds for his moves that are to come later, ones that speak of a return to the origins of the Church. And also of an authentic pope who goes on being himself, convinced that to be a good shepherd you must stay with your flock, be humble like your flock, and be a shepherd "with the odor of the sheep."

Notwithstanding the titanic mission that has arrived so unexpectedly, Pope Francis hasn't lost his sense of humor, his irony. "God forgive you, you don't know what you've done," he says to his "brother" cardinals after supper in the dining room of the Casa Santa Marta. At breakfast, the Indian Cardinal Telesphore Toppo greets him with a respectful, "Good morning, Holy Father!" The reply is immediate: "Good morning, holy son!"

On the morning of March 14, they want to take the new pope to the tailor's. He can't go on wearing black trousers under the white soutane, or cassock. But for him, wearing a pair of white trousers is like wearing pajamas. He should also go to the shoemaker; he can't go on wearing his worn-out, orthopedic black shoes. Bergoglio doesn't say no, that he will never change them. With a smile he says, "Not for the time being," and leaves matters to solve themselves later on.

First, he has more important things to do—such as paying homage to the Virgin in the Basilica of Santa Maria Maggiore, one of the four papal basilicas in Rome. The object of his devotion is the Byzantine icon *Salus Popoli Romani* (Protector of the Roman People) of the Virgin and Child, venerated by more than one pope. One can perhaps see as a sign of what is to come in the fact that Jorge Bergoglio has always visited her on every journey to Rome. This time he doesn't wear a clergyman's suit; he is dressed in white, as pope. And he is surrounded by photographers and television cameras: it's his first public outing after his election. To reach Santa Maria Maggiore, which is very near the Argentine embassy in Piazza dell'Esquilino, he has once again refused the official limousine. "I want an ordinary car that doesn't attract attention, and the minimum possible bodyguard," he informs his assistants courteously but firmly.

During his first twenty-four hours as leader of the 1.2 billion Catholics in the world, Pope Francis makes it clear that he is used to organizing himself, without delegating. When an official suggests that he send an assistant to pick up the personal belongings he has left in his room at the Casa Internazionale, where he stayed before the conclave, he refuses. He wants to take care of it himself, pay his bill, and say good-bye to the hotel staff. So, on his return from Santa Maria Maggiore, the pope stops at the Casa Internazionale in the central Via della Scrofa. This creates a great to-do. The pope has come back to pay the hotel bill! He says good-bye to the staff, one by one, who seem to have gone crazy at this unexpected visit. He takes his leave saying, "Pray for me."

During his first hours as pope, even before appearing on the central balcony of St. Peter's Basilica for the *habemus papam* announcement, Pope Francis starts making telephone calls. The first is to Pope Emeritus Benedict XVI, who has been in seclusion since February 28 at Castel Gandolfo, where he has followed the whole electoral process on television. "I'm happy that it's you who has taken up the reins of the Church," says the Pope Emeritus to the new pope. The Argentine pope assures him that he will soon visit him. Obviously, they have many things to talk about.

But so as not to feel alone in a virtual cage, he also calls his sister María Elena and the many friends he has in Rome, Buenos Aires, and other parts of the world. He doesn't know if the phones are controlled, but from his room in the Casa Santa Marta he communicates with the whole world. He goes on phoning during the following days: to a priest, a friend of his who lives in a remote village in northern Argentina whose birthday it is; to his newspaper deliverer, to tell him to stop delivering papers; to his dentist,

with whom he had an appointment; to his shoemaker, who makes orthopedic shoes; to the nun who cooked Patagonian lamb for him; to his secretaries. At the other end, the person he's phoned often believes this is a
joke and says, "Give up—stop playing the fool." At the beginning nobody
believes that he is calling his friends directly. How come? Doesn't he have
a secretary who makes the calls for him? But it's clear that he wants to
go on looking after himself as he has done all his life: by himself, without
intermediaries.

During his telephone calls, Pope Francis reveals that he hasn't lost his
sense of humor. When he calls a Bishop friend of his at dawn to wish him
a happy birthday, he says: "Here, from Rome, I'm the pope" (in Italian).
After greeting and chatting with him, the Bishop pretends to complain:
"But couldn't you have called me at a more decent time?" And Pope Francis
replies, "That's your problem!"

On March 15, two days after his election, he hears that his old friend
Cardinal Jorge Mejía, age ninety, has had a stroke. He immediately decides
to visit him in the Roman nursing home where he is a patient. Evidently,
this creates confusion, but it also confirms that there has been a change
in the atmosphere. He talks to the patients in intensive care and blesses
them, prays with the community of nuns at the hospital, and thanks everybody for their work. "You, too, pray for me, and thank you for your work
with the sick and the suffering," he says, to applause.

As indicated by Vatican protocol, at five o'clock on the afternoon of his first
day as pope, he must go back to the Sistine Chapel (where he had been
elected less than twenty-four hours before) to celebrate his first Mass *pro
Ecclesia*, for the Church, before the cardinal-electors.

That morning an assistant had brought to his room the Latin text he
was supposed to read. "Thank you," says the pope, with a shy smile, even
though he has already decided not to read a Latin text written by others
and that says things he doesn't want to say.

Later, before the same fresco of the *Last Judgment* that has witnessed an election that will change the history of the Church, the former Cardinal Primate of Buenos Aires, reading nothing but speaking from the heart, delivers a first, fundamental homily. Concisely, simply, and directly, he outlines the agenda of his pontificate: to return to the essential foundations—to the original, purer, more essential form of the Church—"to walk, to build, to profess Jesus Christ crucified."

"When we do not profess Jesus Christ, we profess the worldliness of the devil, a demonic worldliness," he adds. Without mentioning it, the new pope refers to the "disfigured face" of the Church, which Pope Emeritus Benedict XVI also exposed with his resignation of February 11. A resignation due to the physical weakness of an already old, tired, and fragile man, but according to many also owing to an internal situation about to explode, with struggles for power and obvious enmities between many curia officials involved in Vati Leaks. It could not have been pleasant for the gentle Benedict XVI to discover that he had been betrayed by Paolo "Paoletto" Gabriele, the butler who helped him dress every day and with whom he chatted at times during his solitary meals in the pontifical apartment. It was during these meals, as Paolo Gabriele himself recounted at his trial in the Vatican, that he realized that Benedict XVI, shut inside his pontifical apartment and more interested in his essays on theology, was totally misinformed. He didn't know what was happening around him.

"My wish," says Pope Francis, in that first homily, "is that all of us, after these days of grace, will have the courage, and I mean courage, to walk in the Lord's presence, with the Lord's Cross, to build the Church on the blood of the Lord, shed on the cross, and to confess its only glory: Christ crucified. And so in this way the Church will go forward. I wish to all of us that the Holy Spirit, with the prayer of the Madonna, our Mother, grant us this grace: to walk, to build, to confess Jesus Christ crucified. So be it."

Pope Francis is a tsunami. It becomes clear when on Saturday, March 16, he receives an audience of the six thousand journalists from eighty-one countries who covered his election. During the meeting in the famous Sala Nervi, or Paul VI Audience Hall, of the Vatican, the Argentine pope imposes an absolutely informal atmosphere. Spontaneous, modest, intelligent, and with a sense of humor, he wins over the representatives of the world's media, whom many would deem to be the most skeptical and godless race on the planet.

No one had ever heard a pope tell the secrets of the conclave so naturally and admit to having been elected with a majority much higher than the seventy-seven votes necessary for the two-thirds quorum. No one had ever heard a pope repeating, many times, that he is, first of all, the "Bishop of Rome."

"From a strictly theological point of view, the fact that he wants to present himself from the very beginning, and with insistence, as the Bishop of Rome is already an indication of how he understands the exercise of the papacy," stresses Archbishop Víctor Manuel Fernández, Rector of the Pontifical Catholic University of Argentina. In his speech, Pope Francis points out the pressing need to put Christ at the center of the Church once more. "Christ is the shepherd of the Church, but his presence in history passes through men's freedom: among them one is chosen to serve as his vicar, Peter's successor," he says. "Christ is the center. Christ is the fundamental reference, the heart of the Church. Without him, Peter and the Church would not exist or have a reason for existing."

"Some people didn't know why the Bishop of Rome had chosen to be called Francis. Some had thought of Francis Xavier, of Francis de Sales, even of Francis of Assisi. I'll tell you a story," he says, putting aside the text he has in front of him and improvising. During the conclave, next to him in the Sistine Chapel was the Brazilian Cardinal Cláudio Hummes, Archbishop Emeritus of São Paulo and Prefect emeritus of the Congregation for the Clergy, "a great friend," Pope Francis says in a conspiratorial tone of voice.

"When things got a little dangerous, he comforted me," he said, provoking laughter among his public of fascinated journalists. "And when the votes went up to two-thirds, there was the usual applause, because the pope had been elected. [Hummes] hugged me, kissed me, and said, 'Don't forget the poor!' And that word got inside me: the poor, the poor. Then suddenly, in relation to the poor, I thought of Francis of Assisi. Then, while the ballot count went on, I thought about wars, while the count went on, till the end. And Francis is the man of peace. And so, the name came to me, to my heart: Francis of Assisi. For me he is the man of poverty, the man of peace, the man who loves and guards the created world; at this time we don't have a very good relationship with the created world, do we? He's the man who gives us this spirit of peace, this poor man." And then he exclaims, "Oh, how I would like a Church that is poor and for the poor!" to loud applause.

Pope Francis says that some cardinals made a few remarks: "But you should have called yourself Adrian, like Adrian VI, who was a reformer, and we need to reform"; "No, no, your name should be Clement"; "But why?"; "Clement XV—that's how you'll pay back Clement XIV, who suppressed the Society of Jesus!"

The pope also finds agreement when he comments on the immense work done by journalists during the past few days. "You've worked, eh? Yes, you certainly have!" And then he invites all of us to get to know the true nature of the Church better and its path through the world "with its virtues and its sins" and to discover the spiritual motivation that guides it, which is the most authentic clue to understanding it. "Your work demands study, sensitivity, experience, like so many other professions, but it also implies a particular attention to the truth, to goodness and beauty, and that brings us very close together because the Church exists to communicate these things: truth, goodness, and beauty 'in person' as it were," he says.

He ends by charming everyone present with the warmest and most tolerant blessing ever remembered as being imparted by a pope. Speaking in his *porteño* (from Buenos Aires) Spanish for the first time since being elected, he says, "Since many of you don't belong to the Catholic Church, others are not believers, I'm giving this blessing to you in silence, to every one of you, respecting each one's conscience, but knowing that every one of you is a child of God. May God bless you."

In the course of the first months of his pontificate, he will often speak of silence, an essential instrument of Jesuit spiritual exercises. He uses it first on the historic evening of March 13, after his election, when from the central balcony of St. Peter's Basilica he asks the crowd to bless him in silence. He will ask for silence once again on the sunny first Sunday of June, during the Angelus, when he invites the hundred thousand people present to pray for the fallen in all wars, for their families, and for the wounded. And once again in the historic vigil of fasting and prayer for peace in Syria on Saturday, September 7. On every such occasion, the silence is commanding, impressive, indispensable, alive.

I'm in one of the front rows of Paul VI Audience Hall. I'm a member of a group of fifty media operators privileged to greet Pope Francis. My heart is pounding; I'm meeting him for the first time since his election, even though we've talked on the phone. Yesterday he actually phoned me on my birthday; I told him that his election was my best gift. Now, each of us fifty mounts the steps to the stage slowly, in single file.

Monsignor Lucio Adrián Ruiz, of Santa Fe, Argentina, who directs the Vatican Internet Services and whom I interviewed some time ago, has already passed by; he looks very moved. He gives the Holy Father an iPad, which I doubt he'll ever use. Then it's the turn of Monsignor Eduardo García, Auxiliary Bishop of Buenos Aires, just off the plane (bringing with him another pair of the Holy Father's black shoes), who kneels before him and then rises and hugs him hard, sparking applause. Then come my colleagues Virginia Bonnard of the magazine *Ciudad Nueva*, who gives him a *mate* (which I find out later was her own); and Sergio Rubin of the daily paper *Clarín*, who is known to everybody because his book *The Jesuit*—written with Francesca Ambrogetti, a friend of mine since I apprenticed at ANSA, Italy's news wire, in Buenos Aires—is practically the only existing book on Bergoglio; then Alicia Barrios.

A giant screen on the right transmits pictures of the people greeting the pope. I can't believe I'm there too. I look back and see a Swiss Guard wearing the famous Renaissance-style uniform with yellow, blue, and red stripes, standing in the middle of the aisle dividing the Paul VI Audience Hall. A short way behind him is Gerry, my husband; he, too, would have liked to greet Padre Jorge, but he's glad that at least I have this privilege.

As the pictures on the giant screen change, there are ovations. Here is Pope Francis greeting everyone approaching him, with affection and a smile. There's also a blind journalist with a guide dog, which Bergoglio pets. I don't know if it's all a dream, reality, or something else. I only know that it's all very exciting.

Before me is Hiroshi Miyahira, a veteran Japanese journalist. When it's his turn, he bows in perfect Japanese style and asks Pope Francis if he intends to go to Japan. Padre Jorge, dressed in white, smiling, answers that he has already been to Japan in 1987, that he doesn't know, he'll see. He greets him humbly, also bowing his head. It's my turn. I feel that I'm about to weep and fall into Pope Francis's arms. I'm tremendously moved but maintain self-control. I'm standing before the pope but also before Padre Jorge dressed as pope. Without thinking, because it comes from my bursting heart, I seize his arms and tell him to go on being as he is, that he's doing fine, that he mustn't change, he must stay the way he is, that I'm with him, that he's not alone.

Consistent with his desire for a Church that is poor and for the poor, Pope Francis decides to go on living in the Santa Marta residence, a guesthouse built by John Paul II within the Vatican so that the cardinals taking part in the conclave should have a minimum of comfort (not like in 1978, when they were crammed into claustrophobic cells). The new pope doesn't want to lodge in the apartment on the third floor of the Apostolic Palace, a kind of ivory tower. He wants to stay in touch with his flock.

Since 1903, when Pius X settled on the third floor of the Apostolic Palace, every pope has lived in the papal apartment. Preceding popes, dating back to the fourteenth century, had always lived in other parts of the Apostolic Palace and the Vatican—for example, where the museums are now.

Shortly after his election, accompanied by the Cardinal Secretary of State, Tarcisio Bertone, and other officials, Pope Francis visits the stately apartment that was locked and sealed at the beginning of the "vacant see." Passing through the rooms, he exclaims, "But three hundred people could stay here!" He doesn't hide his fear at the idea of living in this opulent place, which has nothing to do with his almost monastic style of life.

The apartment, totally restructured under Benedict XVI, has ten rooms, including a medical suite, a chapel, a kitchen and dining room, and decorated drawing rooms with spectacular sixteenth-century marble floors. Although he undergoes some pressure to change his mind, because his living at Santa Marta would be an inconvenience, Pope Francis is to use this apartment only to appear at the window of the study every Sunday for the Marian prayer of the Angelus; he will use the second floor of the Apostolic Palace to receive heads of state and other dignitaries.

The Domus Sanctae Marthae, the official name of the Santa Marta residence, is a few meters away from the Basilica of St. Peter and from the Paul VI Audience Hall. It's a five-floor building with 106 suites, twenty-two single rooms, an apartment, and a number of reception rooms. Here, in the common rooms, the dining room, or the elevator, the pope may run into clergy passing through Rome—which is a way of not losing contact with the outside world. "It isn't just a question of not wanting wealth; it's that I feel the need to live among people. Living in isolation wouldn't do me good. I'm staying at Santa Marta for psychiatric reasons," the pope has explained on several occasions.

Santa Marta has become the pope's headquarters. His suite, Room 201 on the second floor, becomes his bunker and main studio. Simple, white walled, a little bare—a picture of St. Francis, crucifixes, a little statue of Our Lady of Luján and other images of the Virgin on small tables—the suite is composed of a small living room, a study, a room with a big dark-wood bed, and a bathroom. It used to be reserved for important visitors, so when he receives the Patriarch of Constantinople Bartholomew I, who used to have it, Pope Francis says, "I'm sorry, I've stolen your room."

On the same floor live his two private secretaries: the Maltese Canadian Monsignor Alfred Xuereb, whom Bergoglio "inherits" from his predecessor, and Father Fabián Pedacchio Leaniz, age forty-nine, an Argentine who arrived at the Congregation for Bishops in 2007 with Bergoglio's consent, an expert in canon law, and a fan of the River Plate soccer team.

From the first day, Pope Francis celebrates Mass every morning at seven o'clock sharp in the Santa Marta chapel. He invites Vatican officials among others, and at the end of the service he sits on one of the benches at the back of the chapel and prays, like an ordinary person, among nameless ordinary people.

Francis always surprises the Swiss Guards, who have had to move there to protect him. Once more rebelling against protocol, he tells them to sit down instead of standing all the time on their guard duty, or he offers them a brioche.

"You can't imagine the faces that the cardinals in the Sistine Chapel made when they heard that the new pope was to be called Francis," reveals Cardinal Angelo Comastri on the morning of Sunday, March 17, while welcoming the pope, who is celebrating his first public Mass at the Vatican's parish Church of St. Anne. Gerry and I are there, and the atmosphere in the crowded church is impressive. The new pope's call for mercy, in his simple and clear homily, touches everyone. Shortly after, the pope who has come from the ends of the world amazes his guardian angels by leaving the Vatican walls to greet and kiss the faithful, like a parish priest of the people.

He exceeds all expectations at his first Angelus from the study window of the Apostolic Palace. Speaking in his Argentina-accented Italian that charms the Romans, he starts with a simple, "Brothers and sisters, good morning." An ordinary greeting like the historic "Buona sera" (Good evening) that followed the *habemus papam* announcement. And then he says good-bye with an equally simple, but totally unlike the usual Vatican stiffness, "Have a good Sunday and enjoy your meal!"—words he will go on using regularly.

Pope Francis receives an ovation from the beginning to the end of his appearance, which lasts only twelve minutes—twelve minutes during which he speaks of the mercy and patience of God and tells amusing stories. There are moments of impressive silence filled with prayer and meditation—and then applause.

On the fifth Sunday of Lent, he comments, simply and clearly, on the Gospel episode of the woman taken in adultery, the woman Jesus saves from a death sentence. "Jesus' attitude is striking: we do not hear words of scorn, we do not hear words of condemnation, but only words of love, of mercy, which are an invitation to conversion," he says.

Pope Francis speaks spontaneously, off the cuff. He tells of reading a book about mercy by the German Cardinal Walter Kasper, a "very smart" theologian, which has really done him a lot of good. "But don't think I'm promoting my cardinals' books! Not so!" he jokes. "Cardinal Kasper said that feeling mercy changes everything. And it's the best thing we can feel: it changes the world. A little mercy makes the world less cold and more just," he insists, and he tells a story that faithfully reflects popular wisdom on the concept of mercy. "I remember when I had just become a Bishop in 1992, the Madonna of Fátima arrived in Buenos Aires and a great Mass was celebrated for the sick. I went to hear confessions at that Mass. Nearly at the end of the Mass I got up because I had to go and administer confirmation. An elderly woman came to me, humble, very humble, over eighty years old. I looked at her and told her: 'Grandmother'—because that's how we address our old ladies—'Granny, do you want to confess?'"

"Yes."

"But if you haven't sinned—"

"We all have sins."

"But perhaps the Lord hasn't forgiven them."

"The Lord pardons everything."

"But how do *you* know that, dear lady?"

"If the Lord didn't forgive everything, the world wouldn't exist."

"And I had a great urge to say to her: 'Tell me, lady, have you studied at the Gregorian?' [the Jesuit-run Pontifical Gregorian University], because that is the wisdom granted by the Holy Spirit—the inner wisdom focused on the mercy of God. Let's not forget this word," he urges. "God never tires of forgiving, never! [A person might say,] 'Well, Father, what's the problem?' Well, the problem is that we get tired of asking for forgiveness. He never tires of forgiving but at times we get tired of asking for forgiveness," he says regretfully.

The atmosphere in St. Peter's Square is electric. The Catholic Church, shaken after many years of crisis and scandal, depressed, closed in on itself, seems to have reawakened. The people in the square are exultant, euphoric, full of hope. They feel that Pope Francis is "one of us." Yes, the pope is one of us, like us, who speaks like us and understands what we feel. Among the hundreds of banners that flood the square, where the blue and white ones of Argentina are beginning to be a standard feature, one reads: "Padre Bergoglio, sei il nostro orgoglio" (Father Bergoglio, you are our pride). But the one that attracts the most attention reads, "Francis, go repair my house."

Archbishop Jorge Mario Bergoglio riding the subway to his office in Buenos Aires, Argentina.

Above: Chilean Cardinal Ricardo Ezzati Andrello (left) receiving his beret upon his appointment as Cardinal.

Above: Carrying his briefcase, Pope Francis boards the plane to World Youth Day in Brazil.

Jorge Bergoglio, Provincial Superior of the Jesuits in Argentina, celebrates Mass with (left to right) Victor Zorzín, Rector of the Colegio Máximo; Andrés Swinnen, Master of Novices; Carlos Cravena, Minister of the Colegio Máximo; and Hipolito Salvo, former Provincial in Argentina.

API/Gamma-Rapho/Getty Images.

Right: The future Pope Francis following his ordination to the priesthood in 1969.

Franco Origlia/Getty Images.

Right: In an undated photo, a young Jorge Bergoglio poses for the camera.

Bottom: The Bergoglio family (left to right) standing, brother Alberto Horacio, Jorge Mario, Óscar Adrián, and sister Marta Regina. Sitting, sister María Elena, mother Regina María Sivori, and father Mario José Francisco.

Franco Origlia/Getty Images.

API/Gamma-Rapho/Getty Images.

Jorge Mario Bergoglio, left, and his brother Óscar following
their First Communion in 1942.

Pope Francis waving to the crowd from the Popemobile as he arrives in St. Peter's Square for his weekly audience on October 30, 2013.

Pope Francis with the author Elisabetta Piqué.

Above: A child removes Pope Francis's white zucchetto, or skullcap.

Left: Pope Francis hugs a group of Spanish children who traveled from Madrid to see him at his general audience on June 25, 2014.

Wind blows away Pope Francis's white zucchetto, or skullcap, as he leaves this general audience.

Unannounced, Pope Francis has lunch with Vatican workers in their cafeteria.

Pope Francis celebrates Mass at the Basilica of the National Shrine of Our Lady of Aparecida, the Patroness of Brazil, during World Youth Day 2013.

Pope Francis washes the foot of a man at the Don Gnocchi Foundation Center in Rome on Holy Thursday, April 17, 2014. The Pontiff washed the feet of twelve men and women with disabilities.

# 14

# Deep-Seated Changes

No, Francis's changes are not just cosmetic. "It's as if what's happening is a sex change," a European monsignor confesses to me one day, opening his eyes wide and raising his eyebrows while referring to significant changes made in such a short time. The Argentine pope is a strategist. He knows exactly what he wants. Anyone who thinks he doesn't know how to keep the helm of Peter's boat steady in the middle of the storm is mistaken.

Unwittingly, Bergoglio had for some time been preparing to lead the Catholic Church. Like a shepherd who takes care of his sheep, but also reading, studying, and gathering information. Some members of the Roman Curia believe that being in Buenos Aires, 7,500 miles away, Bergoglio was too far from Vatican affairs.

But those who know him are aware that he followed closely what was happening. Through his friends he has access to a network of firsthand information. He has always known what was happening. When the Vati Leaks case blows up, Bergoglio isn't surprised. He knows very well that the Church is made up of sinners—human beings who can fall to the temptations of evil, career ambition, power, sex, money. Corruption exists everywhere. And the Vatican is no exception. Also, in the Vatican corruption is a mortal sin, he thinks.

Pope Francis knows perfectly well the details of the Viganò case, which broke in 2011; this situation symbolized so well the curia's going adrift; the smell of rot had reached intolerable proportions. The television program *The Untouchables*, hosted by Gianluigi Nuzzi, brought the scandal to light at the end of January 2012. Nuzzi is the same journalist who months later wrote the best seller *His Holiness: The Secret Papers of Benedict XVI* and the earlier book *Vaticano S.p.A* on the Vatican's shadowy finances. In one of the episodes of the show, he revealed that in 2011 a high-ranking prelate, Monsignor Carlo Maria Viganò, wrote a letter to the pope denouncing the "corruption" in the administration of the world's smallest state. Viganò, a native of Varese, age seventy-one at the time, had in 2009 been appointed by Benedict XVI the secretary-general of the Vatican Governorate (the body dealing with the awarding of contracts), to bring order to the accounting system, which had become a virtual black hole.

Viganò took the lid off a cauldron of unheard-of intrigue and corruption. So much so that the television program defined his action as a kind of *mani pulite* (clean hands) operation, which earns him many enemies in the Vatican Curia, where plots are hatched to have him transferred to another assignment a safe distance from Rome.

On March 27, 2011, Viganò wrote an explosive letter to Pope Benedict in which he tried desperately to demolish an "internal conspiracy." "My transfer would provoke perplexity among those who believed it was possible to reform so many situations of corruption and abuse of office," he wrote in his letter. "I could never have imagined finding myself confronting such a disastrous situation, known to the whole curia."

But there was no turning back. A month later, Viganò was nominated nuncio (Vatican Ambassador) to Washington, DC—certainly a very important post but one that reflected the classic Vatican mechanism *promoveatur ut amoveatur*: promotion for removal.

Viganò—who also wrote inflammatory letters to the Cardinal Secretary of State Tarcisio Bertone—had discovered that the Vatican was always working with the same group of suppliers and firms, who were getting paid double the normal rate, without any requests for bids and hardly any transparency—hence the losses of the Vatican Governorate. A good example of this state of affairs is the Christmas tree and giant crib set up in St. Peter's Square at Christmas 2009, which had cost an astronomical €550,000. The following year, Viganò drastically reduced the cost to €200,000, and he did the same thing for other extravagant amounts of money that had been invested in the famous, beautiful Vatican Gardens. He also discovered the existence of a higher-up "management committee" run by four important names in the world of Italian finance.

Viganò's *mani pulite* operations were successful: the governorate's budget changed from a deficit of €8 million to a profit of €34.4 million in just one year. But he affected too many special interests. And so began the intrigue, the anonymous letters, and the unsigned articles in *Il Giornale*, an Italian daily: they are all against him. All of this is what culminated in his unwanted golden exile in Washington—an appointment generally considered a top pick for a Holy See diplomat.

As former Archbishop of Buenos Aires, Bergoglio knows of this case and of others that cause him the same revulsion. His objectives, then as always, are clean-up, transparency, and decentralizing the government of the Church.

"Inconsistency between the faithful and their pastors, between what they say and what they do, between words and way of life, undermines the credibility of the Church," Pope Francis preaches in a homily on April 14, 2013, during the ceremony in which he, as the new pope, "takes possession" of the Basilica of St. Paul Outside the Walls. "Let us all remember it well: you can't announce the gospel of Jesus without the actual witness of your life. Anyone who listens to us and sees us must be able to read in our actions what he hears from our mouths and give glory to God! I now recall some advice that St. Francis of Assisi gave to his brothers: preach the gospel and, if necessary, use words. Preach with your life, with your witness."

In the general congregations—the preconclave meetings—the cardinals insisted on the urgent need to clean things up, to promote transparency and reform of the curia, a body that recently had not been of help to the pope but rather had sunk him into a web of intrigue that soiled the image of the Vatican and the Church. The Roman Curia must begin to be regulated according to the Second Vatican Council; it must be modernized and restructured—with fewer departments and greater harmony—and it must adapt itself to the times we live in.

One of the earliest decisions of the Jesuit pope—who listens attentively, takes note, and then acts—is to create a council of eight cardinals, the so-called G8 of the pope, to help him govern the universal Church and reform the Roman Curia.

The decision is announced on April 13, exactly a month after his election, with a communiqué from the Secretariat of State: "The Holy Father Francis, taking up a suggestion made during the general congregations preceding the conclave, has set up a group of cardinals to advise him on the government of the universal Church and to study a project of revision of the Apostolic Constitution *Pastor bonus* [published in 1988 by John Paul II] on the Roman Curia."

According to the analysts, this decision is the first response of the Argentine pope to the recent Vatican scandals. But actually it is an action that goes far beyond the scandals: it confirms that Pope Francis wants to change the way the universal Church is governed. It's a step toward the implementation of the model of Church government called for by the Second Vatican Council: less centralized, more collegial, and based on the principle of subsidiarity—that is, problems should be dealt with at the most immediate or local level consistent with their solution.

Pope Francis chooses one cardinal from every continent and one from the Roman Curia. As coordinator he appoints the seventy-year-old Honduran Cardinal Óscar Rodríguez Maradiaga, Archbishop of Tegucigalpa, a Salesian. The eight cardinal advisers, who include two native English speakers—Seán O'Malley (United States) and George Pell (Australia)—constitute a virtual board of directors. The Argentine pope chooses personalities of a certain importance and with varying tendencies. Among the eight there are, in fact, as many conservatives as progressives. As in Buenos Aires as Archbishop, so too as pope, Francis does not want to be surrounded by people who think like him, by "yes-men."

There are only two Italians in the G8. To represent the curia, the pope appoints Cardinal Giuseppe Bertello, age seventy, president of the

Governorate of the Vatican City State, a man with considerable diplomatic experience. And he names as secretary Monsignor Marcello Semeraro, Bishop of Albano, whom he has known since the synod of late 2001. Vatican correspondents, as well as bishops and cardinals, are very curious to know who will be the Argentine pope's choice to replace the controversial Cardinal Secretary of State Tarcisio Bertone. Even though many would like to see him removed from office at once, along with others of the so-called Vatican Mafia, Pope Francis, showing kindness and political skill, moves cautiously and avoids inflicting public humiliation—it isn't necessary. So he lets Bertone keep his post for a few more months, even taking him on the first official journey of his pontificate to Brazil.

On August 31, 2013, at the end of a summer without having taken a holiday, Pope Francis announces that his second-in-command will be Pietro Parolin. A fifty-eight-year-old diplomat with broad experience, he has up to this moment been nuncio to Venezuela. His nomination shakes those sectors of the curia that are reluctant to accept change because it is a clear signal of reform. Pope Francis has chosen as his right-hand man not only a younger person—Parolin, fifty-eight, is the youngest Secretary of State since the times of Eugenio Pacelli (later Pius XII)—but above all he is averse to the power games within the Vatican. After five months and eighteen days of consultation and reflection, Pope Francis decides in favor of someone with a profile similar to his own: a pastor open to dialogue, in line with the winds of change he has brought about.

Born on January 17, 1955, in Schiavon, near Vicenza, Italy, ordained in 1980 and a graduate of canon law, Parolin joined the diplomatic service of the Holy See in July 1986. He knows several languages—besides Italian, he speaks French, English, and Spanish. He has worked in the pontifical missions in Nigeria and Mexico, and since 1992 he has worked in the division of the Secretariat of State devoted to foreign affairs. It was while he had this role, which included maintaining relations of the Holy See with Argentina, that he met the Archbishop of Buenos Aires.

In 2002, John Paul II appointed him deputy undersecretary for foreign relations of the Vatican, and in 2009, after being nominated Archbishop, he was sent as nuncio to Venezuela, during the difficult Hugo Chávez period. When he left for Venezuela, he had such a good reputation that many people expected him to return one day to the Vatican to take up a post of great responsibility, perhaps as Cardinal Secretary of State, though few thought it would happen so quickly.

I got to know Parolin personally in 2006, in the middle of the conflict between the Argentine episcopate and a certain sector of the Roman Curia that, through the former Ambassador Esteban Caselli, had intervened in the nomination of bishops. I asked him to meet with me so I could try to understand the position of the Vatican. Parolin accepted: he received me in an office of the Secretariat of State, was very courteous, and—obviously off the record—discussed the matter with me.

Apart from the G8, Bergoglio makes it clear what type of Church he wants, even before he is elected pope. In his brief speech during the general congregations, on Thursday, March 7, a speech that amazes his audience of cardinals, he says, "There are two images of the Church: the evangelizing Church, which goes out of itself, the Church of God's word, which listens and proclaims faithfully; and the worldly Church, which lives within itself, by itself, for itself. This consideration must illuminate possible changes and reforms to be carried out for the salvation of souls."

From the moment he becomes pope, he makes it clear that he wants the Church to go back to its origins. He wants an essential, poor Church, without superfluous ornaments, one that is not self-referential, which goes out of itself and goes to the peripheries. The pope outlines his program of government on March 19, 2013, during the solemn Mass marking the beginning of his Petrine ministry, when he affirms, "Power is service." He continues, "When exercising power, even the pope must always enter more deeply into that service which has its radiant summit in the Cross; he must give humble service, open his arms to guard all of God's people, especially the poorest, the weakest, the smallest. Only the one who serves with love knows how to be a guardian."

Before two hundred thousand people and delegations from 132 countries (among which the Argentine group, headed by President Cristina Kirchner, stands out), the pope also asks that everyone who holds posts of responsibility please be "guardians" of creation, of "God's plan written in nature, guardians of their fellow men, of the environment."

"Let us not allow marks of destruction and death to accompany the way forward of this world of ours. But in order to be protectors we must also watch over ourselves," says the new pope, stressing that "hate, envy, and pride degrade life."

"So guarding means keeping watch over our emotions, our heart, because our good and bad intentions, those that build and those that destroy, come from there. We must not be afraid of goodness, of tenderness," he says.

From the beginning Pope Francis has the courage to break with old traditions. His Fisherman's Ring—symbol of the Petrine ministry, which he will use only rarely—will no longer be gold but plated with silver. The ceremony of inauguration will no longer be called the Mass of "enthronement," because "there is no king here," as Father Federico Lombardi says, just the Mass initiating the Petrine ministry. The pope will not want to wear luxurious vestments; he will prefer ordinary, discreet ones, modest like himself.

During the Mass initiating the pontificate, an Argentine *cartonero* (cardboard collector), Sergio Sánchez, occupies a post of privilege next to heads of state and government. This is a new message from Pope Francis to the powerful of the world.

Similar scenes occur at Wednesday's general audiences, which attract to St. Peter's Square numbers of faithful as never before. A smiling pope greets the personalities who have come to occupy privileged positions at the audience—but later he also finds time to comfort the sick, the suffering, the strangers. That's when you can see him truly in his element, authentic, while he greets countless anonymous sick people, some in wheelchairs. He devotes more time to them than to the powerful of the earth; he hugs them and lets himself be hugged, warmly, which inspires applause. He blesses their holy pictures, their rosaries; he encourages and consoles them. In a few minutes he changes their lives and makes them feel happy, he makes them understand that it is true, that God exists, that God is love and mercy.

Pope Francis also decides to use the same coat of arms, slightly modified, and the same motto he chose when he was ordained Bishop in 1992. In its simplicity the new part of the coat of arms will consist of the symbols of pontifical dignity, a miter between two keys of St. Peter (one of gold, the other of silver, linked by a red cord like the coat of arms of Pope Emeritus Benedict XVI).

Otherwise, the coat of arms will remain more or less as before: a blue background, at the top the symbol of the Society of Jesus, a sun with the monogram *IHS*, for *Iesus hominem salvator* (Jesus, Savior of humanity). Further down on the left, there is a star, symbol of the Virgin Mary, mother of Christ and of the Church, with eight rays, representing the eight beatitudes. On the right is a lavender flower, indicating St. Joseph, patron of the universal Church. By including these images in his coat of arms, the pope shows his special devotion to the Virgin and to St. Joseph.

The motto, too, is the same one he chose when he was first ordained Bishop: *Miserando atque eligendo.*

During those first days, every speech and every homily reflects the type of pope he wants to be: a pope who puts the Church back on its feet, attracts the lost sheep, engages in dialogue with other religions and with today's world.

On March 22, when he receives the diplomatic corps accredited to the Holy See in the magnificent Sala Regia, he invites the representatives of 180 states present to make a journey together. He urges them to negotiate, to build peace, to construct bridges, to fight against material and spiritual poverty. "One of the titles of the Bishop of Rome is 'pontifex'—that is, the builder of bridges, with God and people. I really hope that the dialogue between us will help build bridges between all people, so that every person can see in another not an enemy, not a rival, but a brother and sister to welcome and embrace." "We cannot build bridges between people while forgetting God. But the opposite is also true: we cannot have true relations with God while ignoring others," he affirms. "That's why it's important to intensify dialogue with the various religions, I'm thinking in particular of Islam ... and it's also important to intensify encounters with nonbelievers, so that differences that separate and wound may never get the upper hand," he goes on.

Having always had excellent relations with the other religious communities, mainly the Jewish and Muslim communities, from his years as Archbishop Primate of Buenos Aires, Pope Francis confirms that he intends to continue on this path. In fact, on the second international trip of his pontificate to Amman, Bethlehem, and Jerusalem, at the end of May 2014, he becomes the first pope to include an interreligious component in his entourage: two Argentine friends, Rabbi Abraham Skorka and the Muslim leader Omar Abboud. This is a strong message of peace in one of the most conflictive regions of the world.

At his first Palm Sunday Mass, before 250,000 people in St. Peter's Square, he denounces for the first time corruption, greed for power and money, divisions, injustices, wars, violence, economic conflicts that hit the weakest, crimes against humanity and against creation. And he begs, "Don't let them steal the hope that Jesus gives us!" "Never be sad men and women: a Christian must never be sad! Never let yourselves be discouraged!"

During his first Wednesday general audience, Pope Francis repeats that following Jesus means "learning to come out of ourselves, to go to meet others, to go toward the peripheries of life, be the first to move toward our brothers and sisters, especially the ones who are far away, forgotten, who most need understanding, consolation, help."

The following day, Holy Thursday 2013, in his homily at his first Chrism Mass as Bishop of Rome, he comes back to the same theme. And in another crucial sermon (the one he had prepared for the Chrism Mass in Buenos Aires, convinced that he would not be elected pope) he earnestly urges priests to be pastors with "the odor of the sheep": "The priest who doesn't go out of himself, who mixes little with people, loses the best part of the people, the part that is able to activate the deepest part of our priestly heart. He who doesn't get out of himself, instead of becoming a mediator, gradually becomes an intermediary, a manager. . . . That is the explanation for the dissatisfaction of some, who end up being sad and transformed, as it were, into collectors of antiques or novelties, instead of being shepherds smelling of sheep, shepherds in the middle of their own flock, and fishers of men." "I ask you: be shepherds smelling of sheep, they must be smelled!"

On the afternoon of that same Maundy Thursday, in an act that is fundamental for understanding how he wants to change the Church and the papacy, Pope Francis passes from words to action. Even though it's something he has always done in Buenos Aires, he becomes the first pope in history to wash and kiss the feet of two women and two Muslims. They are among the twelve young people in the juvenile detention center at Casal del Marmo in Rome. "I do it with my heart, because it's my duty. As a priest and as a Bishop I must be at your service," says the Argentine pope, who insists that what he is giving is "a caress from Jesus."

In the second general audience of his pontificate, April 3, 2013, Pope Francis highlights the "primary, fundamental role" of women. It's another breath of modernity for a Church that usually relegates women to secondary roles. Though nobody believes that Pope Francis will open the doors to women priests—as he will say clearly in a press conference given on the plane during his return from Brazil—he might give women more important tasks. Actually, he is to include several women in different commissions created to clear up the dark finances of the Vatican. Besides, it is obvious that his relationship with women differs totally from the one that prevails in the Vatican. He's not afraid of kissing them as a way to say hello or of embracing them, like a good shepherd.

During this audience he recalls that it was they who, according to the Gospels, were the first to believe in the resurrection of Christ. "The first witnesses of the birth of Jesus are shepherds, simple and humble people, and the first witnesses of the Resurrection are women. And this is fine! And this is, in part, the mission of women—of mothers, of women! To give witness to their children, to their grandchildren, that Jesus lives, he is alive, he has risen!" exclaims Francis. "Mothers and women, go ahead with this testimony!" he cries, leaving his written text and drawing applause.

Aware that the scandal of pedophile priests has damaged the image of the Catholic Church as never before, Pope Francis, who is repelled by these crimes, on April 4 makes it very clear that he will be uncompromising, that he will act decisively against cases of sexual abuse of juveniles by priests, following the line of zero tolerance established by Benedict XVI.

Francis spells it out after giving a hearing to Monsignor Gerhard Ludwig Müller, Prefect of the Congregation for the Doctrine of the Faith, the department dealing with this terrible matter. Francis asks him to act "with decision against cases of sexual abuse." He asks him to promote measures to protect minors, help for those who have suffered "such violence" in the past, and trials for the guilty. He stresses the importance of the commitment of the episcopal conferences to formulate and implement the necessary directives in this field, which he defines as "important for the witness of the Church and its credibility."

"The Holy Father has assured that the victims of abuse are present in a particular way in his attention and his prayers for the suffering," says a Vatican communiqué.

It is the first time that the Argentine pope refers, even if indirectly, to the scourge of the sexual abuse of minors by clergy, which branded with fire the pontificate of Benedict XVI. Although the scandal made headlines in the United States at the end of 2000, during Pope Benedict's pontificate it also spread in Europe, especially in Ireland and Germany, where devastating reports were published revealing not only abuse but also cover-ups by high ecclesiastical authorities. Benedict XVI, who has asked for forgiveness and expressed sorrow and shame for these incidents, approved new directives and a zero-tolerance policy in line with the one started by John Paul II. In 2006 he punished the Mexican priest Marcial Maciel Degollado, founder of the ultraconservative Legion of Christ movement, who had abused a number of minors and is an emblematic case of degeneration and crime within the Church. In addition, Pope John Paul II met with the victims several times.

In May 2011, the Congregation for the Doctrine of the Faith granted the episcopal conferences around the world one year to adopt policies in the fight against pedophilia; these policies make collaborating with civil justice mandatory. The new prosecutor of this department, Father of Malta Robert Oliver, who replaced Bishop Charles Scicluna, recently stated that it is obligatory for all bishops to turn to civil authorities in the case of the sexual abuse of minors committed by members of the clergy, "even though every country has its own legislation."

According to Oliver, during the past three years (2009–2012) the Vatican has received six hundred reports each year of sexual abuse of minors. Most of these crimes took place between 1965 and 1985. The scandal of pedophile priests also touched the conclave. The Scottish Cardinal Keith O'Brien did not take part in the conclave after admitting that he had "behaved improperly" with four priests, though not as minors. On the other hand, the U.S. association of victims, Survivors Network of Those Abused by Priests (SNAP), also accused twelve cardinal-electors of having covered up cases and asked that they not be admitted to the conclave.

On May 16, 2013, Pope Francis punishes O'Brien, demonstrating that he will not hesitate a moment to clean up the behavior of priests. With a very concise communiqué, the Vatican states, "For the same reasons for which he decided not to take part in the last conclave and in agreement with the Holy Father, O'Brien is to leave Scotland for some months of 'spiritual renewal, prayer and penitence.'" The Vatican, without specifying where he will be sent, adds, "Any decision on the Cardinal's future destination will be agreed on with the Holy See."

A few days earlier, on May 5, on the occasion of the Regina Coeli (the prayer that replaces the Angelus after Easter), Pope Francis speaks publicly on the subject of violence against children. Before more than one hundred thousand people who have gathered in St. Peter's Square despite the rain, and taking the opportunity to celebrate the International Day of Children Victims of Violence, he recalls in particular "how many have suffered and suffer now because of abuse. . . . I want to assure them that they are present in my prayers, but I also want to say very firmly that we must all commit ourselves clearly and with courage to ensuring that every person (and especially children, who are among the most vulnerable) is always defended and protected."

On December 5, 2013, he accepts a proposal from his "G8" advisers and decides to create a special commission for the protection for children and the pastoral care of victims. In March 2014, the Vatican announces the names of the first eight members of the commission: four are women, including Marie Collins, an Irish victim who was abused as a child by a priest while she was hospitalized. Another significant member is Cardinal Seán O'Malley, one of the pope's eight advisers and Archbishop of Boston who knows the subject very well from dealing with it in his own diocese.

On April 11, 2014, Pope Francis surprises the world by personally asking pardon for this terrible scandal. "I feel I must take responsibility for all the evil that some priests, a sufficient number of them, did to children." Addressing a delegation of the International Catholic Child Bureau, he says, "I feel I have to take on myself the responsibility to ask pardon for the damage that they have done by the sexual abuse of children. The Church is aware of this damage. It is a personal and moral damage done to these children by men of the Church." And he assures everybody, "We will not go backward in terms of dealing with these problems and the sanctions that must be imposed. On the contrary, I believe that we have to be even stronger. There is no messing around when it comes to children."

Francis makes another strong "mea culpa" on July 7, 2014, when he celebrates Mass for six survivors of clergy sex abuse (three men and three women, from United Kingdom, Ireland, and Germany) and meets each of them afterward in Casa Santa Marta. "Before God and his people I express my sorrow for the sins and grave crimes of clerical sexual abuse committed against you. And I humbly ask forgiveness," Francis says in his homily. And he goes further: "I beg your forgiveness, too, for the sins of omission on the part of Church leaders who did not respond adequately to reports of abuse made by family members, and by abuse victims themselves. This led to even greater suffering on the part of those who were abused and it endangered other minors who were at risk."

On April 6, 2013, with his first appointment in the Roman Curia Pope Francis surprises everyone by nominating the Superior of the Franciscans, the Spaniard José Rodríguez Carballo, as secretary of the Congregation for Institutes of Consecrated Life and the Societies of Apostolic Life, which supervises the nine hundred thousand men and women religious in the world. This is another signal of change. Carballo, age fifty-nine, is the general minister of the Franciscan Order of Friars Minor (OFM), which has fifteen thousand friars in 113 countries; his position makes him the successor of the Order's founder, Francis of Assisi. Carballo was one of the main concelebrants, together with the Superior General of the Jesuits, Adolfo Nicolás, at the inaugural Mass of Pope Francis's pontificate on March 19, 2013.

Carballo, the Spanish Franciscan, replaces Joseph Tobin of the United States. Tobin had also been Superior General of a religious order, the Redemptorists, but unlike Carballo, he had left his post a year before being appointed secretary to the Vatican congregation by Benedict XVI. Carballo—formerly head of the International Union of Superiors General, a position that led to his nomination—is now the right-hand man of the Brazilian Cardinal João Braz de Aviz, who is reported to have strongly criticized the Roman Curia and its scandals in the preconclave meetings, provoking applause from many cardinals. Carballo is expected to play a leading role in easing the tensions and healing the wounds opened in 2012 between the Vatican and a group of nuns in the United States known as the Leadership Conference of Women Religious (LCWR), who represent more than 80 percent of the approximately 51,600 women religious in the United States. In April 2012, the Congregation for the Doctrine of the Faith censored and imposed sanctions on this group of nuns because it considered them too liberal and not fully observant of Catholic doctrine. The "dissident" sisters were accused of having incorrect opinions on the priesthood and homosexuality and of promoting "radical feminist issues incompatible with the Catholic faith." Pope Benedict XVI had appointed the Archbishop of Seattle, Peter Sartain, to supervise a reform of this leadership group over the following five years. Before his resignation, there were rumors in Rome and in the United States that Pope Benedict XVI was about to appoint a conservative North American prelate as secretary of the Vatican congregation for religious to carry out the hard line against the "rebellious" nuns. But nothing of the kind happened. And now the experts' interpretation is that Pope Francis's decision to appoint the Superior of the Franciscans as secretary of the congregation that supervises religious throughout the world marks a change in line with a more pastoral vision, open to dialogue, in order to overcome tensions.

A certain détente can already be noted in an audience that Pope Francis grants to 1,900 women religious from different orders around the world in early May 2013 in the Paul VI Audience Hall. He invites the nuns to be "mothers," not "spinsters." "Forgive me if I speak this way, but this maternity is important in the consecrated life, this fruitfulness, the joy of spiritual fruitfulness which must enliven your existence," the pope says.

Before this, only two weeks after being elected pope, Pope Francis nominates his successor to the Archdiocese of Buenos Aires. With the appointment of Monsignor Mario Aurelio Poli, sixty-five-year-old Archbishop of La Pampa, formerly his Auxiliary Bishop in Buenos Aires, the pope once more surprises everyone. The church insiders in Buenos Aires were betting on other names. No one expected this appointment. And yet it was another strategic choice. According to people who know Poli, he is a person "in the likeness" of Bergoglio: low profile and with great pastoral activity to his credit. Besides, Poli doesn't believe he is anyone special, either, as Bergoglio would say.

# 15

# The Pearls of Santa Marta

They had never behaved so well during Mass. They had never been woken up at a quarter to six in the morning without protesting. It's Saturday, May 11, 2013, and my children, Juan Pablo, nearly eight, and Carolina, five and a half, know that they are going to meet Padre Jorge for the first time as pope, now dressed in white.

Thanks to an idea of a colleague and the intercession of Juan Pablo Cafiero, the Argentine Ambassador to the Holy See, a group of Argentine journalists living in Rome, together with their spouses and children, will have the privilege of attending the morning Mass that the pope celebrates in the chapel of the Casa Santa Marta at exactly seven o'clock.

The homilies that the pope delivers during these Masses, inspired by the Gospel of the day and broadcast daily by Vatican Radio, are crucial to the understanding of what he is aiming at in his pontificate. In these homilies, which he delivers without notes, speaking from the heart, he gives precise indications of his proposed line of action. The people working in the curia, the ambassadors accredited to the Holy See, the journalists and experts in Vatican affairs, scrupulously analyze these homilies, which are truly pearls of wisdom.

Under a gray sky, at 6:40 a.m. we are all in front of the Petrine gate, through which you usually go to enter Paul VI's Audience Hall, to the left of St. Peter's Basilica. Ambassador Cafiero and his wife, guest list in hand, accompanied by a couple of Swiss Guards and a group of Argentines, about twenty-five people, including six children, walk toward the Casa Santa Marta.

On arrival there, the pope's secretary, Alfred Xuereb, welcomes us and leads us into the chapel, a simple modern structure. In the row of pews on the left there is already a group of Vatican gendarmes in blue uniforms. Since he was elected, the Argentine pope celebrates Mass every morning before groups of laypeople who work at the Holy See, from sweepers and gardeners to the printers of the *L'Osservatore Romano* and outsiders, like ourselves, who ask to attend. Altogether there are about eighty people.

"He wants laypeople to attend the morning Mass, not just priests and nuns; otherwise it would become a clerical gathering," says a foreign Bishop who has worked in the curia for many years.

At exactly seven o'clock, wearing a simple chasuble and his ordinary black shoes, accompanied by two priests who will celebrate the Mass with him, the pope appears. He is very absorbed. Silence reigns, and for most of the Argentine journalists present, the moment is deeply emotional. Juan Pablo and Carolina sit in the front row—our tactic to make sure they behave themselves. They've known Padre Jorge since they were babies; he baptized them. They keep as still as statues during the whole homily. Gerry and I, seated behind them, don't need to intervene to make them behave.

As always, Francis speaks in a simple, direct, deep way. He conveys passion and energy. He speaks about the wounds of Jesus, which must serve to bring us out of ourselves and go toward Jesus—with a prayer that shouldn't be boring—but also to reach those who really have wounds, the poor and the suffering.

At the end of Mass, a priest comes up to Juan Pablo and Carolina to congratulate them on their good behavior. "Well done!" he tells them. In the meantime, Pope Francis disappears to take off his chasuble. He returns at once, dressed in white, to sit down on a bench at the back of the chapel and pray a little, in silence, among the people; this practice has become another of his habits.

A few minutes later, standing in the hall next to the chapel, Padre Jorge greets those of us privileged to attend the Mass; he greets us one by one, like a host, a good shepherd, a parish priest, devoting a word, a friendly comment, an embrace, or a kiss to each of us.

My colleague and friend Cristina Taquini, very excited, gives the pope a beautiful blue and white poncho made of vicuña wool from Catamarca, sent by Dalmacio Mera, the vice governor of the province of Catamarca in northwestern Argentina.

Juan Pablo and Carolina give the pope drawings. "How lovely they are!" he tells them, bending down to look at them, to give them a kiss and caress them with great tenderness. Carolina, who has an album with picture cards of Pope Francis, has drawn a fine portrait of him, dressed in white, with his silver cross and spectacles. Juan Pablo has drawn something similar, but there is also a soccer field, players, and the words "San Lorenzo 6, River 0."

One of Pope Francis's priorities is to clean up and reform the Roman Curia, the central government of the Church; but even more important is the moral and spiritual reform of the curia itself and the universal Church, the reform of attitudes and ways of thinking and acting.

In his Masses at the chapel of Casa Santa Marta, the pope denounces intrigues, treason, gossip, calumny, slander, careerism, ambition, and corruption—the last, in his opinion, being worse than sin.

"I don't know why, but some people derive a dark pleasure from gossip and malice," he says about slander. "Every time we repeat a malicious remark, we are acting like Judas. When Judas betrayed Jesus, his heart was closed, he didn't feel love or friendship. . . . We ask for forgiveness for what we do to our friends, because Jesus is in that friend. And we ask for the grace not to speak ill of anyone. And if we realize that someone has a fault, let's not do judgment with our tongue but pray for the Lord to help him."

During another Mass, in a spontaneous reflection, he defines the Second Vatican Council as "a beautiful work of the Holy Spirit." But he warns that after fifty years some want to "go backward" or transform the council into "a monument." For this reason he says it is opportune to ask ourselves "if we have done everything which the Holy Spirit told us to do in the Council, in the continuity of the Church's growth." This reflection is crucial to the understanding of Pope Francis's vision of a central but also controversial topic. Historians and faithful have come out, sometimes very harshly, in favor of either continuity or reform. In his homily, Pope Francis asks if the faithful have done everything the Second Vatican Council asked for. "No. We celebrate this anniversary almost as though we are erecting a monument to the council, but we are mainly concerned that it should not disturb us. We don't want to change. I'd say there's even more to it: there are rumors that some want to turn back. That's called being stubborn, that's called wanting to tame the Holy Spirit, that's called becoming foolish and slow of heart," he declares.

In another Mass, Pope Francis leaves the clerks of the Institute for the Works of Religion (IOR, widely known as the Vatican Bank), who are present that day, petrified. He wishes that the Vatican Bank, which has been at the eye of the storm for years, would become transparent. He speaks of the risk the Church runs of becoming "a little bureaucratic" and changing into an nongovernmental organization (NGO). And he reminds people that "the Church is not an NGO. It's a love story." The pope stops, looks at the faithful attending, and exclaims: "But there are some of the staff of the IOR here! Excuse me, will you?" He goes on: "Everything is necessary, offices are necessary, but they are necessary only to a certain point—as assistance to this story of love. But when the organization takes first place, love declines and the Church, poor thing, becomes an NGO. And that is not the path." These words, reported by Vatican Radio and in the afternoon's *L'Osservatore Romano*, curiously do not mention the employees of the IOR. Self-censorship?

During the Mass on the feast day of St. Mark the Evangelist, the pope stresses that Christ, before ascending to heaven, bids the apostles to announce the gospel "until the end of the world," not only in Jerusalem or in Galilee. "The horizon is wide and, as you can see, this is the missionary Church. The Church goes forward with this preaching addressed to everyone, everywhere in the world. But it doesn't go forward alone: it goes with Jesus," Pope Francis declares.

On the morning of Saturday, April 27, he denounces a Church and a community that is "closed in and sure of itself," one that lives on slander, "which looks for security in money, or through agreements with power, and pronounces wounding words, insulting and condemning. . . . Maybe they have forgotten their mother's caresses [from] when they were small."

At another morning Mass, on May 3, he once more attacks the internal battles of a Church "without courage." "When the Church loses courage, a lukewarm atmosphere enters. The lukewarm, the lukewarm Christians, without courage. And yet we have the courage to get involved in our petty little affairs, our jealousies, our envies, in careerism, in going selfishly ahead. The Church must be courageous! We, all of us, must be courageous in prayer, challenging Jesus."

On May 16, he launches a strong attack against the bishops and priests who give way to the temptations of money and vanity, and instead of being shepherds are transformed into "rapacious wolves." The pope admits that both bishops and priests can fall prey to temptation and therefore need prayers. "What are the temptations of the bishop and priest?" he asks. Quoting St. Augustine, he identifies the two main ones: "'Wealth, which can be transformed into avarice, and vanity.' . . . When the bishop, the priest, exploits the sheep on his own behalf, when a priest, a bishop, follows money, he isn't loved by the people, and that is a sign. And he himself comes to a bad end," he says.

Pope Francis's words make one think of the Vati Leaks scandal and the accusations of corruption in the Roman Curia itself. They also make one think about those black Mercedes with chauffeurs that some cardinals use in the Vatican. Some live alone in apartments of thousands of square feet with spectacular views of the Eternal City, treated almost as princes, perhaps with a four-wheel drive in the garage.

"St. Paul didn't have a bank account; he worked. And when a bishop, a priest, follows the path of vanity, he acquires the spirit of careerism, and does great damage to the Church. And in the end he even becomes ridiculous, because he boasts; he likes being seen, being all-powerful. And the people don't like this!" Pope Francis states.

Pope Francis is to expand on these subjects of careerism and luxurious lifestyles on Saturday, July 7, 2013, while speaking without a prepared text to six thousand seminarians and novices from sixty-six countries in the Paul VI Audience Hall of the Vatican. "It hurts me to see priests or nuns with the latest model of cars. . . . You mustn't do this! It's better to cycle, or use a smaller car—think of the children who are dying of hunger!"

The pope speaks with passion. And he calls on young future religious to live lives consistent with their preaching and teaching. "Don't you feel disgust when you meet priests or nuns who are not authentic?" he exclaims, denouncing the hypocrisy and deceitfulness found at times in the clergy. "We must be consistent, authentic, we are preaching the gospel by example, not by words," he declares, to applause and ovations. He also asks future priests and nuns to be joyous, to convey joy: "There is no saintliness in sadness! St. Teresa used to say that a saint who is sad is a sad saint! No priests or nuns with long faces!" he exhorts. "Don't be bachelors and spinsters; have pastoral fruitfulness!" he urges them, explaining that celibacy and the vow of chastity should be the way for priests and nuns to be fathers and mothers, but of their flocks.

As he usually does during his Masses at the chapel of Santa Marta, Pope Francis also denounces idle talk, gossip, jealousy, envy, and ambition that can often be found in church communities, where many speak ill of others. "I've done it too, eh . . ." the pope admits, speaking frankly. Then he says good-bye, asking, "Please, pray for me. I am a sinner."

In the following Masses at Santa Marta, Pope Francis criticizes "drawing-room Christians." "The well-bred, upper-class ones" who lack apostolic fervor, who don't have the courage to disturb "the things that are too calm in the Church." And, as he always did when he was Archbishop of Buenos

Aires, he rails against the corrupt, whom he distinguishes from sinners and defines as "the anti-Christ."

"Sinners, yes; corrupt, no!" he declares in a homily on June 3, 2013, arguing that it's not necessary to dwell too long on sinners "because we all are." "We are familiar with ourselves from inside and know what a sinner is. And if one of us doesn't feel this way, let him go to be examined by a spiritual doctor, because there's something wrong," he says. Before being ordained Bishop, during his exile in Córdoba, Argentina, Bergoglio had already written an article on this subject, which was published as a book in 2005: *Corruption and Sin: Reflections on the Theme of Corruption*. There he emphasizes that one must not confuse sin with corruption: sin can be forgiven; corruption can't.

Commenting on the Gospel of the day about the wicked vinedressers, the pope criticizes another figure represented by those who want to "get possession of the vineyard and have lost their relationship with the master of the vineyard—a master who has called us with love, who protects us, but then gives us freedom."

And he presents an X-ray of the corrupt: "They were sinners like all of us, but they took a step further, as if they had become consolidated in sin: they don't need God! But this is only an illusion, because in their genetic code this relation with God exists. And since they can't deny this, they create a special god: they themselves are god, they are the corrupt," he explains. He warns that the corrupt are "a danger for us, too"—that is, for the Catholic Church.

Perhaps it is not a coincidence that among the people attending the morning Mass that day are some "gentlemen of His Holiness." This is an honorific title instituted by Paul VI in 1968, granted to laymen, mostly Italians (but there was also one Argentine, the former Ambassador Esteban Caselli) as a reward for their work in favor of the Catholic Church. The Papal Gentleman—there are more than 140 of them—depend on the Prefecture of the Casa Pontificia and can have an account at the Vatican Bank. What do they do? Dressed strictly in tailcoats, often decorated with gold medals, crosses, and sashes, they have the honor of serving His Holiness.

How? When he receives the visits of heads of state or other personalities, the "gentlemen" accompany the illustrious guests through the sumptuous corridors and halls of the Vatican, escorting them to the Holy Father.

Pope Benedict XVI had decided to suspend this type of nomination after the emblematic case of Angelo Balducci, gentleman of the pope and former head of Italy's Superior Council of Public Works, who was involved in 2010 in a terrible corruption scandal as well as a homosexual prostitution racket with links to the Vatican, discovered through wiretapping by investigators.

In line with his predecessor Benedict XVI, Pope Francis freezes these nominations. "He considers these ceremonial posts to be archaic, useless, and sometimes downright harmful," according to the Italian daily *Corriere della Sera*.

Two days later, he raises the stakes by adding, "Hypocrisy is the language of corruption." In another homily he condemns corrupt hypocrites, flatterers who hope to get on in life with the aid of "sweet words." He asks Christians to put aside "socially educated language" and to speak clearly, like children, who are not corrupt.

With the same informality shown in Santa Marta, during an audience on June 7 with eight thousand priests and former students of Jesuit schools, held in the Paul VI Audience Hall, after the usual welcome speeches, Pope Francis is about to read a written text. But suddenly he stops and says, "I've written this, but it's five pages long! A bit boring . . . Let's do something: I'll read a brief summary and then give you the written text. Then there'll be the chance for some of you to ask me a question and we can have a little dialogue. Do you like that, no? Yes? Good. We'll do it that way."

Later, Teresa, a six-year-old girl, using the familiar address "you" rather than the formal address, with this very informal Argentine pope, asks, "But did you want to be pope?" The former Archbishop of Buenos Aires replies quickly with another pearl of wisdom: "Do you know what it means if a person doesn't love himself very much? A person who wants, who has the desire to be pope, doesn't love himself. God doesn't bless him. No, I didn't want to be pope."

# 16

# Two Popes in the Vatican

"Mommy, you promised that when they elected the pope you could play with me again." That's what my son Juan Pablo, nearly eight, says to me. He's cross because, since February 11, the day of Benedict XVI's resignation, I've been going crazy trying to be a journalist and a mother at the same time. The Pope Francis hurricane is upon us; it reaches my home, my life, and my family too. "Yes, Juampi, I did tell you that I'd spend more time with you once the pope had been elected, but I didn't know it would be Padre Jorge," I answer. Juampi and Caro experience at firsthand the frenzy of the last months: from the resignation of Pope Benedict XVI to the conclave; from the *habemus papam* announcement to the beginning of Pope Francis's revolution, now in full stride.

When we all went together to Pope Benedict XVI's last Angelus on Sunday, February 24, 2013—when there was also a general election in Italy—it left a big impact on Carolina. In St. Peter's Square, where one hundred thousand people had come from all over Italy to salute the pope, there was a mood of mourning. Among the crowd, people were crying, praying, taking photographs, or filming the moment that, to all intents and purposes, was historical.

"The Lord has called me to 'go up the mountain' to dedicate myself even more to prayer and meditation. But that does not mean abandoning the Church," says Pope Benedict XVI in his German-accented Italian during his last appearance at the window of the papal apartment in the Apostolic Palace.

"Is the pope dead?" Carolina asks me more than once, grasping perfectly the essence of the moment. Juan Pablo, better informed, tells her no, that Benedict XVI is the first pope in six hundred years to resign, and that he'll go to Castel Gandolfo, the castle you can see dominating the shores of Lake Albano, where we sometimes go swimming in summer when it's hot.

On February 28, the day of Pope Benedict XVI's final exit from the Vatican and the start of the "vacant see," Carolina follows the spectacular live program broadcast minute by minute by the Vatican Television Center. From the balcony of our apartment she can see passing in the distance the white helicopter taking him to the residence at Castel Gandolfo. She can hear the city's bells ringing in chorus to salute him. She watches the almost-surreal images of an old and fragile pope saying good-bye: "I'm simply a pilgrim starting on the last stage of his pilgrimage on this earth."

Sitting in an armchair in front of the television set, Carolina cries in silence.

Even the children are personally experiencing the period before the conclave. They ask every priest-friend who visits in our home if he can become the next pope. "No, he's a Bishop, not a Cardinal, he can't become pope. Padre Jorge could," Juampi explains to Caro, almost foreseeing the change that no one expects.

They are both in front of the television on the evening of the *habemus papam* announcement of March 13, when they see Padre Jorge dressed in white emerging on the balcony of St. Peter's Basilica. The election creates a revolution at home. For Gerry and me, it's as if we've been catapulted into a story that's greater than us.

Now Juampi and Caro pray every evening for Benedict XVI, whom they would like to see one day—they are fond of him—and of course they pray for Padre Jorge, or now Pope Francis.

Cardinal Jorge Bergoglio never watches television, but on the evening of February 28, the fifteenth anniversary of his taking over as Archbishop of Buenos Aires, he finds himself by chance in the home of friends who are watching live the end of a chapter of the Church's history. So he sees the final scenes of Benedict XVI's pontificate. He sees the Swiss Guard in their striped uniforms with their halberds closing the heavy wooden doors of the palace at Castel Gandolfo. He probably can't imagine that the next pope to enter that residence will be himself.

The clock has not yet struck eight, the time when, as provided for by Benedict XVI himself, the *sede vacante*—the vacant see—is declared. Benedict XVI ceases to be pope; his Vatican apartment is sealed and his Fisherman's Ring annulled (done so by breaking its seal).

Earlier on that same day, followed minute by minute by the television cameras of the Vatican Television Center in a remarkable broadcast, the ceremony in the majestic Sala Clementina of the Vatican begins. There Pope Benedict XVI salutes the cardinals and his principal collaborators—a public that includes his successor, as the German pope underlines.

"During these eight years we have lived with faith wonderful moments of radiant light on the Church's path, together with moments when clouds were gathering in the sky," says Pope Benedict XVI, referring to the many crises that have marked his pontificate.

He says this again during his last, moving general audience on Wednesday, February 27, when he admits that during his pontificate, "there have been times when the waters were stormy and the wind contrary, as throughout the history of the Church. The Lord seemed to be sleeping. But I have always known that the Lord was in this boat. I have always known that the boat of the Church does not belong to me, but to him, and that the Lord will not let it sink."

Without mentioning the intrigues, divisions, and power struggles in the Roman Curia revealed during the preceding year, which he had denounced a few days earlier, speaking of the "disfigured face of the Church," Pope Benedict XVI issues an urgent call for unity. He asks the College of Cardinals to act like an orchestra, in which "diversities, expressions of the universal Church, always contribute to a superior and concordant harmony."

Benedict XVI salutes, one by one, the 144 cardinals from around the world present at the ceremony. Among them is Bergoglio, who received the most votes, after Ratzinger, at the 2005 conclave.

A few hours later, just before 5 p.m., the Vatican Television cameras show another unthinkable picture: the pope, still wearing the Fisherman's Ring and leaning on a cane, leaves his apartment in the Apostolic Palace forever—the apartment that his successor will never occupy.

In the San Damaso Courtyard, the Vatican guards, nuns, officials, bishops, monsignors, and many laypeople who work in the Vatican await him; they are all lined up, their faces distraught. A long bout of applause breaks out, full of emotion, when the former guardian of orthodoxy during the pontificate of John Paul II arrives in the Renaissance-era courtyard and, shyly and with restraint, says good-bye to those who kneel before him for the last time, weeping and kissing his hand. At that moment his private secretary, Georg Gänswein, who is to accompany him in his new life of retirement from the world, also has tears in his eyes.

The bells of St. Peter's Basilica begin to ring. You can already hear the noise of the white helicopter as Pope Benedict XVI is escorted by black cars to the heliport, across the Vatican Gardens. The television cameras show the faithful in St. Peter's Square and the neighboring buildings with banners reading *grazie, gracias, danke, thank you.*

The conclusion is swift. At 5:07, as shown by the big clock in San Damaso Courtyard, framed by the Vatican's television cameras, the helicopter takes off. The "papacopter," as it has been nicknamed on Twitter, flies over the Tiber River, the Roman Forum, and the Coliseum while evening falls on the Eternal City, under a reddish sky. Rome's churches salute him with their bells. After twenty minutes, which pass in what seems like a few seconds, the helicopter lands in the gardens of the Castel Gandolfo residence. Benedict XVI, who an hour or two later will be called "Pope Emeritus," greets the local authorities serenely and approaches the palace where he has spent many summers; written books, encyclicals, and sermons; read; studied; and played the piano. Another crowd awaits him here with banners and placards. One reads, "Your humility has made you great." A few minutes later, smiling, Benedict XVI appears for the last time as pope. "Long live the pope! Thank you! Be-ne-det-to!" cries the crowd, moved to tears.

"A heartfelt thank-you. As you know, tonight at eight, I shall no longer be the pope. I'm simply a pilgrim starting on the last stage of his pilgrimage on this earth," he says, interrupted once more by applause. "I wish with all my inner strength, with my heart, with my love, with my prayers, with my reflections, to work for the common good of the Church and humanity." At the end of an ovation, he imparts his last blessing as pope and says once more: "Thank you, good night, thank you." Benedict XVI turns and vanishes behind the heavy curtains of the balcony of the Castel Gandolfo palace. It is the end of an era.

Confined in a golden self-exile, Benedict appears for the first time before the world together with his successor on Saturday, March 23, 2013. It is an unprecedented meeting. The two popes—one emeritus and the other in service, both dressed in white, one more fragile, with a light jacket over his vestments and without a cape—embrace at the steps of the helicopter that has brought Pope Francis from the Vatican to Castel Gandolfo.

Pope Francis is aware that he would never have taken Peter's throne without the "revolutionary and courageous" resignation of Benedict XVI, which has shaken the foundations of the Catholic Church, and from the first moment he shows the Pope Emeritus the love of a son. He telephones him immediately after being elected, and during his speech to the world from the balcony of St. Peter's Basilica, the first thing he does is to ask for a prayer "for our Bishop Emeritus, Benedict XVI, that the Lord may bless him and the Madonna protect him."

A few days later, on March 19, Pope Francis calls to wish him a happy St. Joseph's Day—it's his feast day and the day of his own ascent to the papacy. And at once, though some would have preferred the two popes not meet, he insists on going to greet his predecessor in person.

Pope Francis refuses to use a kneeler placed purposely for him in front of the altar. "We are brothers," the Argentine pope says to Benedict XVI, inviting him to sit next to him on one of the wooden pews in the chapel of the residence. Ignoring the groups of ultratraditionalists who would be outraged by the "sacrilege" of two popes together, Pope Francis manages this unprecedented stage in recent Church history in the most natural way.

"The last time there were two or three popes together, they didn't talk, but fought to see which of them was the true pope. During the Western Schism, there were three of them," says Pope Francis, provoking laughter, during the press conference granted during the flight to Rome on his return from Rio de Janeiro on July 28, 2013. "There's something that distinguishes my relationship with Benedict XVI: I really care for him. I've always cared for him, for me he is a man of God, a humble man, a man who prays. I was so happy when they elected him pope. When he resigned, too, it was the example of a great man, a man of God, a man of prayer. Now he lives in the Vatican and there are some who ask, 'But how can that be, two popes in the Vatican—doesn't he get in your way, doesn't he rebel against you?' No, for me it's like having a wise grandfather at home. When there is a grandfather in the family, he is venerated, loved, listened to. He is a prudent man, he doesn't interfere," he adds, and he insists, "For me these words say everything: it's like having a grandfather in the house; he's my dad. If I have any difficulty or something isn't clear to me, I can call him."

The pope and the former pope won't appear on the balcony of the palace at Castel Gandolfo on that historic March 23, as many of the faithful had hoped. They talk for three-quarters of an hour in private and have lunch together. The pictures released by the Vatican show the two of them, in harmony, with a big white box and an envelope on a little table between them. Everyone thinks of the top-secret dossier concerning the Vati Leaks case, entrusted to three cardinals, which Benedict delivers to Francis. This will be confirmed by the pope himself during the press conference on the plane, on his return from Rio de Janeiro. When I ask him if he was scared at the sight of that dossier, he replies, "No. I'll tell you a story about the Vati Leaks dossier. When I went to see Pope Benedict XVI, after praying in the chapel we sat down in the study, and I saw that there was a big box and an envelope. Benedict XVI told me, 'In this box there are all the declarations of the witnesses. And the summary and final conclusions are in this envelope. Here they say this . . . and that . . .' Benedict knew everything by heart. It's a big problem but I'm not scared."

After immense media speculation, on May 2, 2013, Benedict XVI, appearing more fragile, returns to the Vatican. Two popes will live, in peace and harmony, in the shadow of St. Peter's dome. On that day Pope Francis receives him at the door of the Mater Ecclesiae monastery, a recently restructured building where the Pope Emeritus has chosen to live, and welcomes him home with a warm embrace.

Benedict and Francis move to the monastery chapel to pray together. "He is happy to come back to the Vatican since he intends to devote himself, as he announced on February 11 last, to the service of the Church, mainly through prayer," a Vatican communiqué announces formally.

As he prepared to resign, Benedict told the world, "I'm not going back to a private life, a life made of journeys, meetings, receptions, conferences, and so on. I'm not abandoning the cross; I'm staying in a new way near the crucified Lord. I no longer bear the authority of office for the government of the Church, but in the service of prayer I'm staying, so to speak, in St. Peter's enclosure. St. Benedict, whose name I bear as pope, will be a great example for me in this. He has shown us the way for a life that, actively or passively, belongs totally to the work of God."

In the shadow of St. Peter's, however, things turn out differently. The physical proximity between the two popes living in the Vatican—Santa Marta and the monastery where the Pope Emeritus lives are a mere ten minutes' walk apart—leads to a collaboration resulting in Pope Francis's first encyclical, *Lumen fidei* ("The Light of Faith"). This document will mark history as the first written "by four hands."

Even if he signed it, Pope Francis makes clear that this work is written almost entirely by his predecessor, to which he has made a small contribution. In this way, he pays homage to his German predecessor.

Reading *Lumen fidei*, one realizes that the style and contents are characteristic of the former pope. The hand of Benedict XVI, the esteemed theologian, is particularly evident when the document refers to the relationship between faith and truth and between faith and reason, problems that have always concerned him. There are quotations from Nietzsche and Dante, but also from authors such as T. S. Eliot and Dostoevsky and from the theologian Romano Guardini, who is much appreciated by Pope Francis.

Dated June 29, feast day of the apostles Peter and Paul—witnesses of the faith—and published on July 5, the encyclical begins with an invitation: "There is an urgent need, then, to see once again that faith is a light." After placing the theological virtue in its historical context, on the basis of Scripture, it stresses that "faith is not a private matter, an individualistic notion or a personal opinion" but comes from listening to the word of God and is destined to become a proclamation.

"Let us refuse to be robbed of hope or to allow our hope to be dimmed," it exhorts toward the end. This sentence is typical of Francis, who also adds that "the light of faith" does not "make us forget the sufferings of this world," quoting the examples of Francis of Assisi and Blessed Mother Teresa of Calcutta.

During the crowded Vatican press conference at which this first encyclical of the Argentine pope, published less than four months after his election, is presented, Monsignor Gerhard Ludwig Müller, Prefect of the Congregation for the Doctrine of the Faith, is asked why it bears only Francis's signature. His answer is categorical: "We don't have two popes, only one; that is why there aren't two signatures: the encyclical is a witness of unity."

In fact, Pope Francis's first original work, written during the summer in Casa Santa Marta (he does not go on holiday) comes out later, in November 2013, in the form of the apostolic exhortation *Evangelii gaudium*, "The Joy of the Gospel." In this document, considered to be the program for his pontificate, Francis calls for a missionary transformation of the whole

Church, a renewal of the Church, and a "conversion of the papacy." And he invites everyone, religious and laity alike, to be daring and creative in rethinking the objectives, structures, styles, and methods of evangelization.

But on the morning of July 5, the day of the publication of the encyclical *Lumen fidei*, Pope Francis puts the spotlight on Benedict by inviting him to the inauguration ceremony of the new monument to St. Michael the Archangel, during which he entrusts the city-state of the Vatican to St. Joseph and St. Michael. So the two popes appear together once more, taking hands and embracing with great affection.

On the same day, the Vatican announces that two much-loved popes of the last half of the twentieth century, John Paul II (1978–2005), the "traveling pope," and John XXIII (1958–1963), the "good pope," will be proclaimed saints together on April 27, 2014.

"I believe that celebrating the canonization of both together is a message for the Church: these two were really good," Pope Francis explains during the return flight from Rio. For the canonization of the Polish pope, beatified on May 1, 2011, and proclaimed saint in record time, Pope Francis has approved a second miracle made through his intercession. It's the case of Floribeth Mora Díaz, from Costa Rica, who on the night of John Paul II's beatification was inexplicably cured of a brain aneurysm. The great novelty is that Pope Francis has decided to canonize John XXIII (Angelo Roncalli), who died fifty years earlier and whose cause for sainthood had been frozen, without the recognition of a second miracle.

Although he had been elected at age seventy-six—the same age as Bergoglio—as a "transitional" pope, John XXIII, the "peasant pope," compared by many to Pope Francis on account of his closeness to the people, revolutionized the Church by convening the Second Vatican Council. Roncalli was beatified in September 2000, during the Jubilee Year, by John Paul II. Then, in a decision similar to Francis's, John Paul II beatified John XXIII and Pius IX, the last pope-king, in the same ceremony.

With his spontaneity, Pope Francis, who is in regular contact with Pope Emeritus Benedict and meets him on special occasions, convinces the "grandfather" of the Church, as he calls him, to come out of his cloister and return to St. Peter's Square on April 27, 2014, to participate in the historic double canonization ceremony of these two great popes, both of whom Benedict knew and loved. This memorable day, marked by the presence of two living popes and two recent ones now proclaimed saints, will go down in history as "the day of the four popes."

Two months earlier, in February 2014, again encouraged by Pope Francis, the Pope Emeritus had surprised everybody by suddenly appearing in St. Peter's Basilica to attend the consistory at which his Latin American successor created his first batch of cardinals.

People are unlikely to ever forget the emotional, prolonged round of applause that erupted in the basilica as the fragile, humble, Emeritus Bishop of Rome, walking with the aid of a cane, entered the basilica for the first time since his resignation. It was a stunning moment.

# 17

# The Resistance

Pope Francis is immediately accused of being a populist and a demagogue by a conservative and ultratraditional minority, which believes that his informality—he is "too Argentine," folksy, very "Evita," too much "peace and love"—secularizes and diminishes the figure of the Supreme Pontiff, who until now has been seen as an absolute monarch, infallible and hardly accessible.

In spite of this opposition, ever since the election of the first Latin American pope, a kind of miracle has happened in the Vatican. Thousands of the faithful, tourists, and the simply curious invade St. Peter's Square every Wednesday for the general audience—provoking even worse traffic jams in Rome—and every Sunday at noon for the Marian prayer of the Angelus. Such numbers have never been reached before with such regularity: four times the usual number of people—one hundred thousand instead of twenty-five thousand.

On Sunday, from the window of the study in the papal apartment on the third floor of the Apostolic Palace, where he doesn't want to live (secluded up there, he thought he might become depressed), Pope Francis greets his public with the by-now famous words "Good day, brothers and sisters!" and likewise takes leave of the crowd with the equally well-known "Have a good Sunday, and enjoy your lunch!" This behavior is held to be "demagogic" by some dissident groups in the Roman Curia that bear a grudge. Some of them start calling the new pontiff, "Mike Bongiorno." Mike Bongiorno (1924–2009) was a popular Italian TV personality, born in the USA, who used to begin every program by greeting his audience with the words "Allegria! Allegria!" (Cheer up! Cheer up!) This disparaging nickname says everything. But it's not the only one. Some officials of a Eurocentric curia call the pope "El Argentinito," or "the Little Argentine."

"It's only logical that there's resistance to change. It happens in any administration of any government in the world, when, after years of the status quo, someone new, someone from outside, turns up," a Vatican Archbishop admits. "Even if, for reasons of state and faith, the curia adjusts to the new directives," he adds.

The flow of ecstatic people arriving at the Vatican is impressive. In the crowd are many nonbelievers. "I'm an atheist, but I like this pope a lot," Susana, an Argentinian tourist, confesses to me one day. She is wearing an Argentine soccer T-shirt and carrying a flag of Argentina. She had planned this trip to Europe a long time ago. And now she feels she can't miss coming to support her fellow countryman who is giving a lesson in humanity to the whole world.

Now, on Wednesdays and Sundays, Via della Conciliazione must be closed to traffic because of the enormous flood of people. Even the Pope-mobile in which Francis travels through the square to greet the faith-ful—the white jeep that every day ends up full of presents (scarves, caps, T-shirts) people have thrown to him—has been forced to leave the Vatican's borders and go down Via della Conciliazione so that everybody can greet him, if only for a second. Something of this kind has been seen only at significant events, such as the funeral of John Paul II (April 8, 2005), John Paul II's beatification (May 1, 2011), and the beatification of Mother Teresa of Calcutta (October 19, 2003).

The "Francis effect" has provoked a boom in Confessions and full churches throughout the world and a significant influx of tourists to Rome, which had been hit by the most serious economic crisis since World War II. If in February the religious souvenir shops on Via della Concili-azione were closing down, they are now reborn and offering medals, imi-tations of Pope Francis's silver cross, key chains, rosaries, candles, posters, and T-shirts with the face of this pope who comes from the other end of the world. Argentines living in Italy suddenly find themselves rediscovered. "Now everybody congratulates us; it's as if they've realized that we Argentines can give something to the world besides footballers and television soap operas," they say proudly. "Thanks to Francis, we've gone up in status," comments an Argentine seminarian studying in Rome.

Francis's resonance with people increases as the days go by. If sometimes he was shy, now, dressed in white and with a smile that was not often seen in Buenos Aires, he's become a wizard of communication. During the Regina Coeli prayer on April 21, 2013, the "populist" pope engages in a dialogue—so far unprecedented in the Vatican—with the hundreds of thousands of pilgrims in the square.

"Today there are so many young people here. I'd like to ask you: have you ever heard the voice of the Lord asking you to follow him? Have you heard it? I can't hear you!" he shouts, putting his right hand around his ear.

"Yes!" answers the crowd in chorus.

"Have you wanted to be the apostles of Jesus?" the pope asks them again.

"Yes!" the multitude shouts back.

"Young people must put their lives on the line for great ideals. Do you think so too? Do you agree?"

"Yes!" replies his public, full of enthusiasm. "Francis! Francis!" they shout with elation at the end.

"Thank you for your greeting, but greet Jesus too. Shout loudly, 'Jesus!'" Francis goes on, showing that though his detractors accuse him of being a demagogue, he wants to avoid any kind of "pope mania." And the crowd obeys.

"Jesus! Jesus!"

Similar scenes are repeated many times, with young people who really listen to him, who shout "Jesus! Jesus!" as the Popemobile passes. Although many people don't know it, when he was a simple priest in his beloved Argentina, he behaved in the same way. When Jorge Bergoglio was a parish priest in San Miguel and then Bishop and Archbishop, he interacted with his flock, asking questions, involving them. And this is what he does as pope. In the general audience of June 12, when he comments that "it is enough to open a newspaper" to see the presence of evil, of the devil in action, but that "God is stronger," he asks the seventy thousand people listening to him under a merciless sun: "Do you believe that God is stronger? Let's all say it together: God is stronger!" Once more he gets a response from his listeners.

This kind of scene is hair-raising for the ultratraditionalist and conservative sectors that have a different vision of the Church and of how a pope should behave. "They say that I'm a populist because I'm with the people? Well, then, yes, it's true—of course I'm a populist!" the pope says to the people around him. As always, he is well-informed and aware of the criticism.

"Let's hope they let him act." "Will he be able to resist, alone against everyone, in that nest of vipers?" "No, he won't, the curia will gobble him up in a mouthful." During the first days of the collective love affair with the Argentine pope who "is one of us, speaks like us, and is simple like us," it's usual to hear in Rome such phrases in bars, shops, and among small groups of people.

After the revelations of the struggles for power and money, thanks to the secret documents revealed through Vati Leaks, it's understandable that people in the street wonder whether the Argentine pope will actually manage the urgently needed cleanup of the Church's central government.

"I think they will poison him, as they did John Paul I; this pope is too pure and humble, one must be careful," my baker tells me.

In the streets, the people—in a faithful reflection of that popular wisdom that Bergoglio has always respected—feel that this pope from the end of the world could provoke a real earthquake in the Vatican. Hence the belief that Pope Francis could be assassinated.

"And how will they do it, by offering me a cup of tea?" he always jokes when someone tells him to be careful because his life might be in danger.

"When some monks tried to poison St. Benedict in the sixth century, he blessed the goblet of poisoned wine and it broke into a thousand pieces," a monsignor from the curia reminds me. Francis is aware that, apart from the enthusiasm he has inspired in the world, there are sectors, albeit small ones, that don't appreciate him at all. But he stays calm; he is convinced that God put him where he is, and that the Virgin, St. Joseph, and St. Teresita are protecting him and will go on protecting him as long as Divine Providence wills it.

The well-known Italian correspondent on Vatican affairs, Marco Politi, is the first to expose the internal resistance. According to Politi, it is certainly the determination shown by Pope Francis that generated the reactions inside the ecclesiastical structure. "Demanding a poor Church and blameless priests means challenging the lifestyle and behavior of thousands of 'hierarchs' great and small," he writes in the Italian daily *Il Fatto Quotidiano*. Besides, for the Holy See this could mean making public its real estate value, calculated by Italy's financial newspaper *Il Sole 24 Ore* at one billion euros in Italy alone, as well as publishing—as is done already in Germany—the budgets of the dioceses in Italy, which are usually reluctant to do so. It also means drastically reforming the Vatican Bank, as the pope is determined to do.

A certain resistance is also beginning to be noticed among some of the more famous Italian journalists. Giuliano Ferrara, editor of the conservative daily *Il Foglio*, considered a "pious atheist" (communist in his youth, he is now on the political right, and stridently defends what he considers the Catholic traditions) writes an open letter to Pope Francis, titled "Father, I'm Afraid of Tenderness." He is playing on the words of a homily given during the Mass inaugurating Pope Francis's papacy, when Francis invited the faithful not to be afraid of tenderness.

"I'm one of the few who is afraid of tenderness, and among the very few who believe that a part of divine mercy is also judgment and the exercise of authority," writes Ferrara, champion of the fight against abortion, which has been legal in Italy since 1978 if it takes place within the first ninety days of pregnancy.

"For me it would be instinctive to write to you now, not very humbly, that 'enjoy your lunch' is not good theology, that the pardon, patience, and friendship of God for men are part of a plan for creation illuminated by incontrollable freedoms that must be sternly disciplined," Ferrara affirms, recalling that Bergoglio once said, "Having an abortion is killing a being that can't defend itself." Ferrara would now like to hear him say those same words "with an attitude of coherence, clarity, and truth."

In the Vatican there are those who believe that the traditionalists—who cannot stand Francis's many moves outside the norm—will calm down only if the pope speaks out clearly against abortion and same-sex marriage.

Even though his position on many delicate issues had already been expressed when he was Archbishop of Buenos Aires, Pope Francis refers to abortion for the first time in public during the Regina Coeli prayer on May 12. After greeting the members of a crowded March for Life who have arrived in St. Peter's Square, he invites his audience to "keep their attention alive on the very important subject of the respect for human life from the moment of conception" and to "guarantee the legal protection of the embryo, protecting every human being from the very first instant of their existence."

As he had already done at other times, Pope Francis avoids using the word *abortion* and referring to issues of sexual morality, both of which are the obsession of right-wing sectors he has always detested because they think "from the belt down" and not about people's daily lives.

"In my opinion, subjects like abortion and the meaning of marriage are not political, but doctrinal and moral, and all of us bishops, including the Bishop of Rome, must talk about these matters," says the Archbishop of Philadelphia, Charles Chaput. This Franciscan prelate, in an interview with John Allen of the *National Catholic Reporter*, stresses that right-wing Catholics in the United States complain because Pope Francis is not more combative on these subjects. "Right-wing Catholics are not very happy about Francis's election, and it will be interesting to see how he treats them," Chaput says.

During his return trip from Rio de Janeiro to Rome, when the Brazilian journalist Patricia Zorzan Alves, from Rede TV, asks Pope Francis why during the World Youth Day he didn't express his opinion on abortion or same-sex marriage, he replies: "The Church has already expressed itself perfectly in this connection. It wasn't necessary to come back to it, just as I didn't speak about fraud, falsehood, or other things about which the Church's doctrine is clear."

"But it's a subject that interests young people," she responds.

"Yes, but it wasn't necessary to talk about it, but about positive things that open the way to young people. Isn't that true? Besides, young people know the position of the Church perfectly well."

"What is the position of Your Holiness, can you tell us?"

"It's the position of the Church. I'm a son of the Church."

The ultraconservative sectors vent their fury on the Internet, on websites and blogs where—besides accusing Francis of being a demagogue, a populist, and wanting to diminish the role of Supreme Pontiff—they charge him with "pauperism," being attracted to poverty.

From the beginning these people don't like the pope's refusal to wear the traditional vestments such as the mozzetta—the short red cape that he turned down when he made his appearance on the central balcony of St. Peter's Basilica on the evening of the *habemus papam* announcement—the red slippers, and the white trousers under the soutane. Nor do they appreciate the fact that he renounced wearing the gold pontifical cross around his neck, preferring to go on using his bishop's silver cross, given to him by Quarracino, and insisting on calling himself the "Bishop of Rome."

Furthermore, his decision not to live in the apartment on the third floor of the Apostolic Palace provokes great outcry. Not only because he has rejected an implicit tradition, which, in the minds of many, desacralizes the papacy, but also because of the confusion created among the forty-some priests who usually lodge in the Casa Santa Marta, which has been transformed into a kind of fortress protected by Swiss Guards and gendarmes, and because of the fears for his safety caused by his living there.

"How can I love a pope who doesn't want to be pope and doesn't even want to be called pope?" writes Katrina Fernandez, a U.S. conservative blogger.

But criticisms don't come only from bloggers. "The pope should live in that apartment, where he would be much more protected. In the Casa Santa Marta, under the Vatican walls, next to a Roman neighborhood, he is too vulnerable. He could easily be the victim of a car bomb. . . . It's impossible to defend him from an attack there," comments an official of the Secretary of State. "Not counting the fact that after Vati Leaks, his papers and documents aren't safe at Santa Marta," he adds anxiously.

The Romans who live on the other side of the Vatican walls near Santa Marta are not happy either. Used to parking in the space near the Vatican residence, they can no longer do so since Francis has come to live there. Complaints are not confined to parking problems, which are easily solved by parking instead in a square on the Janiculum, five minutes away and always half empty. It also appears that the electronic protection system surrounding the pope's current residence stops certain mobile networks from functioning, which infuriates their users.

"We only hope his apartment on the third floor of the Apostolic Palace isn't added to the Vatican Museums," says a commenter at the traditionalist Latin Mass site, who calls Pope Francis *Papa piacione* ("the charmer pope"), an expression that refers disparagingly to a person who is always smiling and gets on well with everybody.

The chief concern of the conservative sector is that Pope Francis may annul the *Summorum Pontificum*, the 2007 decree in which Benedict XVI rehabilitated the ancient Latin Mass. This is very unlikely.

When he gave these indications to restore the Latin Mass, Benedict XVI was looking for reconciliation with traditionalists in the Catholic Church who had never stomached the liturgical reform of 1970, a result of the Second Vatican Council, which involved a great revolution: Mass celebrated in native languages, with the priest turned toward the people. Thanks to

*Summorum Pontificum*, since September 14, 2007, it is possible to celebrate the Mass freely, without a special bishop's dispensation, according to the old rite decreed by St. Pius V after the Council of Trent (1542–1563) and updated by John XXIII in 1962.

The ten articles of this apostolic letter by the former German pope (a refined theologian famous for his love of the Gregorian chant; his attachment to tradition; and his rejection of liturgical abuse, such as the Mass as a show) lay down that the earlier Latin rite can also be used during marriages, baptisms, ordinations, funerals, and occasional celebrations such as pilgrimages.

According to the papal decree, if a stable group of the faithful wishes to have the old Latin Mass celebrated, "the parish priest should willingly accept their request." If such a group "has not had its request satisfied by the parish priest," it should inform the Bishop, who, according to the document—obviously written in Latin—is "warmly" invited to grant their wish.

Well aware that this big change would provoke contrasting opinions and strong resistance from major episcopal conferences such as the French and German ones, Pope Benedict XVI added to the decree a letter addressed to all the bishops in the world. Here he justified his decision to recuperate the Latin Mass, and he categorically denied that it meant a step back or a blow to the Second Vatican Council.

But Pope Francis is too intelligent and doesn't move in the way the ultra-traditionalists fear. Far from being contrary to the use of Latin, from the first day of his pontificate he celebrates parts of the Mass, if not the whole, in the traditional language of the Roman Church. During his first canonization, that of more than eight hundred martyrs beheaded in Otranto in 1480, and two Latin American nuns—the Columbian Laura Montoya y Upegui (1874–1949) and the Mexican María Guadalupe "Lupita" García Zavala (1878–1963)—it is significant that Latin is used not only in the canonization rite (as is usual) but also in the celebration of the Eucharist. At that event, only in his homily does the pope use Italian and Spanish.

In that same Mass, Vatican correspondents note that the pope, when referring to the eight hundred people who, "having survived the siege and invasion of Otranto, refused to deny their faith and died confessing the risen Christ," eliminates with a stroke the references to the Ottoman Empire present in the published text and handed to journalists in advance. Pope Francis, politically savvy, remembers what happened after Benedict XVI's *lectio magistralis* at Regensburg in September 2006, in which he offended followers of Islam. Pope Francis does not want to repeat similar lapses.

Pope Francis is also criticized for certain liturgical innovations, starting with the "silent blessing" that he imparted to journalists during the March 16, 2013, audience, which he did out of respect for non-Catholics and nonbelievers.

However, he causes a sensation when, on Maundy Thursday 2013, he washes the feet of two Muslims and two women in the Casal del Marmo juvenile detention center. The international traditionalist Catholic blog *Rorate Coeli* recalls that only "chosen men," and not women or Muslims, should have been admitted to the washing of the feet. The same blog is shocked when after the Angelus of Sunday, August 11, 2013, Pope Francis greets Muslims at the end of Ramadan, publicly calling them "brothers," as Paul VI and John Paul II had done before him. "Muslims are brothers like Cain and Abel!" declares the *Rorate Coeli* site.

"Personally, I've found a number of aspects of this papacy annoying from the very start, and I'm not the only one," writes Jeffrey Tucker, editor of the blog *New Liturgical Movement*, which detests Pope Francis's style.

Pope Francis is criticized by those who love the traditional liturgy when, taking ceremonial possession of the Basilica of St. John Lateran, he appears with Paul VI's antique crosier, also used by John Paul II but that Benedict XVI had stopped using in 2008, when he replaced it with another model with a gilded cross at the top. For traditionalists, this is a slap in the face. But a few days later, in another ceremony, Pope Francis surprises them again by carrying Benedict XVI's gilded staff, a gift received by Pius IX in 1877 and used from time to time by John XXIII during the Second Vatican Council.

The idea of a two-headed Church, the unprecedented coexistence of two popes in the Vatican, is also a cause for anxiety, if not indeed fear.

Besides the opposition of groups on the extreme right, in some circles upset by a "streetwise" pope, it is said that Pope Francis doesn't have the intellectual, theological, and philosophical stature of his predecessors. These groups accuse him of always repeating the same things. These circles are not aware of the pope's extensive Jesuit education.

The Italian Cardinal Gianfranco Ravasi, president of the Pontifical Council for Culture, echoes the perplexities of some intellectual circles in an interview for "Vatican Insider" on May 5, 2013.

To the question "What did the cardinals see in their Argentine brother to make them elect him?" Ravasi answers, "We Western pastors have an expressive way and a very precise method of analysis, but which is not capable of direct contact with the grass roots, who are not much based on arguments but require testimony and stimulus. Our pastoral letters are often really documents with theological and scientific support. Now, however, we need the national-popular element, that wide horizon that feeds only on television but has its problems. Pope Francis has an influence on simple people who need a direct language and a presence close to daily life. On the other hand, even people indifferent to religion feel attracted by this new pope. Perhaps it will be the intellectuals who start having reservations."

Some find this implicit criticism annoying. "Ravasi's interview reveals a European tendency not to look beyond Europe and a scanty knowledge of the churches of Latin America, where there are many intellectuals devoted to philosophy and theology; it also betrays a tone of superiority and contempt," says Father Carlos Galli, former deacon of the Faculty of Theology of the Pontifical Catholic University of Argentina (UCA).

"The people who criticize Francis say that he speaks to the emotions and not to the intelligence, that his style is pleasant but doesn't touch difficult questions, a simple style of a low intellectual level. Obviously they don't know Bergoglio, who has had an impressive formation in many fields. Some charge that Francis's closeness to people is populism. I think this is a theoretical mistake and also a practical one. The theoretical mistake is to think that everything popular is populist. The practical mistake is to believe that he makes all those gestures of pastoral affection only for show, because that's not how it is, he makes them because he has always acted this way," Galli adds.

It's understandable that there is criticism. There was some at the start of the pontificate of the first pope to come from Eastern Europe, John Paul II, and also of the German pope Benedict XVI. But the objections to Francis come from a minority that prefers the status quo and is opposed to change. In other words, resistance comes from within the Church. Christians—Protestant and Orthodox—Muslims, and Jews are fascinated by this pope who comes from the ends of the world and evidently knows how to build bridges. He shows this clearly in May 2014 during his historic visit to the Holy Land and in the prayer for peace in the Holy Land that takes place two weeks later in the Vatican Gardens, attended by the presidents of Israel and Palestine, Shimon Peres and Mahmoud Abbas, a dream come true.

On March 29, 2013, during the celebration of the Lord's Passion in St. Peter's Basilica, a very moving rite in which at the beginning he prostrates himself before the altar for a few minutes in a sign of adoration and penitence, the Argentine pope receives strong and significant support from the Capuchin preacher of the Pontifical Household.

"This Good Friday, in the presence of the new successor to St. Peter, there could be the beginning of a new life," says Father Raniero Cantalamessa, in his homily. Cantalamessa, who mentions a short story by Franz Kafka, supports the renewal of the Church that the pope aspires to. "We must do everything possible so that the Church may never look like that complicated and cluttered castle described by Kafka, and the message may come out of it as free and joyous as when the messenger began his run. We know what the impediments are that can restrain the messenger: dividing walls, starting with those that separate the various Christian churches from one another, the excess of bureaucracy, the residue of past ceremonials, laws, and disputes, now only debris," he says.

"In the Book of Revelation," he continues, "Jesus says that he stands at the door and knocks. Sometimes, as noted by our Pope Francis, he does not knock to enter, but knocks from within to go out. To reach out to the 'existential peripheries of sin, suffering, injustice, religious ignorance and indifference, and of all forms of misery.'"

"As happens with certain old buildings. Over the centuries, to adapt to the needs of the moment, they become filled with partitions, staircases, rooms, and closets. The time comes when we realize that all these adjustments no longer meet the current needs, but rather are obstacles, so we must have the courage to knock them down and return the building to the simplicity and linearity of its origins. This was the mission that was received one day by a man who prayed before the Crucifix of San Damiano: 'Go, Francis, and repair my Church.'"

Cantalamessa, who obviously does not belong to the minority against the "populist" pope, ends his homily with these words: "May the Holy Spirit, in this moment in which a new time is opening for the Church, full of hope, reawaken in men who are at the window the expectancy of the message, and in the messengers the will to make it reach them, even at the cost of their lives."

# 18

# A Left-Wing Pope?

It's six o'clock in the evening. The pope has just finished writing a note and wants somebody to copy it on the computer. He looks for an official in the Vatican offices, but by now there is no one there. However, the lights are on. Francis starts to switch them off, room by room. And he is angry: "With all this waste of light a priest in Latin America could live for a month!"

The scene was observed and reported by people close to the pope. And it's totally believable. When he lived in an apartment on the third floor of the Buenos Aires metropolitan curia, in the middle of winter, during weekends, when he was alone in the building, Padre Jorge didn't switch on the central heating. An electric space heater was enough for him.

The scene of Francis switching off the lights in the Vatican tells us a lot about him. His arrival means the beginning of a new, different style, even for the internal administration, the economy, and the shadowy finances of the Holy See.

His wish for a "poor Church for the poor" immediately revolutionizes the Vatican. In the Roman Curia, which in the main adjusts itself to the new wind blowing from the south, silver rings and crucifixes suddenly become fashionable. Gold chains and crucifixes (worse still if studded with jewels) are no longer worn. Better give them to the poor, or in any case, keep them locked up in a safe.

The new policy of austerity the pope imposes with his decision to live at Casa Santa Marta, in keeping with his simple style—with no limo or

Mercedes Benz, he travels in an ordinary car, a blue Ford Focus—begins to be noted in real facts.

With one stroke of the pen, the *villero* ("shantytown") pope decides to abolish the bonus given to the three thousand officials of the Vatican whenever there is a change of pope. After such a disruption in the Vatican City State's functioning, it is standard procedure to compensate personnel for overtime work and the greater effort required. For example in 2005, when John Paul II died, Vatican officials received about $1,300 each, besides a check for about $671 after the election of Benedict XVI. Pope Francis decides to devote this sum, more than $8 million, to charities for the most needy. But that is only the beginning.

He wants to set an example, starting at home. He intervenes in the Vatican Bank, which has been at the center of many scandals during past decades, suspected of shady operations, such as money laundering. Pope Francis has only one objective: transparency. Before intervening in a concrete way, he decides to cut the bonuses paid to the five cardinal members of the bank's oversight committee. Although it is not a very big sum (a total of about $33,550 a year for each one, according to the Italian press), it is another important signal. Spirituality follows a different path.

Before tackling the Vatican Bank and the Vatican's financial system by setting up different pontifical commissions to examine the facts and then take action, Pope Francis—famous in Argentina for denouncing corruption, poverty, the increase in social inequality, and the excesses of both untamed capitalism and statism—prepares the ground. And he makes known his views on economic matters.

On May 16, two months and three days after his election, in his first important speech on the world financial crisis, he makes a relentless analysis. With a firm tone he denounces "the dictatorship of an economy without face or human goal," one that results in "daily insecurity with fatal consequences." Then he rails against "the imbalance promoted by the absolute autonomy of the markets and financial speculation," and "pervasive corruption and selfish tax evasion, which have reached worldwide dimensions."

Calling for "an ethical financial reform" that at the same time promotes an economic reform that works for everyone, he invites the world's ruling classes to change their attitude and put themselves "truly at the service of the common good of their peoples."

"The pope exhorts you to impartial solidarity and a return to ethical values in favor of man in financial and economic actuality," he says during a harsh speech on the occasion of the presentation of credentials by the ambassadors of Kyrgyzstan, Antigua and Barbuda, Luxemburg and Botswana to the Holy See, a message addressed in reality to the international community. "The financial crisis we are going through makes us forget its origin in a deep anthropological crisis, and in the negation of man's primacy," the pope affirms.

"Today a human being is thought of as a commodity, to be used and then thrown away," he denounces, criticizing the growing gap between rich and poor. While the income of a minority of people is growing exponentially, that of the majority is decreasing. He invites experts and rulers to consider the words of St. John Chrysostom: "Not to share your goods with the poor is to rob them and deprive them of life." These words cause a great sensation in the Vatican, where many tremble: Will the pope sell the priceless properties of the Holy See? Will he stop devoting resources to the activities of the many Vatican departments?

Two days later, on May 18, during a prayer vigil on the eve of Pentecost before more than two hundred thousand faithful, he answers many of these questions. He tells them that the real crisis today is that "if the investments of the banks decline, it's a tragedy; but if people die of hunger, if they have nothing to eat, that doesn't matter! That's our crisis today!"

"Today it is not news if a homeless person dies, nor is it news that so many children haven't enough to eat. Today a scandal is news. And that is serious," he says regretfully, explaining that "a poor Church for the poor goes against that mentality."

When on May 21 he visits a group of nuns from Mother Teresa of Calcutta's Missionaries of Charity, who run a refuge for the poor in the Vatican, Pope Francis denounces "untamed capitalism, based on the logic of profit at any cost, of giving in order to get, of exploitation without seeing the person involved," the consequences of which "can be seen in the crisis we are living through."

On May 24, during an audience for those taking part in a plenary assembly of the Pontifical Council for the Pastoral Care of Migrants and Itinerant People, he rails against human trafficking, "a despicable activity, a disgrace for our societies that call themselves civilized," which takes place in a culture where "the fetishism of money reigns."

On June 5, on the occasion of World Environment Day, Pope Francis returns to this issue. He launches an earnest appeal to respect the creation and oppose the "culture of waste" reigning in today's world, where "money gives the orders." "Food that is thrown away has in effect been stolen from the table of the poor man, the one who is hungry. Consumerism has persuaded us to get used to the superfluous and the daily waste of food, so we no longer know how to give it its right value, which goes well beyond mere economic parameters."

"Today it isn't men who give orders; it's money! God, our Father, has given the task of guarding the earth not to money, but to us. Yet men and women are sacrificed to the idols of profit and consumption; it's the culture of waste. If a computer breaks down it's a tragedy, but poverty, the plights of so many people, end up as part of normality. . . .

"If somebody dies it isn't news, but if the markets lose ten points it's a tragedy! So people are discarded as if they were rubbish."

According to a report by the United Nations Food and Agriculture Organization, which has its headquarters in Rome, 1.4 billion people waste food, while 870 million people—one out of eight in the world—are victims of malnutrition. When on June 20 he receives the participants of the thirty-eighth session of the FAO, Pope Francis says, "It's well known that the current production of food in the world is sufficient, yet there are millions of people suffering and dying of hunger: that, dear friends, is a real scandal."

In addition to his experiences in Argentina's shantytowns, the pope has always paid attention to the world, being concerned about disasters, famine, and the poverty that wars leave behind—wars he defines as "madness, the suicide of humanity" and that, too, are the result of the power of money.

"In history we have so often seen that the powerful ones of this world want to solve local problems, economic problems, economic crises . . . by war," Francis charges during a Mass on June 2, 2013, with the Italian families of those killed in various wars. "Why? Because for them, money is more important than people! And that is just what war is, an act of faith dedicated to money, to the idols of hate, to the idol that makes you kill your brother, kill love." He affirms something very similar on the day after the vigil of fasting and prayer for peace in Syria, when during the Angelus he denounces arms trafficking, which lies behind every conflict.

"There is always the doubt: this war here or that war there—because everywhere there are wars—is it really a war because of problems or is it a commercial war to sell arms in illegal trade?" he asks.

Moved by the loss of lives that occurs every year, to general indifference, in the sea around the island of Sicily, where thousands of desperate Africans, fleeing from war and poverty, drown while trying to escape by boat, the pope overnight decides to visit the island of Lampedusa, a symbol of the dramatic plight of immigrants and refugees.

As his personal secretary, Alfred Xuereb, from Malta, reveals, the pope wishes to "weep for the dead" of Lampedusa, the twenty thousand people who have lost their lives in tragic shipwrecks over the past twenty-five years. Lampedusa is an Italian island of six thousand souls south of Sicily, closer to Africa than to Italy. As a port of entry into Europe, it is a perfect image of one of those existential peripheries of the world that the pope calls on us to give attention to.

This is the first journey of Francis's pontificate, a lightning-fast trip on July 8, 2013, a little more than four hours, which Europe perceives as a punch in the stomach. The pope, son of immigrants, sends from there a vibrant *j'accuse* against the world's indifference.

In a forceful sermon, which rocks much of the political class of the European Union—a fortress inaccessible to non-EU immigrants because of its restrictive migration policies—the pope speaks without beating around the bush about the plight of hundreds of thousands of desperate people who board the boats of death in search of a better future. "These brothers and sisters of ours were seeking to leave difficult situations to find a little peace and serenity; they were looking for a better place for themselves and their families, but they have found death. How often these seekers find no understanding, no welcome, no solidarity! And their voices rise up to God!"

Evoking a passage from the Bible, in which God asks Cain, "Where is your brother?" Pope Francis (who has been a professor of literature) wonders: "Who is responsible for this blood? In Spanish literature there is a play by Lope de Vega that tells how the inhabitants of the town of Fuenteovejuna kill their governor because he was a tyrant, and they do it in such a way that no one knows who performed the execution. And when the king's judge asks, 'Who killed the governor?' everyone answers: 'Fuenteovejuna, Sir.' Everyone and no one! Even today this is a crucial question: who is responsible for the blood of these brothers and sisters? No one!"

The pope's second journey in Italy, on September 22 of the same year, takes him to Cagliari, Sardinia, to venerate the Madonna of Bonaria, who gave her name to his beloved Buenos Aires. On this occasion he rails against "an economic system that leads to tragedy because it has as its center an idol called money.... Here too, in this second island that I visit, I have found suffering, suffering due to lack of work, which deprives you of dignity. Where there is no work, there is no dignity!" he exclaims.

Pope Francis's words, which turn the spotlights of the whole planet onto the cemetery of the Mediterranean Sea and the plight of unemployment as no one has done before, obviously thrill the Catholic flock, but also atheists, nonbelievers, and pacifists. His cries against a global political leadership that is indifferent to the dramatic situations of millions of outcasts shock Italy's political right. "It's easy to open Italy's doors while living in the Vatican," comments Cristiano of the xenophobic Northern League party, after the pope's trip to Lampedusa. "Why not take the immigrants to live in the Vatican, which is big enough, instead of bringing them into Italy, where we are dying of hunger?" agrees Luigi, from Milan.

It's not only the Northern League that rebels against Francis's *j'accuse*. The politicians of former Prime Minister Silvio Berlusconi's People of Freedom party also criticize the pope of the poor: "A religious sermon is one thing; the management of the state is quite another," says member of parliament Fabrizio Cicchitto. Journalists of a number of conservative dailies such as *Il Giornale* and *Il Foglio* are of the same opinion, and they accuse Bergoglio of not understanding that globalization and the free market guarantee "the emancipation and liberation of the peoples of the Third World."

The social and economic definitions of Pope Francis—who was named "Person of the Year" by *Time* magazine and by the Italian *Vanity Fair*, and whose image has graced the covers of many weeklies and magazines throughout the world—provoke a certain disquiet in the world of high finance. Although there is nothing new in the Catholic Church expressing itself on the subject of economic and social justice—during the past hundred years, different popes have expressed their vision through their encyclicals—the first Jesuit pope's anathema against the idolization of money does not meet with Wall Street's approval. Nobody understands whether he is a conservative or a progressive, because as a good Jesuit he can't be easily pigeonholed.

This disquiet about him comes out clearly if one talks to professionals in the financial world or reads articles like the one published at the end of March 2013 by *Forbes* magazine, the most important magazine for investors and businesspeople, titled "Pope Francis's Economics: Yes, He Has a Left-Wing Vision of the Free Market."

"The pope attacks the order of the market because he finds it 'faceless' and 'without human objectives.' He is right: the market hasn't got a face," writes Jerry Bowyer in the article. "But that's only because it's got seven billion faces. It doesn't have one human objective, because it has seven billion human objectives."

Pope Francis's ideas on the economy—already expressed in Buenos Aires and in the Aparecida Document—provoke perplexity not only in financial circles. They don't go down well with some members of the clergy either. "Since he started talking about a poor Church for the poor, the faithful have been donating less money. . . . And how will we survive without charity?" a Bishop from Eastern Europe complains in confidence.

But the pope, aware of playing a difficult game, continues undaunted. "Francis wants to break down the wall between the North and South of the world, just as John Paul II wanted to bring down the Berlin Wall between East and West. Opposing the 'globalization of indifference' is the main geopolitical and spiritual mission of the poor Church for the poor, the new 'cold war' that he must win over selfishness," explains a Vatican official.

On August 15, when he celebrates the Assumption of the Virgin with a Mass at Castel Gandolfo, Pope Francis once more shows that he prefers deeds to words. He doesn't go by helicopter—why such a waste?—but in the modest blue Ford Focus in which he always travels.

Harshly attacked at the end of 2013 by conservative sectors in the United States who accuse him of being a Marxist for criticizing capitalism and the current global financial system, which he expressed in the apostolic exhortation *The Joy of the Gospel* (*Evangelii gaudium*), Pope Francis dots the *i*'s and crosses the *t*'s in a pre-Christmas interview in *La Stampa*.

"There is nothing in the exhortation that one does not find in the social teaching of the Church. . . . I do not speak from a technical point of view, but I sought to present a photograph of what is happening," he explains.

And he returns to denounce the so-called trickle-down theory of economics, according to which the free market generates greater equity and social inclusion. "The promise was that when the glass is full it would overflow and the poor would benefit. However, what actually happens is that when the glass is full, as if by magic, then it [the glass] becomes even bigger and so nothing comes out for the poor. That was the only reference to a specific theory. And that does not mean being a Marxist!"

Pope Francis goes further and states, "The Marxist ideology is erroneous. However, in my life I have known many Marxists who are good people, and so for this reason I do not feel offended [at being called one]."

# 19

# The Gay Lobby: Is the Honeymoon Over?

It is the beginning of June 2013. For the second time this year I am called by the producers of *Porta a porta*, the RAI 1 TV program that is one of the most widely followed political talk shows in Italy, anchored by the influential journalist Bruno Vespa. The show will feature the first three months of Pope Francis's papacy, and they would like me to be there. The program is shot at the Via Teulada studios in Rome on the evening of Tuesday, June 11. On the very same day, the French news agency AFP releases a flash news item: "The pope admits to corruption and the existence of a 'gay lobby' inside the Roman Curia." A veritable bombshell.

It is early morning in Argentina, but at the editorial office of *La Nación* online, they immediately see the news. Nati Pecoraro asks me to check the information. So I visit the little-known progressive Chilean website Reflexión y Liberación, which is the source of the news. There I can read the transcript of a private and evidently very confidential audience the pope granted on June 6 to the leadership of the Latin American and Caribbean Confederation of Men and Women Religious (CLAR) at the Casa Santa Marta. "In the curia there are saintly people, but there is also a current of corruption, it's true. . . . There is talk of a 'gay lobby' and that's true too. We will have to see what we can do," the pope said, according to the Chilean portal.

Although it is not news that there are both corruption and gay men in the Vatican, it is unheard of for a pope to say this without mincing his words. In addition, the fact that the press office of the Holy See does not issue an immediate reaction flatly denying the version given by the Chilean site is surprising; it smacks of admission.

When I get to the *Porta a porta* studios a few hours later, I am surprised to note that none of the invited guests is commenting on the news of the day. Soon after the beginning of the taping, after 6 p.m., a frightened-looking assistant brings Vespa a communiqué from an Italian press agency that, belatedly, reports this news item.

The host cuts short the taping to get more information. Since I am the only one in the know on the set, I immediately explain that it is about information appearing on a Chilean site that is apparently reporting the words of the pope himself. Vespa, a veteran journalist, understands that it will prove impossible not to talk about this during the program, which will air this same evening, because the matter is too important. Without a moment's hesitation, he decides to include the news.

So, if only for a few minutes, the question is referred to during the program. The guests, authoritative experts on Vatican affairs and authors of several books—the Catholic writer Vittorio Messori; the *Corriere della Sera* journalist Massimo Franco; the already-mentioned Vatican correspondent Marco Politi; Gian Franco Svidercoschi, former deputy director of the *L'Osservatore Romano*; and Father Antonio Spadaro, director of the prestigious review *La Civiltà Cattolica,* and a Jesuit, who, months later, will publish a groundbreaking interview with the pope—remain cautious. They don't dare say much because "it remains to be seen whether the pope actually said those things." Indeed, the Chilean site that publishes the transcript of the audience doesn't detail the circumstances, nor does it list the questions posed to the pope.

Leaving this aside, during the program, Vittorio Messori (author of the interview book with John Paul II, *Crossing the Threshold of Hope* and considered the "prince of Italian Vaticanists") says something surprising. Close to conservative circles in the curia, Messori questions the statement made by the Holy Father that very same morning: "St. Peter didn't have a bank account." Messori says, "With all due respect, as a Catholic and an admirer,

I wouldn't want him to slip into a kind of demagogy." However, the most disturbing moment comes when he shows his concern for the revolution triggered by the Argentine pope who wants "a poor Church for the poor" and who lashes out against clericalism. "I hope he is an all-around Jesuit and is in possession of the virtue of prudence and knows when to stop in time."

"For example, about the IOR [Vatican Bank]," continues Messori, "a pope who sees the reality cannot ignore that the biggest religious institution of the world needs a financial institution. In this respect I don't think we will see it all dismantled, because I believe St. Ignatius with his charisma will stop him in time."

Messori's words clearly reflect the terror felt by part of the Roman Curia, that Pope Francis may abolish the IOR, also called the Vatican Bank, "whose negative image tarnishes the pope's message," as its German chair Ernst von Freyberg readily admits in an interview with me on May 29, 2013, at the bank's headquarters, the famous Torrione di Niccolò V, which in olden times housed a Vatican jail.

By recognizing the existence of a "gay lobby," which amounts to a sort of public secret, Pope Francis does away with a taboo, opening up questions about who belongs to such a lobby. And he is criticized.

After Benedict XVI unexpectedly stepped down, the daily *La Repubblica* in an article assured readers that the three-hundred-page secret report the pope had asked three cardinals to draw up after the Vati Leaks scandal mentioned sins connected to corruption, power, and sex, and the existence of a so-called gay lobby within the Roman Curia.

"This incident may mark a sort of 'transition' in the young history of this pontificate, from a 'honeymoon' period, lasting about 90 days, in which the Pope's refreshingly direct words have been greeted with appreciation and generally without criticism, to a period in which those remarks have begun to elicit calls for greater clarity and theological precision in order to avoid perplexity and confusion among the faithful," writes Robert Moynihan, editor of the U.S. Catholic journal *Inside the Vatican*.

"As to the gay lobby, the pope hasn't discovered anything new, but speaks the language of truth. They can poison him; he isn't safe in there and is already rather isolated. He is risking his life—they can kill him," comments Paolo Farinella, a parish priest from Genoa who is famous for his outspokenness.

"The Pope's Words Are Making the Curia Tremble," headlines *La Stampa*, informing readers that for some time accusations and counter-accusations, anonymous letters, and gossip have been circulating on the alleged homosexuality of some prelates inside the sacred palaces. "That of being a homosexual is the most widely used accusation to destroy adversaries," the article emphasizes.

"Strange things have happened inside the curia," admits Monsignor Marcelo Sánchez Sorondo, chancellor of the Pontifical Academy of Sciences. He is from Buenos Aires like the pope and has lived in Rome since 1971. When consulted on the existence of a gay lobby, he says, "All men have original sin and a twofold nature, divided between good and evil. It happens in the Church at large and it may also happen in the curia. What I don't know, even if the pope said it himself, is how widespread the problem is. Saying that there is a lobby that affects the governance of the Church seems a little strong, but there is something in it. Francis will change things. Besides, it's simple: those who are happy with the pope want the Church to go forward with evangelization and with what the pope is proposing, which, ultimately, is what is already in the Gospel. Those who are unhappy... well, there must be a reason if they are unhappy."

"The problem isn't only the gay lobby, but the fact that a clergyman leading a double life may be blackmailed," writes Vittorio Messori in *Corriere della Sera*. And he adds, "The fact that there are homosexuals within the Church has been known for some time, but I don't know if there are lobbies that operate to support careers and protect their members." Messori takes advantage of the article to further substantiate his disapproval of the pope's statement he considers demagogic: "St. Peter didn't have a bank account."

In an interview in *Il Fatto Quotidiano* that gives rise to controversies among Catholic historians—several will disprove him—Messori states, "The poor church is rubbish. Jesus wasn't a down-and-out." He goes even further: "Let us not talk nonsense. Jesus had money, even a treasurer who then betrayed him, Judas Iscariot. When he was crucified, the guards noticed his tunic was sewn from a single piece of fabric, a rare luxury. Jesus dressed Armani."

Pope Francis starts taking his first steps in the Vatican Bank affair, a minefield, in mid-June 2013. As he will reveal during the press conference held on his return flight from Rio de Janeiro, the pope would have liked to tackle the matter later. But he was unable to defer it.

"I thought I would deal with the economic aspect next year, because it isn't the most important aspect I needed to deal with. But the agenda changed because of the circumstances you all know and that are public. These things happen when in the office of government someone goes in a certain direction and gets hit by a fastball coming from the other side—he must stop that ball. Isn't that so?" the pope says.

After his first hundred days as St. Peter's successor, Pope Francis will undertake a series of actions aimed at eliminating all the rotten apples not only in the Vatican Bank but also within the economic and administrative bodies of the Holy See; these scandals tarnish the image of the Catholic Church. In less than two months he sets up three commissions: one that starts investigating the Vatican Bank (on June 26), another to audit and reconcile the administrative, economic situation of the Holy See (on July 19), and a third to step up controls on Vatican finances (on August 8).

A cleanup has started, and measures are set up that make some circles significantly far from happy. For example, a decision is made to freeze the bank accounts of the postulators for the causes of saints, who are suspected of receiving significant sums of money to advance the beatification or canonization of one or another figure—big business in the Vatican.

"I wish IOR was the only problem Francis had to solve!" a non-Italian Archbishop tells me off the record, stating that over the past few decades of curial mismanagement, episcopal appointments have been virtually bought and sold. In other words, groups that donated large sums to fund church projects apparently used their influence to have particular candidates appointed as bishops. Are we talking about simony?

Despite the concrete actions undertaken by Pope Francis to start changing things, some continue to complain that he isn't doing anything. "In Italy, when nobody wants to solve a problem, they set up a committee," comments a skeptical monsignor who asks not to be named.

But let us proceed chronologically. On June 15, Francis does something that will soon prove a major headache and will be used against him: he chooses Monsignor Mario Salvatore Ricca as the new interim prelate of the Vatican Bank. This is an important appointment: Ricca, age fifty-seven, is the director of the Casa Santa Marta and is considered one of the pope's trusted men.

On Saturday, June 22, the pope decides at the last minute not to attend a concert to be broadcast live by RAI on the occasion of the Year of Faith. This is considered by Italian Vaticanists as a slight against the Roman Curia. This absence on the part of the Argentine pope, who until then had always been reliable and punctual (although never one to go to concerts or other society events) is met with astonishment. Indeed, some even think he has an unexpected health problem.

"There's no need to worry about the pope's health. All engagements on tomorrow's agenda are confirmed. Bergoglio didn't go to the concert because he gave priority to some work commitments he had in the afternoon," Father Federico Lombardi, spokesman of the Holy See, reassures observers. The following day, the pope's absence at the concert is on the front page of every Italian paper. They publish the emblematic shot of an empty white armchair, surrounded by bishops and cardinals looking puzzled.

"I am no Renaissance prince who listens to music instead of working" is the pope's explanation, according to some Italian media. It will be revealed later that since more than one hundred nuncios—the Vatican's ambassadors in the world—had come to Rome to see him during those very days, he had had to receive one of them on an urgent matter.

In the audience with the nuncios, the pope says things that are not wholly well received and are interpreted by some as a reprimand against their lifestyle. "Giving in to the worldly spirit, especially for us pastors, exposes us to ridicule," he declares.

However, ecclesiastical circles are most shaken when he reminds nuncios—who play a crucial role in the nomination of bishops—what the criteria are for selection. "In the delicate task of carrying out the inquiries leading to the choice of bishops, make sure candidates are pastors who are close to the people. This is criterion number one: pastors close to the people. One may be a great theologian, a beautiful mind; let him go and teach at the university, where he will do much good! Pastors! We need them! May they be fathers and brothers, mild, patient, and compassionate; may they love inner poverty as freedom for the Lord and external poverty as shown by a simple and austere life; may they not have the psychology of a prince. Make sure they are not ambitious, that they are not seeking to become bishops."

As of June 26, the minority that accuses Pope Francis of "too much talk and no action" must take a step back and keep quiet. Determined to turn it into a transparent body, the pope sets up "a papal reporting commission" on the Vatican Bank, consisting of five members. Among them is only one Italian, Cardinal Raffaele Farina, who will chair, and one woman, Harvard professor Mary Ann Glendon, former U.S. Ambassador to the Holy See. There is a Spaniard, Monsignor Juan Ignacio Arrieta Ochoa de Chinchetru, of Opus Dei, who will coordinate the committee; Monsignor Peter Wells, a U.S. diplomat from the Secretariat of State who will be secretary; and French Cardinal Jean-Louis Tauran, who on March 13, 2013, had announced the election of an Argentine pope.

The commission "was born of the desire of the Holy Father to know better the legal position and the activities of the Institute so as to harmonize it with the mission of the universal Church and of the Apostolic See in the wider context of the reforms that institutions supporting the Apostolic See should undertake," affirms a communiqué from the Secretariat of State. "The commission is tasked with collecting information on the institution and to submit its findings to the Holy Father," the communiqué adds. It is circulated together with the "chirography," a document handwritten by Francis himself, which details the commission's functions.

This action follows in the footsteps of Benedict XVI, "having listened to the opinion of several cardinals, that of brothers among bishops as well as other advisors, and in the light of the need to introduce reforms within the institutions supporting the Apostolic See," Pope Francis writes. It is clear he wants to understand what goes on in the Vatican Bank and that he doesn't trust the information that its directors may have given him.

The commission will inform him directly and regularly, and he will have access to all the papers of the Vatican Bank, whose managers can no longer refuse handing over information under the pretext of protecting professional confidentiality, as they have done previously on several occasions.

The Vatican Bank controls assets amounting to 7.1 billion euros and nineteen thousand bank accounts. The deaths of Roberto Calvi, responsible for the bankruptcy of Banco Ambrosiano, and that of the Mafia-linked banker Michele Sindona seem to support the suspicion of corrupt dealings, which have been weighing on the bank for decades.

On June 28, two days after the ad hoc commission is created to review it, the Vatican Bank is back in the eye of the storm. Monsignor Nunzio Scarano, a Vatican prelate and former official of the Administration of the Patrimony of the Apostolic See, is arrested and brought to the Roman prison of Regina Coeli on charges of corruption, fraud, and slander. The news travels around the world.

With him, Giovanni Zito, a former secret agent, and Giovanni Carenzio, a financial broker, end up behind bars as well, following an investigation by the Italian Financial Police on the attempted illegal importation of capital, which ran parallel to a second inquiry into the Vatican Bank undertaken by Rome's Prosecutor's Office in 2010, based on suspected money-laundering activities.

According to taped phone conversations, Monsignor Scarano, age sixty-one—nicknamed "Don Five Hundred" for his passion for five-hundred-euro banknotes—Zito, and Carenzio tried to import from Switzerland twenty million euros in cash, the fruits of evading taxes. The operation, which was never realized, was to benefit some friends of the prelate, the d'Amicos, important ship owners in Salerno, where Scarano comes from.

In the view of the investigating magistrates, Scarano used the Vatican Bank "as a quick and safe tool to carry out banking and financial transactions dodging, if not breaching, the tax-related anti-money-laundering regulations." Under investigation from the Salerno Prosecutor's Office as well, published telephone conversations reveal that Scarano talked in a code: he used "books" to refer to millions of euros. "The more books you bring, the better," he tells Giovanni Zito, the secret agent involved.

As a consequence of the Scarano scandal, on July 1, the first heads start rolling at the Vatican Bank. Director Paolo Cipriani and deputy director Massimo Tulli resign from their posts. If Scarano was able to use the Vatican Bank as he wished, it was because management allowed it or failed to make the necessary checks. In actual practice, Scarano was on very friendly terms with both Cipriani and Tulli: according to tapped telephone conversations they addressed each other using the Italian term of familiarity for "you."

Cipriani and Tulli also had been under investigation by the Rome Prosecutor's Office since 2010 for a transfer of twenty-three million euros from the Vatican Bank to other banks in a suspected case of money laundering.

Cipriani had previously taken on Ettore Gotti Tedeschi, former president of the Vatican Bank and member of Opus Dei, who had been sacked abruptly in 2012. According to secret letters circulated during the Vati

Leaks scandal, he had sent a psychiatrist to observe Gotti Tedeschi. The psychiatrist subsequently submitted a report describing him as a man with psychological disturbances.

In the midst of this earthquake and on the eve of Pope Francis's first international trip, to Brazil, the Ricca scandal erupts. The Italian weekly *L'Espresso* reveals that the prelate, one of the pope's trusted men, appointed by Francis to an important position within the bank, allegedly had had a scandalous past involving homosexual activity when he worked at the nunciature in Uruguay between 1999 and 2004, a past that allegedly had been hidden from Francis to make him more vulnerable to attack.

According to the press, an invisible hand had supposedly stolen the documents on the turbulent events in Ricca's past from the in-house Vatican dossier that exists for every member of the diplomatic service. In the Ricca file there is no report stating that he lived in the Montevideo nunciature with a captain in Switzerland's army named Patrick Haari; or on the fact that one day he had been attacked in a gay nightclub; or that, on a different occasion, he was saved by the fire department from an elevator in which he'd been locked in with a teenager.

A mere week after Ricca had been appointed prelate at the Vatican Bank, these details started emerging, but they were first considered slander. "He, the pope, was kept in the dark about the relevant information that may have stopped him from appointing Battista Ricca as prelate in the [bank], had he known about it in time," writes Sandro Magister, who reports on the Vatican for *L'Espresso*.

During the lengthy press conference that Pope Francis granted reporters, including myself, on the flight back from Rio, he answers a question on the Ricca case: "As for Monsignor Ricca, I did what is prescribed by canon law, that is, *investigatio previa*. This investigation revealed nothing of what they accuse him of, we found nothing," a totally serene Francis affirms. "But I would like to add something else about this: I see that often inside the Church, beyond this case and in this case too, people look for the sins of youth, and this is then published. Not crimes, mind you, crimes are of a different nature: abuse of a minor is a crime. No, sins. But if a person, a layperson or a priest or a nun, committed a sin and then repented, the Lord forgives, and when the Lord forgives, the Lord forgets, and this is important for our lives," he says.

"Then, you spoke about the gay lobby. So much is written about the gay lobby. I still haven't found anyone with an identity card in the Vatican with 'gay' on it. They say there are some there. I believe that when you are dealing with such a person, you must distinguish between the fact of a person being gay and the fact of someone forming a lobby, because not all lobbies are good. This one is not good. If someone is gay and is searching for the Lord and has good will, then who am I to judge him? The Catechism of the Catholic Church explains this in a beautiful way, saying, 'No one should marginalize these people for this, they must be integrated into society.' The problem is not having this tendency—no, we must be brothers and sisters to one another, and there is this one and there is that one. The problem is in making a lobby of this tendency: a lobby of misers, a lobby of politicians, a lobby of masons, so many lobbies. For me, this is the greater problem. Thank you so much for asking this question."

During the same press conference, the pope says he doesn't know what will happen with the Vatican Bank. "Some say that it may be better if it is a bank, others if it is a support fund, others that it should be closed down. I don't know. I trust the work of IOR [the Vatican Bank's] people, who are working on this in the commission as well. The president [von Freyberg] stays, while the general manger and his deputy [Cipriani and Tulli] have resigned. But I can't tell you how the story will end. We find, we search; we are human. We must find the best, but the characteristics of IOR—be it a bank, a support fund, or anything else—must be transparency and honesty," he affirms.

Keeping his sense of humor, Pope Francis also speaks of the scandals related to Monsignor Scarano. "Within the curia there are saintly persons, and there are some who are not so saintly, and the latter make the most noise. You know that a tree crashing down makes more noise than a forest that is growing. And I am hurt when these things happen. But some people give rise to scandals—some. We have this monsignor in jail, I believe he is still in jail; and he didn't go to jail because he is a saintly person. These are scandals that hurt."

When he is asked whether he thinks his changes will be met with some resistance, the pope answers diplomatically, "If there is a resistance, I haven't seen it yet. Maybe yes, there is some, but I haven't noticed. Resistance: in four months you can't find that much."

Some compare the dynamics of the Ricca case to that of the scandal involving Richard Williamson, the Lefèbvrian Bishop whose excommunication was lifted by Pope Benedict XVI in 2009. The pope had ignored Williamson's revisionist position on the Holocaust because nobody in the curia had alerted him to this. It appears that even now the Roman Curia mechanisms are not functioning properly.

Another case immediately follows the Ricca one. This one involves a woman: Francesca Immacolata Chaouqui, the "Pope's PR." On July 18, 2013, Francesca, age thirty, born of an Egyptian father and an Italian mother, is elected member of a second "reporting commission" (the only woman and the only Italian) set up to review the economic and administrative structure of the Holy See.

The task of this committee is to suggest reforms of the Holy See's institutions with a view to a "simplification and rationalization of existing bodies and establish more targeted economic planning of the activities of all Vatican administrations." In another chirograph (letter written by hand and signed by the pope), the pope explains that, thanks to this group of mostly lay experts in legal economic and administrative matters, he wishes to have strategic solutions put forward in order to improve the management of the Holy See.

In addition to the Vatican Bank, there are other economic bodies that need restructuring. There is the Administration of the Patrimony of the Apostolic See, where Monsignor Scarano, today in jail, worked as an accountant. This is a Vatican office managing real estate and financial investments. Then there is the governorate of the Vatican City State, which manages sizable real estate assets, independent of the Holy See. And then Propaganda Fide, the powerful Congregation for the Evangelization of Peoples, which owns assets amounting to ten billion euro. And that's not all. There's also the Prefecture for Economic Affairs, endowed with planning powers and tasked with writing up Vatican financial statements.

But let's go back to Francesca Chaouqui. The young woman is chosen to take part in the commission. And her past indicts her. An attractive woman, she is a graduate of law school but never passed the Italian examination to practice as a lawyer. She has no economic or administrative background, but she is a lobbyist, close to Opus Dei. She is married to Corrado Lanino, an IT engineer who allegedly has worked for the Vatican.

But this isn't the main cause for concern. Entrusted with public relations for the Italian branch of the multinational consultancy Ernst & Young, Chaouqui reveals an irreverent past on Twitter. In some tweets she will later describe as forged, published by *Il Giornale*, Chaouqui had scathingly criticized Secretary of State Tarcisio Bertone, accusing him of corruption.

Chaouqui closes her account on Twitter at the beginning of August 2013, causing the tweets to disappear. But even more disturbing are the versions according to which she is accused of being a "crow"—that is, a leaker of information out of the sacred palaces of the Vatican. She is allegedly also a very close friend of Gianluigi Nuzzi, author of the book on Vati Leaks. In addition, she is supposed to have passed information to the website Dagospia.com, a site that is extremely well-known in Italy for shedding light on gossip and plots in the Vatican.

Both the Ricca and the Chaouqui cases are signs of how difficult it has been for Pope Francis to clean up the Vatican. The big question in the Chaouqui case is, who were the high-ranking prelates who recommended her? It isn't easy to ban intrigue from the Vatican.

From July to August 2013, months during which popes have often retired to Castel Gandolfo to rest, Francis carries on. On July 11, he signs another *motu proprio*—a decree issued at his own initiative—that reforms the criminal and administrative law of the Vatican, providing harsher sentences for offenses of corruption, money laundering, and sexual abuse of minors.

The *motu proprio* updates old-fashioned legislation based mostly on the Italian criminal code of 1889. The reform provides for a new definition of offenses against minors, which now includes the trafficking of children, child prostitution, child recruitment, sexual violence, sexual acts involving children, and the production and possession of child pornography. According to the previous code, such crimes would normally have entailed at most a prison sentence between three and ten years, Father Lombardi explains. With the reform, the minimum term goes up from five to ten years, and with aggravating circumstances, the maximum term increases to twelve years.

It is a step forward in the fight, begun by Benedict XVI, against the sexual abuse of minors carried out by members of the clergy. Indeed, the new provisions are binding not only for the officials and employees of the Roman Curia but also for diplomatic staff and for those who work in bodies or institutions connected to the Holy See, even if they may not be on Vatican territory.

Furthermore, the reform aligns Vatican legislation with the provisions of several international treaties, signed by the Holy See, against terrorism, torture and war crimes, crimes against humanity, and money laundering. Another new feature is the abolishing of life imprisonment: from now on, in the Vatican City State, the longest sentence anyone may have to serve is thirty-five years.

Another clear sign of Pope Francis's wish to clean up the Vatican is the new legislation's redefinition of offences against public administration in accordance with the UN Convention against Corruption (2003). It also introduces a system of penalties against legal persons or entities—such as the IOR—"in all those cases in which they may profit from criminal activities carried out by their bodies or employees, thereby establishing their direct liability through prohibitive sanctions and fines."

But there is more: according to this decree, revealing confidential information is now an offense. If someone steals secret documents, he or she may be punished with eight years in jail. It is a measure conceived to avoid the repetition of a scandal such as the one involving Pope Benedict XVI's butler, Paolo Gabriele, sentenced to eighteen months in prison for robbery, but who was pardoned by the German pope and is now a free man.

This is a no-holiday August for Pope Francis. Just back from the tiring but productive trip to Brazil for World Youth Day, on Saturday, August 3, the pope meets the reporting commission tasked with investigating the organization of the economic and administrative structure of the Holy See.

To make his position crystal clear, Francis says, "The assets of the Holy See do not belong to the Holy See; they must be used to finance hospitals, leprosariums, shelters for children, and the elderly."

And on August 8, by means of a new *motu proprio* on preventing and fighting money laundering, the funding of terrorism, and the proliferation of weapons of mass destruction, the pope intensifies surveillance of the financial system of the Vatican. From then on there will be more effective controls on all bodies handling money through a new "commission for financial security" consisting of seven members, which will have to coordinate the competent authorities of the Holy See and the Vatican City State so as to prevent financial wrongdoing and money laundering.

At the same time, Pope Francis strengthens the role of the Financial Information Authority, a body set up by Benedict XVI, who gave it the "function of prudential vigilance" over those bodies that carry out professional financial activities. According to a Vatican communiqué, these measures are responses to "the request from Moneyval," the Council of Europe's anti-money-laundering body. Moneyval, which in July had judged the Vatican's anti-money-laundering provisions merely "sufficient," is forced to issue a new verdict. It is obvious that Pope Francis wants good marks, so that the Vatican is finally included among the virtuous states. This is the very aim of Francis's *motu proprio*. And this is why it extends the application of Vatican legislation to all departments of the Roman Curia and the central administration, to all the other institutions depending on the Holy See, and to the nonprofit organizations headquartered in the Vatican, as requested by Moneyval.

The Ricca and Chaouqui cases appear as Pope Francis's first two slip-ups, probably caused by his detractors, but they are understandable. Although he knows the curia much better than many imagine, he has never worked in it and doesn't know its inner mechanisms or the people employed in it. This is why it is crucial that he spend the first few months observing, listening, analyzing, and then deciding. "In Argentina, where he knows the lay of the land, he immediately appointed his successor, Mario Aurelio Poli, and without hesitation designated as Archbishop the Rector of the Pontifical Catholic University of Argentina, Víctor Manuel Fernández. It's obvious, they catapulted him into Rome, from the other end of the world, and he has to get to know people. Because, otherwise, a cardinal may go up to him and say, 'Listen, the best secretary of state is so-and-so,' and Francis doesn't know him. It's like getting married by correspondence. He needs to get to know people, and he's taking all the time it takes," explains Sánchez Sorondo in mid-June 2013. And he adds, "Appointments in the curia are exceedingly complex to make because once appointed it is far from easy to remove someone, so one has to choose well."

Above and beyond the difficulties and traps, rapid as a high-speed train, Pope Francis moves firmly and decisively on the complex, obscure, and all "too Italian" management of the Vatican economy.

On February 24, 2014, he revolutionizes the Holy See's finances with a significant decree that creates a new super-ministry for the economy of the Vatican, the Secretariat of the Economy. He makes clear that there is no turning back, that the page has been turned, that the days of the mismanagement have ended. In fact, he appoints another Cardinal from the ends of the world, George Pell, Archbishop of Sydney, Australia, and a member of the papal G8, as head of this new body.

At the same time, he creates the new Council of the Economy, composed of fifteen members from different nationalities—eight prelates and seven laypeople with expertise in financial affairs. Its task is to give policy directives to the secretariat and to exercise overall monitoring of the economic and administrative activities of the Holy See. He appoints another member of the G8, the German Cardinal Reinhard Marx, as president of this council.

Given the delicate and important nature of the task entrusted to him—to justify, restructure, cut costs, and review not only the finances but also the human resources in the Vatican—Cardinal Pell moves from Sydney to Rome.

Two months later, on April 7, the Vatican announces that Pope Francis will not close the Vatican Bank, as some had expected. Instead, he will complete its transformation in such a way that in the future it will operate with maximum transparency, in accordance with international norms, and provide specialized financial services to the Catholic Church worldwide. In July, the president of the IOR, Ernst von Freyberg, hands over his post to Jean-Baptiste de Frassu, a French banker.

Weeks earlier, the pope dissolves the two pontifical commissions that he had set up in June 2013 to investigate the controversial bank and to analyze the economic and administrative organization of the Holy See (among the members of one of these commissions was the controversial Francesca Immacolata Chaouqui).

By mid-July 2014, Pope Francis's cleanup and reform of the Vatican's finances is beginning to bear fruit.

20

# Fiesta in Brazil

On Monday, July 22, I wake up at dawn. My taxi comes and picks me up at 5:30 a.m. In Rome it is full summer but still dark. I have to be at Terminal 3 of Fiumicino airport at 6:15 a.m. for check-in. Thus starts my journey on Pope Francis's first international trip, to Brazil, on the occasion of World Youth Day, the great coming together of young people conceived by John Paul II.

I am one of seventy-one journalists from all over the world to be admitted onto the papal flight. Flying on the pope's airplane is an immense privilege. It also means paying thousands of euros for a very expensive flight: a round-trip ticket from Rome to Rio de Janeiro costs more than 5,500 euros, four times the normal fare, not because we were in first or business class. For the past few years, flying on the pope's airplane was almost impossible. I never flew with Benedict XVI. To cut costs, I always went on my own.

It is difficult to find an explanation for this astronomical price that Pope Francis—who always traveled in economy class as a Cardinal—certainly doesn't know about. Do we journalists pay the expenses of the retinue of cardinals and bishops? Who benefits?

But it isn't just a matter of financial means. A journalist must first submit a formal application for admission to the Vatican's press office, which grants temporary or permanent accreditation. Since available seats are limited—usually requests exceed plane capacity—a seat is not guaranteed. What criterion is followed to select journalists? I don't know.

At the dawn of my job as correspondent for the daily paper *La Nación*, despite the fact that I had been an accredited correspondent in the Vatican since 1999, when Spanish journalist, Joaquin Navarro-Valls from Opus Dei was head of the Vatican's press office, I was always left out despite my many requests for admission to the papal flight. The reason was that nobody knew me, and I still had to prove myself. However, it was apparent that had I been a journalist from a European or North American paper, instead of one from the end of the world, my place would have been guaranteed.

That same attitude of giving scarce value to the Southern Hemisphere felt within the Roman Curia was reflected in the selection of journalists included on papal flights. Only in June 2001, thanks to the intercession of the Argentine Ambassador to the Holy See, at that time Vicente Espeche Gil, I finally managed to fly on the pope's plane. We went to the Ukraine with John Paul II, who was already very ill.

Now everything has changed. At Fiumicino's Terminal 3, I meet several colleagues who are checking in. Many who before didn't even look at me now greet me with broad grins. Just as the first Argentine pope at the Vatican brought about a "geopolitical" change, thanks to which I was admitted onto the papal flight from the word *go*, so a change in behavior is apparent among Vatican correspondents.

"Do you think he'll talk to us? Will we manage to say hello?" These are the questions many raise with me as we are having cappuccino and croissants at a bar at the airport before boarding the plane. I say yes, he will certainly come and say hello. Bergoglio is well brought up; the same way he says good morning when he starts the Angelus every Sunday, he will undoubtedly come and say good morning to us, too, we who are accompanying him on his first international journey. And it is precisely because he will come and talk to us that the price of the ticket is worth paying.

Unlike some heads of state who have their own private planes, the pope does not own this plane. It is from the Alitalia fleet, and the papal emblem is applied to the fuselage; the same is embroidered on the headrests and cushions. The motto *Miserando atque eligendo* is printed on the cover of the agenda for the trip, which is handed out by the extremely courteous flight attendants; it includes a map showing the route and indicating the distance in kilometers between Rome and Rio (9,201 kilometers, or 5,717 miles in twelve hours and fifteen minutes), in addition to some information about the plane. It is a brand new Airbus 330. It is so new that, to the joy of the journalists, between every two seats there are electric outlets for charging computers and other devices; there's even a USB port.

We journalists sit at the back. But since we are traveling with the pope—or maybe to justify the astronomical ticket price—the service is excellent, much better than in normal economy class. The flight staff is in good spirits and very attentive, and the food is good. We even get a real glass and a real napkin.

While we were completing the check-in for flight AZ 4000, Pope Francis was boarding a helicopter that would take him from the Vatican to Fiumicino Airport. And although he has never liked intercontinental travel, today he seems to be happy. Not only because he is finally leaving the walls of the small papal state but also because, for the first time since February when he came to Rome for the conclave, he is going back to his continent to meet his fellow Latin Americans, his people.

This trip will be his first significant international test, and it presents several challenges. The main one will be telling 3.5 million young people from 178 countries who are taking part in World Youth Day to have the courage to go against the current, not to be afraid to follow Christ.

The second is to revitalize the Church on the continent with the largest number of Catholics in the world. In Brazil, over the past few decades, certain religious sects and evangelical movements have gained ground, drawing many Catholics away from their faith communities. According to the figures of the last census in 2010, approximately 123 million Brazilians said they were Catholics, representing 64 percent of the population, as opposed to 91 percent in 1970. In contrast, the numbers of people identifying as evangelical Christian have been on the rise: from 5.2 percent of the population in 1970 to 22 percent in 2010, amounting to 42.3 million people.

In addition to the progress made by these other denominations, a phenomenon that is also taking place in many other Latin American countries, Brazil faces another challenge common in other parts of the world: many of the million Brazilians who say they are Catholic are not practicing believers.

Francis arrives in a country that's in turmoil. Brazil is shaken by massive protests from young people who want less corruption, less waste, and a fairer distribution of resources. They want fewer million reales spent on events such as the recent FIFA Confederations Cup, the 2014 World Cup, and the 2016 Olympics, and more invested in education, health, and transportation.

Although progress has been made in the fight against poverty, throughout Latin America in general and Brazil in particular conditions of severe social injustice remain, as well as an astounding gap between the rich and the poor. In Brazil a small and wealthy minority moves by helicopter in chaotic metropolises such as São Paulo, while the overwhelming majority still live in destitute neighborhoods and shantytowns (the favelas). According to the 2010 census, in Brazil there are 6,838 favelas, in which 11.4 million people (6 percent of the population) live.

In this context, Pope Francis choosing to visit and spend part of his time in one of the 763 favelas of Rio sends a strong message. He will also visit a clinic for drug addicts and will meet with juvenile delinquents.

His repeated appeals for a simple Church—one close to the poor, one that is consistent with and true to the Gospel—are the topics that the pope of the poor will expound on during his first international journey. This trip will be scrutinized by more than five thousand accredited journalists and will become the ideal stage from which Pope Francis can enchant the world once and for all.

Immediately, as he boards the airplane—which he has specifically asked not be furnished in any particular way (no "papal" bed or other special furnishings)—it is clear that this trip will see the already-high popularity of the Latin American supreme pontiff soar to the stars.

On the runway, the Alitalia plane's engines are running. From our windows we see Pope Francis still on the tarmac, chatting animatedly with Prime Minister Enrico Letta, a practicing Catholic and a former member of the Christian Democratic Party, who has come to see him on his way. As the pope climbs the stairs, our attention is drawn to a black briefcase he carries in his right hand. "It doesn't contain the key to the atom bomb!" he will joke later, when, during an unprecedented press conference on this same plane, he is asked about the mysterious black briefcase. "I carried it because I always do: when I travel I take it with me. What is in it? My razor, my breviary, my diary, a book to read. . . . I took with me one on Saint Teresita [St. Thérèse of Lisieux], to whom I am devoted. I have always traveled with my briefcase; it's normal. We have to be normal. What you are saying sounds a bit strange to me, that the picture [of my briefcase] went around the world. However, we have to get used to being normal. The normality of life," he says.

At 10:29 in the morning (Italian time) the Airbus 330 has already been flying for an hour and a half. At more than thirty thousand feet, it is flying over the African desert. The flight attendants are removing the breakfast trays, breakfast having consisted of a delicious zucchini, bacon, and tomato pie, when among the journalistic fauna a certain frenzy begins, and tripods, cables, cameras, and tablets come out. "The pope is arriving!"

Accompanied by Father Lombardi, Pope Francis, with a slightly frightened, shy face, is coming toward the end of the plane where we, the journalists, are sitting.

Valentina Alazraki, the veteran Mexican correspondent for Televisa, who has been on more than a hundred papal flights (the first with John Paul II in 1979) greets him on behalf of all the other journalists. "We know that journalists are not exactly 'saints of your devotion.' Maybe you think that Father Lombardi has brought you to the lions' den. But the truth is, we aren't that fierce," Valentina tells him, giving him an image of the Virgin of Guadalupe, patron saint of Mexico and known as the "empress" of the Americas. The pope thanks Valentina, kissing her on both cheeks.

When the pope takes the microphone and starts speaking in his Argentine-accented Italian, he visibly relaxes. "Good morning! You said something strange? You are not saints of my devotion? I am here among lions, but not very fierce ones,' ah? Well thanks. I really don't give interviews, not because I don't know how, I just can't, that's the way it is. It is a little difficult for me but thank you for your company," he starts off, promising to answer questions during the return trip. And he says a few words to introduce his first international trip: "A people has a future if it brings forward both elements: the young, who have strength, and the elderly, because they provide life's wisdom. . . . The young, now, are having a hard time. We are kind of used to the culture of throwing things away: this is done all too often with the elderly. But now all these jobless young people are getting hit by this throwaway culture. We have to put an end to this habit of scrapping things! No! A culture of inclusion, a culture of coming together, making an effort to bring everyone into society! This is the meaning I want to give to this visit. I thank you very much, my dear 'saints not of my devotion' and 'not so fierce lions.' But thank you very much, thank you very much."

He stops there and declares he wants to say hello to all seventy-one journalists present, one by one. Pope Francis spends more than an hour warmly greeting everybody. And he leaves many journalists, a skeptical and cynical breed indeed, with trembling legs and tear-filled eyes.

Alexey Bukalov, veteran journalist from the Russian news agency ITAR-TASS, presents him with a book he has written in Italy on Aleksandr Pushkin, an author the pope quoted once. Bukalov reports of the encounter, "He is passionate about poetry and he told me, 'I admire Pushkin but my master is Dostoevsky.'"

Franca Giansoldati, Vatican correspondent of Roman daily *Il Messaggero*, gives him another book, *If Francis Came Back* (*Se tornasse Francesco*) by Carlo Bo. "It is a prophecy on the return of St Francis's true heir, like him. He promised to read it," she tells me.

Javier Martínez Brocal, a Spaniard from "Rome Reports" TV news agency, is unable to hide his happiness. "The pope blessed, by laying his hand on it, a photograph of my brother Pablo, who has been unemployed for the past seven months," he recounts.

Another Spanish journalist, Darío Mentor Torres, from the daily *La Razón*, is very impressed. "I have never been a believer, and I thank you because I have asked myself questions on faith that I had never asked myself before," he says to Pope Francis. "Then pray for me, so that I can keep it [the faith]," answers the pope, gripping his arm hard.

With Brazilian journalists he jokingly refers to the traditional rivalry existing between Argentina and Brazil: "You already have God, who is Brazilian; you also wanted a Brazilian pope? You are never satisfied, eh?"

When it's my turn to say hello to the pope, I get an embrace, two kisses, and the same affection as ever. "Are the kids well?" he asks, and I tell him that Gerry, who couldn't afford this expensive trip, has traveled on his own and is already in Rio. I immediately introduce my friend Irene Hernández Velasco, correspondent for the Spanish paper *El Mundo*, one of those nonbeliever journalists the pope has won over during the four months of his pontificate. I tell him that Irene is the mother of Manuel, my son Juan Pablo's best friend. Irene has brought a package with twelve rosaries, which Francis immediately blesses, in addition to a box with the skullcap she bought in the famous ecclesiastical tailoring shop Gammarelli, to exchange it with the pope's, a favor she was asked by a priest friend of hers. The exchange of skullcaps is an ancient tradition: you buy a white one in the pope's tailor's shop, and you present it to him during an audience. The Holy Father will give his in exchange, as he has done several times during his general audience on Wednesdays in St. Peter's Square.

"Your Holiness, thank you for having started to achieve the miracle so many of us were waiting for, that of a clean Church," says Irene, in a broken voice. Francis answers, "This is just the beginning. Pray for me."

Since she is close to being paralyzed with emotion, I remind her that she must give the pope his skullcap. Smilingly, Francis immediately accepts the exchange, among the flashes of photographers' cameras.

We will realize an hour later that the skullcap is too wide. Vik van Brantegem, assistant to the Vatican Press Office, calls me and Irene and asks us if we can return Francis's skullcap since it is the only one he has on the plane and that the other one falls off. "In any case, he's kept it on for more than an hour," he stresses, raising his eyebrows and trying to console us. Of course we oblige.

"Popes had always seemed to me inaccessible figures, kings in ermine cloaks, and I never would have thought I could tell him the word *cleanup* from the bottom of my heart. But this man inspires a trust that makes you say everything that comes from the heart, he answers gently and encourages you to keep on doing it!" comments Irene, who is sitting beside me and who is quite emotional after meeting the pope.

The atmosphere on the papal flight is very relaxed. Unlike the return trip, the flight to Brazil takes place during the day, and the pope's private secretary, Monsignor Alfred Xuereb, occasionally appears to chat with us. So do a few cardinals of the retinue and even Pope Francis's guardian angels—his guards, fully aware that a complicated visit awaits them. I also chat with Domenico Giani, the head of security for the pope, whom I have known since the time of John Paul II. I ask him if Francis will wear a bulletproof vest. "I didn't even dare suggest it!" Giani responds. "He would have fired me!"

"I am reckless, but I am not afraid. I know that nobody dies before his time comes," the pope will explain to the Brazilian broadcasting company Rede Globo. "When my time comes, it will be the will of God."

As soon as he sets foot on Latin American ground, Pope Francis receives a triumphal welcome. In Rio de Janeiro—where roads have been closed off, presided over by the military—a party breaks out. It will last six days. Ticker tape floats down from several buildings downtown, as if the city were celebrating a World Cup. Thousands of young people declare him a hero as he moves through a euphoric crowd; welcome placards and flags are out, many of them the white and blue of Argentina's flag. The Argentine group, with fifty thousand faithful, is the largest at this first international event of Pope Francis.

Officially received on a red carpet by Dilma Rousseff, president of Brazil, by the Archbishop of Rio de Janeiro Monsignor Orani Joao Tempesta, and by other authorities at the military base of the Galeao-Antonio Carlos Jobim International Airport—and after receiving a gift of flowers from some children—the pope rides in a modest metallic gray Fiat Idea, not an armored limousine, from which, smiling broadly through its open windows, he starts saluting the throngs of people in the road that leads to the center of town. Before going to Guanabara Palace for the official welcome ceremony, with its hymns, ceremonial rites, authorities, and VIPs, Francis wishes to go and salute young people, the true reason for his trip.

The car, very ordinary, without even automatic windows, will become the great symbol, a leading character in a grueling week.

A few weeks before the journey, Francis had gone to visit the Vatican car fleet to personally inspect the two armored Popemobiles. Convinced that a shepherd must be physically close to his sheep, he disrupted established habits once again. "I don't want to be in a glass box. I want to be able to touch, hug, kiss people. Otherwise what's the point of going to Brazil?" he told his assistants, who had no choice but to obey and change plans. "If you go and see someone who loves you very much, a friend who wishes to talk to you, do you go in a glass box? No."

Although he doesn't want to be the absolute pope-monarch of the past, Francis has power and knows full well how to exercise it. "Safety means trusting people. It is true that there is always the danger of a madman doing something, but the Lord is there too! Creating an armored space between a bishop and the people is madness, and I prefer this [other] madness," he will explain during the press conference on the return flight from Rio.

With the windows of the legendary Fiat Idea rolled down, despite the impressive security measures and the several helicopters flying overhead, there is at first a moment of panic. Instead of taking the lane cleared for the purpose, the car leading the pope's convoy moves into the wrong road, closed and full of vehicles. The pope's car remains trapped in a high-risk traffic jam, right in the middle of a tide of people. And it takes twelve minutes to cover a third of a mile. The tension is sky-high among his guards, and their terrified faces say it all. The pope, however, is totally calm. He continues to salute and bless with his hand the people pressing against his small car.

He is in the hands of the Lord, he feels he is doing what God is asking of him; he is serene, smiling, even amused. After four "boring" months at the Vatican, at last some action.

Pope Francis wins Brazilians over with his humility. "I learned that, in order to have access to the Brazilian people, you have to get in from the main door of their immense hearts; please allow me, at this moment, to delicately knock on this door. I ask permission to come in and spend this week with you. I have no gold or silver, but I bring the most precious thing I have been given: Jesus Christ," he says in his first speech, during the welcome ceremony at the Guanabara Palace, where he later arrives by helicopter.

In his speech in front of the president, Francis clearly makes reference to the young Brazilian *indignados*, the young people who had been protesting in the streets for days and weeks for justice and economic opportunity.

"Our generation will show itself worthy of the promise living inside every young person when we will be able to offer them space, protect the material and spiritual conditions for their full development, give them solid foundations on which to build their life, guarantee safety and education so that they can become what they can be, convey to them lasting values for which it is worth living," he says. After recalling that the main reason for his visit is World Youth Day, he underscores the importance of ensuring each young person "a transcendent perspective," "a world worthy of human life," and "the fulfillment of their full potential so that they can be leaders of tomorrow and share the responsibility for everyone's destiny."

The day following the chaotic Rio welcome, the pope rests in Sumaré, the private residence of Río de Janeiro's Archbishop, immersed in green, on a hill 1,300 feet above the city, known as the Cidade Maravilhosa, or Marvelous City. They give him the same room, number 5, that Pope John Paul II stayed in when he was in Brazil, in 1980 and 1997. After an intercontinental flight lasting more than twelve hours, with a five-hour difference in time zones and an emotion-filled welcome, it is logical that he catch his breath.

The weather in Rio is horrible: it's raining and cold, to the great chagrin of many of the thousands of journalists accredited for the event, who would gladly have taken advantage of the free day to go for a dip in the sea at Copacabana Beach.

The pope's wish to go quickly to the Corcovado mountain to pay homage to the imposing Christ the Redeemer statue with open arms, the symbol of the city, is equally thwarted. Francis will have to be content with paying his tribute to the huge statue—124 feet tall, weighing 1,150 tons, and raised up in 1973—with a prayer from the sky each time his helicopter flies close to it during his transfers.

This lack of papal activity leaves room for polemics about his safety. Contrasting accusations fall on the different Brazilian law enforcement agencies tasked with protecting the Church's paramount leader because clearly they have "failed" at their job.

"A pontiff cannot travel in a family car with the windows down. He has run enormous risks," comment some veteran Vatican correspondents in low voices, confessing they had never seen such a degree of uncertainty and lack of control around a pope.

Among the Holy Father's entourage, nobody hides his uneasiness at the pope's clearly expressed wish not to use the armored Popemobile. "He is a shepherd wanting to be with his sheep, but he has to learn to be a pope," say other critics. Furthermore, there are quite a few jokes about the unintentional publicity this matter is offering to Fiat Idea, a car that "evidently can put up with the worst." Father Lombardi tries to smooth things over: "A mistake was made. But we shouldn't dramatize. The pope wasn't worried, even if his secretary Alfred Xuereb was—a lot."

For the people on the streets, the Fiat Idea is a symbol, a powerful, crystal-clear message from a pope who wants to turn everything around. As a matter of.fact, the day on which he is supposed to be resting after a twelve-hour journey, Francis continues to work on the reform of the Roman Curia, a priority of his pontificate. He also meets Cardinal Óscar Andrés Rodríguez Maradiaga from Honduras, Archbishop of Tegucigalpa and coordinator of the G8 (the group of eight cardinal advisors).

Wednesday, July 24. The bad weather of Brazil's winter continues with an extreme cold front, the likes of which hadn't been recorded for forty years, and Pope Francis has to change his plans. Instead of going by helicopter to the Marian sanctuary of Aparecida, 124 miles south of Rio, he goes by plane. This sanctuary did not appear on the agenda that had been created when it was assumed Benedict XVI would make this trip. Francis added it to the program because he feels he has to go and pray to the Black Madonna, patron of Brazil, to whom he wishes to entrust his pontificate. He knows that, one way or another, the Madonna has had to do with his reaching Peter's throne.

I too go to Aparecida. I belong to a group of journalists leaving Rio by bus at five in the morning. A little because of the jet lag and a little because I am afraid I won't get up in time, I am awake at three in the morning. I don't manage to sleep on the bus either. I chat with Father Javier Soteras from Radio María in Córdoba. I contemplate the gorgeous tropical landscape, with mountains, the intensely green vegetation, and the jungle. And I cannot stop thinking of when, in 2007, five months pregnant with my daughter Carolina, I first came to Aparecida.

It is pouring rain in Aparecida as well. The thermometer reading is 50 degrees Fahrenheit, but there are two hundred thousand people waiting, the faithful who, drenched and freezing, have spent the night there to see the pope. Only fifteen people have managed to get into the modern basilica of the sanctuary, where they are waiting for the pope, alternating between chanting and prayers. The atmosphere is festive, the rhythm of a very catchy song calls to "Francis, Francis!"

Just after ten thirty, the pope goes directly to the chapel of the small sanctuary to pray in front of the Black Madonna, which was miraculously fished out of the Paraiba River in 1717. The small statue was found without its head. The fishermen threw their nets again and found the missing part, and with the third throw the net was full of fish.

Inside the basilica, where the cold is terrible, there are video screens showing the live images of Pope Francis inside the chapel, as he is praying to the Madonna for a few minutes that seem eternal. There is an astounding silence. The pope appears highly emotional, almost about to cry; several believers notice it and are in tears themselves. The atmosphere gives one the shivers. Francis entrusts his pontificate to the Aparecida Madonna, asks her to make World Youth Day successful, and "puts at her feet the life of Latin American people."

"Today, looking at the World Youth Day which brought me to Brazil, I too come and knock at the door of Mary's house—who loved and brought up Jesus—so that she can help us all, the shepherds of God's people, the parents and educators, to transmit to our young the values that will make them creators of a fairer, more solidarity-filled and brotherly nation and world. For this reason I would like to recall three simple attitudes: hopefulness, letting oneself be surprised by God, and living in joy," Francis says in a profoundly optimistic homily, like all the homilies of this first international journey.

Having delivered a stirring sermon, Pope Francis steps out onto the balcony of the basilica holding the miraculous Madonna in his hands. He greets the tens of thousands of people who followed the Mass on the big screens. "*Eu no falo brasileiro.* So I will speak Spanish. Thank you so much for being here, thank you wholeheartedly," he says, facing a carpetlike mass of umbrellas and raincoats acclaiming him. And he throws out a question: "Can a mother ever forget her children?" "Nooo!" answer in unison the almost two hundred thousand people there. "The Virgin doesn't forget us, she loves us and takes care of us," he reassures them, finally asking the

Madonna, who had almost moved him to tears, for a blessing for all. And he concludes with an announcement: in 2017 he will come back to Aparecida for the third centenary of the recovery of this miraculous image he venerates.

Inside the basilica, the pope not only warmly greets and embraces rabbis, representatives of Orthodox Christianity, Islam, and other confessions present there. He also kisses and embraces children and people who are on stretchers and in wheelchairs.

Although the encounter is unnoticed in the huge human wave, at a certain point Pope Francis clasps in an embrace Sergio Gobulin, sixty-seven, and his wife, Ana Barzola. He was the one who married Sergio and Ana on November 15, 1975. And it was thanks to him that Sergio managed to escape from the clutches of the military and flee from Argentina. Sergio, who has been living in Pordenone, Italy, since the beginning of 1977, is another one of those unknown cases in which Bergoglio provided help to people who, because they carried out social work in the shantytowns, had been targeted by the military on charges of having terrorist and subversive leanings. When Bergoglio was elected pope and old accusations of his having sided with the dictatorship reemerged, Sergio felt the need to tell his story.

"I can say I am alive because he saved me," says Sergio, a *desaparecido* in October 1976 for eighteen days during which he was savagely tortured. He was released thanks to the intervention of the then-Jesuit Provincial in Argentina, who moved heaven and earth for him and knocked on the doors of several barracks.

"I met Bergoglio because I studied theology, as a lay student, at the Universidad del Salvador, at the Colegio Maximo of San Miguel, in 1969. He was my professor of spiritual theology. But I also had Father Yorio and Father Jalics as my professors," recalls Gobulin, the son of an Italian family that emigrated in 1950 to Villa Constitución, in Argentina's Santa Fe province.

"After the first year of theology, I decided to go and live in a shantytown, Villa Mitre, in San Miguel, where, together with others I started doing different jobs: we set up an evening school for the illiterate, and a dispensary, paved the dust roads, built an aqueduct. It was 1971–72. Even though I was never a Catholic militant, nor did I go to church, because Bergoglio was always a man with an open mind toward other sectors, he stayed with me in the shantytown for three to four days, to have a look at the work I was doing," recounts Sergio, who went with Padre Jorge on the car trips he took in the Santa Fe province. "Once, when traveling alone in the car, he fell asleep and almost had an accident, so he realized it was best to travel with someone else."

After the 1976 coup, trouble and searches started for Sergio, who worked in the printing office of the Observatorio Nacional de Física Cósmica of San Miguel (at the time managed by Jesuits, but transferred to the air force after the coup), and he decided to leave the shantytown. His kidnapping took place in mid-October, when he was twenty-nine years old. "They abducted me for eighteen days. I don't know exactly where I was, probably in the Moreno air base. They left me without food or water and they tortured me; they wanted me to admit I had taken part in terrorist activities. At the time any social work in the poor neighborhoods was considered subversive. When they released me, since I had never lost my Italian citizenship, I was taken to the Italian hospital, and the deputy consul, Enrico Calamai, placed me under the protection of the consulate and called over my wife and six-month-old daughter. I remember the day before my release, during interrogation, an officer who spoke in a cultured way said I would manage to get out thanks to the intercession of a person of the church. When Bergoglio came to visit me at the hospital, he confirmed that he had negotiated in every possible way to have my life spared. He strongly recommended that I leave Argentina."

So Sergio, his wife, and their daughter were repatriated to Italy in January 1977, helped by the consulate. The meeting in Aparecida was casual. Some friends of Sergio's, owners of Friul Mosaic, the company that won the contract to complete the cupola of the Aparecida basilica, asked him if he wanted to come over and follow part of the work and, in the meantime, say hello to the pope during his lightning-fast trip to the largest Marian sanctuary in the world.

The schedule is very busy. After Aparecida, Pope Francis's marathon continues at the St. Francis of Assisi hospital in Rio de Janeiro, another stop he wanted to add on, a further demonstration that he wishes to be close to the marginalized and excluded.

It is still pouring rain and unusually cold. But this doesn't stop thousands of people from waiting for him at the hospital, which he reaches after dark. Francis's visit to the hospital, which holds five hundred beds and specializes in the recovery of drug addicts and alcoholics, in addition to treating the poor, is full of very emotional moments. Crying, the young drug addicts under treatment tell him about their experiences. Francis stands up and clasps in a fraternal embrace each of the young people who offer him their testimony; in a way, they are the "new lepers" of the world. In his speech he refers to the figure of St. Francis.

"God has willed that my journey, after the Shrine of Our Lady of Aparecida, should take me to a particular shrine of human suffering—the St. Francis of Assisi Hospital. The conversion of your patron saint is well known: the young Francis abandoned riches and comfort in order to become a poor man among the poor. He understood that true joy and riches do not come from the idols of this world—material things and the possession of them—but are to be found only in following Christ and serving others. Less well known, perhaps, is the moment when this understanding took concrete form in his own life. It was when Francis embraced a leper. This suffering brother was the 'mediator of light . . . for Saint Francis of Assisi' because in every suffering brother and sister that we embrace, we embrace the suffering Body of Christ. Today, in this place where people struggle with drug addiction, I wish to embrace each and every one of you, who are the flesh of Christ, and to ask God to renew your journey, and also mine, with purpose and steadfast hope," he says. He then concludes: "I would like to repeat to all of you: Do not let yourselves be robbed of hope! Do not let yourselves be robbed of hope! And not only that, but I say to us all: let us not rob others of hope, let us become bearers of hope!"

Rio de Janeiro is transformed. It projects even more vitality and energy than usual thanks to this invasion of young people from all over the world. The majority of Argentines there for World Youth Day arrived after an odyssey of more than fifty-six hours by bus. Only a few arrived by plane. Among them is Alejandro Pavoni, a twenty-seven-year-old seminarian who is having his year of parish experience in the St. Nicolas of Bari Church in Buenos Aires and who is accompanying a group of sixty-eight young people.

Slim, blond, with a beard and brown eyes, Alejandro reveals something incredible. In the middle of 2012, a directive from the Archbishop at the time, Jorge Bergoglio, had reached the Villa Devoto Seminary in Buenos Aires. This hit them like a bombshell: he forbade the seminarian from taking part in the World Youth Day in Rio de Janeiro.

"Since we were not happy about that order, I and four other seminarians asked to talk with our Archbishop, and Bergoglio received us in the curia in December. First he clarified that the question was a matter of opinion and then explained his reasons: 'The World Youth Day is something very beautiful: seeing the pope, being with thousands of young Catholics is very beautiful. But we mustn't pick every beautiful thing; we must be discerning, and it seems to me that at the moment your task is to be in the seminary; a similar trip would distract you,'" he said.

"We listened to him, petrified. And when he finished speaking, he said: 'Come on, react, don't just stand there with folded arms!' Then we started saying that in 2013 we were due to have our parish experience and that it seemed good to us to participate by accompanying the young people who would go," Alejandro recalls. "We left the curia without an answer but with a chink of hope. 'I had thought of two exceptions, but your case had escaped me,' was all Bergoglio told us. But then in the month of February we five seminarians received the news that we could take part in [World Youth Day]," he remembers, smiling. "It is a very strange thing. At the time I didn't know why, but now that I am here I understand how obsessed I was by the idea of coming and I understand why Bergoglio, now the pope, helped me fight for what I wanted. Evidently God wanted me to be here to be present and testify to a new Pentecost in the Church."

# 21

# A Call for Renewal

During the journey to Brazil, Pope Francis is treated like a rock star by the 3.5 million young people from all over the world. But the trip also confirms that St. Peter's successor has been transformed: his smile is permanent. And his energy is inexhaustible. He never tires of greeting, blessing, making gestures with his head or his hands, for example to communicate that it's better not to hand over a baby because it's crying, or making the thumbs-up sign when he sees Argentine banners or the flags of San Lorenzo de Almagro, his soccer team.

He blesses, caresses, touches, and embraces everyone: children, the old, the sick. To the great horror of several European Vatican correspondents, he even takes a *mate* that some unknown compatriots from the crowd offer him—they might poison him! He lets people take photographs of him, give him T-shirts and shoes, catching them as he passes in his open car—quick, dynamic, more nimble than ever. Nobody would ever say that next December 17 this man will be seventy-seven.

"This is the pope we've been dreaming about . . . he's like Christ come back to Earth," I'm told by Clelia, twenty-five, a Peruvian nurse who can't stop crying while the Popemobile passes through the hysterical screams of the crowd, down the main street of Copacabana.

But it's not just the euphoria typical of World Youth Days. During his journey to Brazil, the pope doesn't speak only to the young. In his touching speeches before the Brazilian bishops and the coordinating committee of the Latin American Episcopal Conferences (CELAM), but also before his compatriots, inviting them to "stir things up," he makes the platform of his pontificate clearer than ever: to return to a simple, missionary Church, attentive to the needs of today's world.

During these speeches Francis also engages in some self-criticism. He admits the faults and sins of the Church and identifies clearly what the chief challenges of the moment are, affirming that this is not "an epoch of changes but a change of epoch": inner renewal of the Church and dialogue with the world. Before the Brazilian bishops he speaks explicitly of the exodus of the faithful from the Church that has taken place over the past decades. "Perhaps the Church has seemed too weak, perhaps too far away from their needs, perhaps too poor to respond to their worries, perhaps too cold toward them, perhaps too self-referential, perhaps a prisoner of its own stiff language. Perhaps the world has made the Church seem like a relic of the past, inadequate for new demands; perhaps the Church had replies for man's childhood but not for his adult age," he says.

Francis doesn't confine himself to launching challenges; he also gives answers, gives directions to the Brazilian bishops, although the message is also addressed to the 4,938 bishops throughout the world (according to the 2013 Vatican Yearbook). To reverse the crisis of the Church, it is fundamental to understand that "humility is in God's DNA." And an education of quality for bishops, priests, religious, and laypeople is a priority.

During his meeting with the coordinating committee of the Latin American Episcopal Conferences, he insists on the need for a "change of attitude" and defines as temptations against the missionary discipleship the ideologization of the gospel message, the functionalism "that reduces the reality of the Church to the structure of an NGO [a nongovernmental, non-profit organization], where what is of value is the ascertainable result and statistics" and clericalism. And as he had already done before the nuncios of the whole world gathered in Rome in June 2013, he comes back to outline the profile of a Bishop, "who must lead, which is not the same thing as giving orders."

On Thursday, July 25 in Rio it goes on pouring rain, but it doesn't matter. Today is, in a certain sense, the day of Jorge Bergoglio's return home. In two emotional events that he insisted on fitting into the agenda of the first international voyage of his pontificate, he goes back to embracing the lowest, the excluded, and the marginalized, visiting a favela, or shantytown, north of Rio. A little later, in another event organized at the last minute, but one that cannot be postponed, he embraces thousands of the Argentine faithful, during an emotional meeting in the cathedral of Rio. The poor and his compatriots, a doubly moving reunion.

When he arrives at the favela of Varginha, where in spite of the rain people are waiting for him, singing and dancing in an impressive party atmosphere, he never stops kissing, blessing, touching, and embracing everybody who manages to get near him. He visits the chapel of the Church of San Jeronimo and the home of a family, and he delivers a powerful speech from a platform set up in the favela's soccer field. An enormous banner with the words "Pope of the *villeros*," together with an Argentine flag, stand out.

"From the beginning, in planning this visit to Brazil, my wish was to be able to visit every district of this nation. I should have liked to knock on every door, say good morning, ask for a glass of fresh water, drink a *cafezinho*—not a strong drink like *cachaça*!" he jokes. "I should have liked to talk as to household friends, listen to the heart of everyone, of parents, children, grandparents. . . . But Brazil is so big! It's not possible to knock on all the doors. So I have chosen to come here, to visit your community, which today represents all the districts of Brazil. How nice it is to be welcomed with love, with generosity, with joy," he declares, surely winning over everyone in the crowd.

"But who organized this?" asks the coordinator of a group of young Argentines, without hiding his discontent when he hears that they can't come in with their backpacks. "Twitter!" answers a young priest who with two others organized without notice the pope's meeting with his compatriots. "All the information we've got is on a tweet issued by the Argentine Bishops'

Conference at two in the morning, where they said that the meeting would be at noon and that five thousand people could come in, without backpacks and without flags," he explains, exhausted.

It's five o'clock in the morning, raining, and there are seven more hours to go before the meeting with Pope Francis, and everybody knows that forty-five thousand pilgrims will be left outside the Metropolitan Cathedral of Rio de Janeiro. The building was consecrated in 1979; it has a surprising structure, like a Mayan pyramid, in homage to the populations of the Latin American continent who received the gift of faith from the missionaries.

Chaos reigns, and the crush barriers, which have never been put in place, are lying on the ground. A number of Brazilian police officers, well sheltered and with coffees in their hands, watch thousands of Argentines trying desperately to join the queues of the selected ones.

"Capa de chuva! Capa de chuva!" shout the street vendors, who are making a lot of money selling raincoats. It has rained so much that the so-called Campus Fidei di Guaratiba, twenty-four miles from Rio, where the vigil and final Mass were to take place, has become a sea of mud. And the authorities have decided that these events, which will attract more than three million young people, are to take place on the beach of Copacabana, to the horror of the residents in that part of the city.

The shouts of the vendors mingle with the ever more creative songs of the Argentines, who don't know what else they can do to forget that their legs can't hold them up any more after so many hours standing. "*Asado*! The Pope eats *asado*! *Mate*! The pope drinks *mate*!" they sing proudly.

Carla Ríos, seventeen, manipulates her wheelchair in a thousand ways to get in. She doesn't know if she'll manage. She only knows that she wants to see Pope Francis, and she's sure that he will want to see her. And she's not wrong. When she's already happily in the second row of pews in the cathedral, a Bishop announces that the pope has asked for the sick to be brought in front of the barriers. Clara doesn't know what she'll say to him. She prepares by reciting a rosary.

The hymn of the World Youth Day celebrated in Argentina in 1987 with John Paul II rings out. It's called "Un nuevo sol," or "A New Sun." A Brazilian photographer pesters for the image of the Virgin of Luján (patroness of Argentina) to be moved because he can't frame the pope in his shot. He doesn't realize how upset Argentines would be by what he's asking. Francis looks at the Virgin as a son looks at his mother and kisses her. Argentine euphoria dominates the cathedral of Rio. Smiling, Francis invites the young people to "stir things up," to defend their own values. He denounces how "this world civilization has gone too far," enslaved by money. He once more condemns the "throwaway culture" that affects young and old alike, and he bids them not to lose their faith in Jesus.

"Let me tell you what I hope will be the outcome of World Youth Day: I hope there will be noise. Here there will be noise, I'm quite sure. Here in Rio there will be plenty of noise, no doubt about that. But I want you to make yourselves heard in your dioceses, I want the noise to go out, I want the Church to go out onto the streets. I want us to resist everything worldly, everything static, everything comfortable, everything to do with clerical-ism, everything that might make us closed in on ourselves. The parishes, the schools, the institutions are made for going out . . . if they don't, they become NGOs, and the Church cannot be an NGO. May the bishops and priests forgive me if some of you create a bit of confusion afterward. That's my advice. Thanks for whatever you can do." That is just the beginning of a great speech.

During the meeting with the Argentines, Pope Francis greets, kisses, embraces, recognizes people, feels at home. He also tries to include the immense majority of his compatriots who were left outside the cathedral by waving an Argentine flag in front of them. Accompanying a boy in a wheelchair, the famous Argentine journalist Nelson Castro manages to talk briefly with Francis, who recognizes him in the crowd and greets him.

Castro is struck by the meeting. "He's another person. I interviewed him twice, in 2005, after the election of Benedict XVI, and in 2010, and he said many interesting things, but in such a weary, slow tone of voice that he was ineffective and even boring for an ordinary listener. But now he's another person!" he says. "He's not the man we used to know. The people of the shantytowns say he is, that he used to smile before as well. But we knew him worried, tired, sad. . . . I don't know if it's the Holy Spirit or what, but he's transformed. Bergoglio is a man who has always liked power, in the sense of using it to put himself at the service of others. And now you can see that he's happy. I think that deep inside he hoped for this kind of end to his life because now he's different and he knows how to reach people in an extraordinary way, never seen before."

If Thursday, July 25, is the day of the return home, it's also the day of apotheosis for Pope Francis. When he arrives for the first time at Copacabana Beach for the young people's welcome party—it was to be his first meeting with them—there is an explosion of joy. Ticker tape rains down from the buildings on the main street, decorated to greet the Supreme Pontiff. "We are the pope's young people!" shout hundreds of thousands of enthusiastic young people.

After a procession of flags, Francis stands up and applauds, while the cardinals imitate him, and he once more encourages the young people, who are dejected by the foul weather. "I want to thank you for the testimony of faith you are giving the world. I've always heard that the *cariocas* [the people of Rio] don't like the cold and the rain," he begins, greeting the young people and the authorities. "You are really heroes!" he adds, provoking a first ovation.

He goes back to self-criticism. "You know that in a bishop's life there are so many problems that need to be solved. And with these problems and difficulties a bishop's faith can become saddened. How horrible is a sad bishop! How horrible! Because I don't want my faith to be sad, I've come here to be infected by the enthusiasm of all of you!"

A young person from each continent greets the pope on behalf of all the others. The pastoral pope hugs a Brazilian girl who is moved to tears at the moment of speaking to him. After witnessing representations of the popular religious devotion of Brazil's five regions, the pope, speaking clearly and with passion, invites the young people to start a revolution of faith. "Put Christ in your lives, put your trust in him and you will never be disappointed! You see, dear friends, faith carries out in our lives a revolution that we can call Copernican: it takes us away from the center and puts God there; faith immerses us in his love and gives us safety, strength, and hope. In appearance nothing has changed, but deep down inside us everything changes. When there is God, in our hearts there is peace, gentleness, tenderness, courage, serenity, and joy, which are the fruits of the Holy Spirit. Then our existence is transformed, our way of thinking and acting is renewed; it becomes the way of thinking and acting of Jesus, of God. Dear friends, faith is revolutionary, and today I ask you: are you ready to enter this revolutionary wave of faith?"

Pope Francis speaks with the same passionate force on the following day in front of 1.5 million young people from all the continents who are taking part in an impressive nocturnal Way of the Cross—theatrical and musical—on the Copacabana seafront. The pope rails against the many crosses that Jesus has to bear in this world. And he condemns not only violence, hunger, persecutions, drugs, selfishness, and the corruption of politicians but also against "the inconsistency of Christians and ministers of the Gospel"; in this way he alludes to, without mentioning them, the many scandals that have shaken the Catholic Church in the past few years.

The atmosphere on Copacabana Beach is electric. There are so many people that many have to be satisfied with seeing the pope from far off, on one of the many jumbo screens. "But even just hearing his voice, the power in his words, even if we don't understand Spanish, is a message," says Farid, twenty-eight, who has arrived in pilgrimage from Lebanon with three hundred other young people.

On the morning of that first finally sunny day, Pope Francis hears confession of five young people chosen by lot—three Brazilians, one Italian girl, and one Venezuelan girl—in the impressive "Confessodrome" of Boa Vista Park, which until the eighteenth century was the property of the

Jesuits, then became the residence of Brazil's imperial family, and is now a community park. Every confession lasts about five minutes. The pope sits in a wooden confessional identical to one hundred others set up in the park, which have the shape of the Corcovado. The first of the privileged five confesses through the grating. The others, kneeling in front of the pope, look him in the eyes. "I immediately felt at ease; the pope was smiling, serene, he was looking into my eyes, he conveyed mercy and encouraged me to speak. He used his usual simple and direct language. He helped me a lot; it was a serene dialogue," says Claudia Giampietro, from Pescara, Italy.

The young Venezuelan girl who receives the sacrament of reconciliation takes courage in her hands and gives him a bracelet with the colors of her national flag. A Brazilian boy, who converted to Catholicism a year ago, goes even further: at the end of the confession "he put his hand on the pope's head, as if imparting a requested blessing," some witnesses tell. "While he was greeting everyone," says Claudia, "the Sisters of Mother Teresa who were guiding adoration in the chapel tried to kiss his ring, but he withdrew his hand and asked them to embrace him."

The pope then goes to the Palacio São Joaquim, seat of the archbishopric, to meet eight juvenile offenders detained in various prisons in Rio—six males and two females. In a very moving meeting, the young prisoners speak freely in front of the pope, who blesses some objects and signs autographs. "Never again violence, only love," he urges them.

Afterward, Pope Francis goes to lunch with twelve young people from all continents. He seeks to talk with each of them, asks what they are doing for the Church, and wins them over with his manner. "Don't think that the pope is one of those people who knows everything. The pope has a confessor who guides him in his life," he says. Since at the beginning all the guests are rather nervous before the Supreme Pontiff and speak in low voices, he tries to break the ice by joking—"Please, I ask you to raise your voices. I'm a bit deaf and sometimes even the Holy Spirit has problems in communicating with me," recounts the Mexican Luis Edmundo Martínez.

Before leaving, the pope asks them a number of questions to which they should reply in the silence of their hearts, after profound reflection. "He asked us why, according to us, we were there, lunching with the pope, while there were children dying of hunger in the streets. And he told us that when we had the answer, we would be nearer to God," says an Argentine volunteer at WYD, Marcos Galeano, twenty-three. "Then we were all deeply moved, and the pope gave us all a warm hug."

Saturday, July 27, is the next-to-last day in Brazil. Smiling but firm, speaking in Spanish "to express better what I have in my heart," Pope Francis invites politicians and religious to a culture of encounter. He advises the politicians to listen to "cries demanding justice" and to have "an ethical sense," to "rehabilitate politics" so that it will return to being "one of the highest forms of charity." He asks the priests "to take the faith out into the streets," to think about pastoral ministry at the peripheries, keeping in mind those who are the most distant.

Celebrating Mass in the cathedral of Rio de Janeiro, he invites more than a thousand bishops and priests taking part in World Youth Day to announce the Gospel to young people so that they can find Christ and become the makers of a more fraternal world. He also speaks plainly in Rio's Teatro Municipal, during a meeting with the Brazilian ruling class, including politicians, diplomats, entrepreneurs, and representatives of the cultural and academic world. He reminds them of their enormous "social responsibility" and the fact that the most important thing is dialogue.

"When the leaders of different sectors ask me for advice, my answer is always the same: dialogue, dialogue, dialogue. The only way of growing for a person, a family, a society—the only way to make the peoples' life advance, is the culture of encounter, the culture in which everyone has something good to give and everyone can get something good in exchange. The other person always has something to give, if we know how to approach him or her with an open and willing attitude, without prejudice."

Saturday, July 27, is the day most awaited by the young people. It's the day of the vigil with the pope, originally planned as a pilgrimage to Campus Fidei. Nobody will walk to that rain-flooded field. However, everyone will wander for hours, first to find the all-important pilgrim kit that includes the meals, then somehow to stake out a space on the beach at Copacabana. Pope Francis will arrive at seven in the evening, but from early morning veritable fortresses of tennis shoes, backpacks, and even lunch boxes appear on the scene.

There's time for everything: sunbathing, dancing, praying, singing, and even taking a dip in the sea. There's even time for thinking. Alone and with an absent look. Ashit Macwan, from India, doesn't seem to need anything or anyone. His satisfaction can be read on his face. He's happy to be a Catholic because "Pope Francis is a simple man, a good leader," he says. Why a good leader? "Because he's a simple man."

The Pérez family, too, is happy. Hugo, Nancy, and their two children are Paraguayan, and they say that they jumped with joy at the news that the pope was from Argentina. "Francis is bringing to flower the force that the Church has in Latin America. Now we feel that someone from up there is supporting us," says Hugo. Nancy, four months pregnant, already knows what she will call her child if it's a boy: Francisco.

The hours fly by, and now the music announcing the pope's arrival rings out. In mere moments, the fortresses are dismantled and a tidal wave of young people crowds in front of the barriers. Defending your private space doesn't matter anymore—what matters is to see the pope, to be close to him. "A man who brings us blessings" is about to pass, says Adelmir Da Silva, twenty-seven, a Brazilian, who is there by chance. He works in a bar on the beach, and the barriers are preventing him from reaching his motorbike so he can return home. He has seen Francis passing by for three days and is moved.

Pope Francis begins his message explaining why those 3.5 million young people are not at the Campus Fidei, transformed by the rain into a sea of mud. "Does perhaps the Lord want to tell us that the real field of faith, the real Campus Fidei, isn't a geographical place but ourselves? Yes! It's true!" he exclaims.

There is an outburst of grateful applause, grateful for such clear words. Francis, a pope who's very keen on soccer, uses soccer metaphors. "Here in Brazil, as in other countries, soccer is a national passion. Yes or no? Well, what does a player do when he's called to join a team? He must train, and train a lot. Jesus offers us something better than the World Cup! Jesus offers us the possibility of a fertile life, a happy life. But he asks us to pay for the ticket, and the ticket is that we must train to face all the situations of life without fear, bearing witness to our faith. Through this dialogue with him: prayer. Father, now you will make us all pray, won't you? I ask you, but answer in your heart, not aloud, but in silence: do I pray? Let everyone answer: Do I talk with Jesus, or am I afraid of the silence? Do I let the Holy Spirit speak in my heart? I should ask Jesus: what do you want me to do, what do you want with my life? That is training. Ask Jesus, speak with Jesus. And if you make a mistake in life, if you make a blunder, if you do something wrong, don't be afraid. Jesus, look what I've done! What can I do now? But always talk to Jesus, in good and in evil, when you've done a good thing and when you've done a bad thing. Don't be afraid!" he affirms.

"I ask you to be the builders of the future, to start working for a better world. Dear young people, please, don't look at life from the balcony; immerse yourselves in it. Jesus didn't stay on the balcony, he immersed himself!" he exclaims. "Dear friends, don't forget: you are the field of faith. You are Christ's athletes. You are the builders of a more beautiful Church and of a better world."

Pope Francis leaves Copacabana beach after having led 3.5 million young people in silent prayer for many minutes during the adoration of the Blessed Sacrament. But for the rest of the evening, pilgrims will keep coming noisily to Copacabana.

Before going to sleep, I can't resist going for a walk on the seafront, which has been transformed into an open-air camp. In the midst of that sea of sleeping bags there's also my sixteen-year-old niece Paola, who, when we saw each other, told me that she was living the best moment of her life. I tweet some emblematic pictures, like the one of a priest hearing a girl's confession, sitting on chairs on the pavement, and one of hundreds of young people sleeping on the road because the beach isn't big enough. I go back to the hotel—it's two in the morning—and I meet Antonio Pelayo, longtime Vatican correspondent of Spain's Antena 3, who is also a priest, and a friend of mine. "You who followed John Paul II's pontificate from the beginning, tell me, was that as impressive as this?" I ask. "No," answers Antonio, shaking his head, the cigar between his teeth, "This is much more impressive."

With the second most-crowded Mass in history—more than 3.5 million people, a record number surpassed only by the World Youth Day in the Philippines in 1995—and a strong call to be missionaries, to uproot evil, violence, selfishness, intolerance, and hate, and build a new world, Pope Francis ends his triumphant international journey to Brazil for World Youth Day.

In another moving sermon at the closing Mass, he stresses that the Gospel is for everybody and not only for some. "It isn't only for those who seem closer, more receptive, more welcoming. It's for everybody. Don't be afraid to go and carry Christ to any place, even to the existential peripheries, even to those who seem furthest away, the most indifferent," he exhorts. "Brazil, Latin America, the world, needs Christ. The Church needs you, and the enthusiasm, creativity, and joy which are typical of you. Do you know the best instrument for evangelizing young people? Another young person," says the pope.

Francis also bids us not to be afraid. "Jesus never leaves anyone alone." And not to isolate ourselves. "Jesus didn't call the apostles to live in isolation; he called them to make a group, a community." Finally, he asks young people to serve. "The life of Jesus is a life for others, a life of service. . . . Evangelizing is bearing witness in the first person to the love of God. It means overcoming our selfishness, it means serving by bending down to wash the feet of our brothers, as Jesus did."

At the end of a Mass that is a *fiesta*—with a diversified liturgy that mingles charismatic and other songs with Gregorian chants and sees people moved to tears—an anxiously awaited announcement is made. The next World Youth Day, in 2016, will be in Krakow, Poland, the homeland of the now saint John Paul II, the founder of this great Catholic event. There is an explosion of joy among the Polish faithful.

We journalists who are traveling on the papal plane are already on board when Francis delivers his good-bye speech to Brazil at the Rio airport, during which he doesn't hide his *saudade* (nostalgia) over leaving the continent of his birth. The engines of the Alitalia plane, the same one we came on, are running. Father Lombardi comes down to confirm that Francis will keep the promise he made during the journey here. "He will come to answer questions, I know that we've got enough time, but it's something new, so get yourselves organized," he warns us.

During Pope Benedict XVI's papal journeys, he used to answer a list of questions prepared in advance, and only on the return flight. Now everything has changed. Because it's impossible for all seventy-one of us to ask questions, we organize ourselves by countries and by linguistic groups. My Spanish colleagues, very practical, use an airsickness bag to draw lots; this will determine who will ask the pope questions. Sergio Rubin and I, the two Argentines present on the plane, have been lucky: both of us will be able to ask a question.

Half an hour after taking off from Rio de Janeiro, Francis reappears at the end of the plane. Even though we are all exhausted after such an exacting journey, he looks as fresh as a daisy and is obviously content. He remains standing for an hour and twenty minutes to answer questions of every kind, including the most difficult and delicate ones, without filters, without a parachute, and without censure.

The former Archbishop of Buenos Aires doesn't take advantage of strong turbulence to escape from us. And he shows his sense of humor—more than once his words provoke laughter, as well as transparency, sincerity, and intelligence.

"What does it feel like to be pope? Are you happy?"

"Doing the work of a bishop is a fine thing, it's fine. The problem is when you look for that work: that's not so good, that's not from the Lord. There's always the danger of thinking of oneself as a bit superior to others, not like the others, a bit like a prince. Those are dangers and sins. But a bishop's work is fine—it means helping your brothers and going ahead. The bishop in front of the faithful, to show the way; the bishop among the faithful to help communion; and the bishop behind the faithful, because so often the faithful have the scent of the street. The question was: did I like it? Yes. I like being Bishop, I like it. In Buenos Aires I was happy, so happy! The Lord helped me in that. But as priest I have been happy, as Bishop I've been happy. I say it in that sense: I like it."

"And being pope?"

"That as well, as well! When the Lord puts you there, if you do what the Lord wants, you're happy. That's my feeling, what I feel."

"After such a journey, aren't you exhausted [which is *spossato*, with two letter *s*'s in Italian]?"

"No, I'm not married [*sposato*, with one *s*], I'm single." [Laughter]

"Why do you ask so insistently for people to pray for you?"

"I began to ask it quite often in my work as Bishop, because I feel that if the Lord doesn't help in this work of helping God's people and going ahead, you can't do it. I really feel that I have so many limits, so many problems, also that I am a sinner, and I must ask for this, it comes from within. I also ask the Madonna to pray to the Lord for me. It's a habit that comes from my heart and also a need I have for my work."

"Do you still feel you are a Jesuit?"

"That's a theological question, because Jesuits make a vow to obey the pope. But if the pope is a Jesuit, maybe he should make a vow to obey the Superior General of the Jesuits; I don't know how to solve this question. I feel I'm a Jesuit in my spirituality. I still think like a Jesuit. I don't mean that hypocritically, but I think like a Jesuit."

"At the fourth month of your pontificate, I want to ask you for a short balance sheet. Can you tell us what has been the best thing, the worst thing, and what surprised you most during this period?"

"But I don't know how to answer this question, I really don't. There haven't been bad things. Good things, yes. For example the meeting with the Italian bishops was very good. There was also a sad thing, which struck at my heart, my visit to Lampedusa. When those boats arrive, they are left a few miles away from the coast and they must arrive by themselves. And I find this painful because I think that those people are the victims of a world socioeconomic system.... But the worst thing has been my sciatica—I mean it!—which I suffered from during the first month. It was most painful. I don't wish it on anybody."

Transcribing this hour and twenty minutes of questions and answers deprives many of us of sleep. An intercontinental flight of more than 5,700 miles has never seemed so fast to me. In twenty minutes, we'll land at Ciampino Airport.

We journalists of the papal flight are still working frantically at our texts, immersed in our computers, when suddenly Pope Francis appears again in the aisle of the plane. He greets us, thanks us, and with a smile asks how we are. I say to him, "Padre Jorge, we haven't slept at all—you exaggerated, you've made us work too much!" And he answers, "You asked for it."

# 22

# Toward a Different Kind of World

Since the very night the *habemus papam* was announced, Pope Francis's way of doing things has been conquering the world. But since his triumphant visit to Brazil, he has been at the top of his game, advancing with determination in that revolution of style and substance that he has set in motion to reform the Church.

Although there are pockets of resistance, the overwhelming majority of Catholics—and even non-Catholics and, most surprising of all, nonbelievers—are behind him. Not for nothing has he garnered in the United States the nickname "Teflon Pope": he is so popular that criticism slides right off him, and nothing seems to stick.

The challenges Pope Francis faces are gigantic. Beyond his intended cleanup of the central governance of the Church, beyond making its finances more transparent—both of which are essential if the gospel is to be spread throughout the world—he has many other issues to deal with. These revolve around putting into practice the rich outcomes of the Second Vatican Council that have yet to be realized: greater collegiality, more synodality in the decision-making process of the Catholic Church, and decentralization.

Sooner or later, however, he will also have to tackle burning issues such as the situation of divorced people who have remarried and the ordination of married men (*viri probati*) to solve the problem of the shortage of priests—as well as reconsidering the role of women and laypeople in the life of the Church, and perhaps also the obligation of clerical celibacy.

In the historic interview that Pope Francis gave to the prestigious Jesuit magazine *La Civiltà Cattolica*, published also in *America* magazine on September 19, 2013, he admitted that it isn't doctrine that needs to change but attitudes. "What the Church needs most today is the ability to heal wounds and warm the hearts of the faithful, to bring them closeness, proximity. I envision the Church as a field hospital after a battle," he says, reminding us that the pastors should be close to people who suffer. "The Confessional is not a torture chamber but a place of mercy," the pope remarks, in a phrase that seems like a cold shower to some of the more conservative sectors of the Church. But he goes further:

> Religion has the right to express its own opinions in the service of the people, but through the act of creation God has set us free: we cannot interfere spiritually in someone else's personal life.... We can't keep on insisting only on issues like abortion, gay marriage, or the use of contraception. It can't be done. I haven't talked about these issues much and I've been reproached for that. But if we're going to talk about these things, we need to do so in a specific context. Beyond that, we all know the teaching of the Church, and I am a son of the Church.... The Church's pastoral ministry cannot be obsessed with the transmission of a disjointed multitude of doctrines to be imposed insistently. Proclamation in a missionary style focuses on the essentials, on the necessary things: this is also what fascinates and attracts more. We have to find a new balance; otherwise even the moral edifice of the Church is likely to fall like a house of cards.

If the challenges are enormous, then so too are people's expectations.

"It's true, this papacy has aroused people's hopes, and there are expectations of a new start for the Church like that of Vatican II. After a time of crisis, we all want a new beginning," says the German Cardinal Walter Kasper, president emeritus of the Pontifical Council for Promoting Christian Unity and the author of a book about mercy that was publicly recommended by Pope Francis during his first Angelus. "But we shouldn't overload this new papacy with disproportionate expectations, which will necessarily lead to new disappointments. A new pope can renew the Church, but he cannot invent a new church. Francis's style may differ from that of his predecessor, but his doctrine certainly doesn't. Personally, I'm hoping for a new phase in the implementation of the Second Vatican Council, which has not yet been completed."

The pope's creation of the advisory council of eight cardinals that must help him reform not only the Roman Curia but also assist in the governance of the universal Church confirms the determination of Pope Francis to advance in a collegial way, listening through its members to the voices of the bishops. The pope also intends to proceed in a synodal way: the word *synod* derives from the union of two Greek words, *syn*, "together," and *odòs*, "journey."

Although the concept of synodality is an old one for the Church, it has fallen by the wayside in recent decades. With power ever more centralized in Rome, although synods of bishops have taken place, they have not been listened to by the Vatican. "Decentralization is urgent because, as we have seen . . . all the minutiae of church life around the world, its cultural manifestations, and its diversity cannot be controlled and directed from a central point," argues the Archbishop Emeritus of San Francisco, John R. Quinn, president of the American Episcopal Conference from 1997 to 2000.

His thinking coincides with that of Cardinal Cormac Murphy-O'Connor, Archbishop Emeritus of Westminster, London, who, when speaking of the changes the Church most urgently needs, stressed the importance of the principle of subsidiarity and the need for its implementation. "There are many issues that can and should be decided at the local level. There are issues that are often sent straight to Rome when, in fact, they could be analyzed and resolved by local bishops. The principle of subsidiarity is very important, and implementing it would help the Church with its mission," he insists.

"The Eurocentrism of the past few centuries has definitely come to an end. In the new context, the unity of the Church can only be a unity in plurality and a plurality in unity. This state of affairs does not diminish the role of the Petrine ministry as a sign and instrument of unity; but it does require that the notion of collegiality be brought up to date, as was intended by the Second Vatican Council. The new council of cardinals from every continent is a step in that direction," states Cardinal Kasper.

Pope Francis, advancing with determination on this road, on January 12, 2014, announces the names of the nineteen new cardinals that he will create at his first consistory in February. His choice indicates a clear desire to correct the imbalance of Europeans (especially Italians) and North Americans in the College of Cardinals and to reduce the number of Roman Curia officials who get the red hat. At the same time, he gives a greater voice to the churches of the Southern Hemisphere, including those in Latin America. In particular, he pays special attention to the peripheries of the world, areas hit by poverty and conflict. Thus, he gives red hats to Church leaders in Haiti, Nicaragua, Burkina Faso, the Ivory Coast, and Mindanao in the Philippines.

In addition to affirming the churches of the Southern Hemisphere and seeking to correct the Eurocentrism that presently prevails in the Roman Curia, the pope is also determined to move ahead with decentralization and synodality, as he stated clearly in his document, "The Joy of the Gospel."

Archbishop Quinn stresses that decentralization is not a new idea but is rather the way the Church has functioned since antiquity. "This is why we need to recover the Church's traditional, patriarchal, metropolitan structure, which in the modern world goes by the name of episcopal conferences," adds this brilliant eighty-five-year-old Archbishop, who explores this topic in more detail in his latest book, *Ever Ancient, Ever New.*

Quinn believes that synods, as they have functioned up to now, do not work. "I have taken part in three synods, and I could see that bishops don't feel free to express themselves; they feel inhibited, they can't say what they want to," he confesses to me. The pope has similar thoughts: "Maybe it's time to change the method of the Synod of Bishops, because the current method seems to me to be very static. . . . I would like there to be real consultations, not just token ones," he says in the interview with *La Civiltà Cattolica.*

According to John R. Quinn, the *ad limina* visits—obligatory meetings between bishops and the pope, during which each bishop reports on the state of his diocese—that take place every five years have not been very useful either. On these visits, bishops from all over the world visit different departments of the Vatican and meet the Holy Father.

"It would have been different if the [former] popes had used the *ad limina* visits to meet with the bishops individually, in private, and say, for instance, 'Tell me, what do your priests think of the encyclical I've just written? Have they said anything? How have they reacted to the text?' Or 'What's the biggest problem you encounter in teaching the faith? Do you think you have enough priests celebrating Mass in your parishes? What do you think we should do to solve this or that?' The truly important issues never get talked about in *ad limina* visits," says Quinn, who in 1999 published a book titled *The Reform of the Papacy* in response to John Paul II's encyclical *Ut unum sint* on the commitment to ecumenism.

To achieve greater collegiality and decentralization, a reform of the Roman Curia is necessary. And indeed, Pope Francis, who has always called himself the "Bishop of Rome," is undertaking this very matter.

"The Roman Curia has a long history, and in the past it has had to adapt to new situations, challenges, and needs. Many in the curia carry out their work competently and efficiently, with great modesty. Blanket criticism would be unfair. But like the Church, the curia, too, must constantly renew and reform itself. It isn't—and can't be—an intermediate level of governance between the pope and the bishops," argues Cardinal Kasper. Will Francis run into resistance in the Roman Curia? "Of course, it's only normal, but there is a sense of awareness, which is more or less shared by all, that some changes are inevitable and necessary."

In this regard, Quinn is even more categorical: "If Francis doesn't transform the curia, not only will everything else come to nothing, but he himself will also be affected by it. I don't like saying things like this because I know a lot of very holy, humble people in the curia. But what I mean is that the curia as a system, as a structure, has long been a great obstacle to the life of the Church."

The issue of divorced people in the Catholic Church who remarry, "especially in the modern and postmodern Western World, is an urgent pastoral challenge," admits Cardinal Kasper. But the German theologian stresses that the fact that remarried divorced people are ineligible for communion is a complex issue. "The specific situations those people are in vary greatly. That is why they need to be considered on a case-by-case basis. Personally I'm in favor of a solution that differentiates each situation and recognizes that marriage between Christians is a representation of the fidelity of God in Jesus. As such, a second marriage cannot be a sacrament while the first partner is still alive. But that doesn't mean that these people should be excluded from the Church and the grace of God, who is always faithful in his mercy," he adds.

When Gian Guido Vecchi, the Vatican expert at *Corriere della Sera*, asked Pope Francis about this delicate issue during the flight from Rio to Rome, he also said it was a complex issue but one that should be analyzed and reconsidered.

"It's a topic people always ask about. Mercy is greater than the case you mention. I think that this is the time for mercy. This change of epoch, when the Church is having so many problems, like corruption or clericalism, for instance, has left many wounded. And if the Lord doesn't tire of forgiving us, we have no other choice: take care of the wounded, before all else. The Church is our mother and must walk the path of mercy. She must find mercy for everyone. This is a *kairos*—a moment—for mercy," says the pope, anticipating what he will later repeat in the interview in *La Civiltà Cattolica*. After observing that the Orthodox churches have different practices, he also admits that the problem needs to be analyzed within the context of pastoral care for marriage.

In regard to the question of the divorced and remarried, on the plane from Rio the pope tells a revealing anecdote: "My predecessor [as Archbishop of Buenos Aires], Cardinal Quarracino, used to say that half of all marriages were null because people get married without being mature enough to do so, without realizing it's for life, perhaps for social reasons.

And all this comes into the pastoral care of marriage. We also need to review the legal problem of the nullity of marriages, because it's too much for the ecclesiastical courts to deal with. The problem of the pastoral care of marriage is difficult."

Indeed, the pastoral care of marriage and the family is one of the topics Pope Francis is discussing with his eight cardinal advisors from different continents. He has already organized throughout the Church a consultation on the family, held a consistory of cardinals on this in February 2014 at which he invited Cardinal Kasper to give the keynote talk, and has called two synods to focus on this subject in October 2014 and 2015.

For Quinn, Archbishop Emeritus of San Francisco, above and beyond the question of whether people who have divorced and then remarried can receive communion, the issue that needs to be discussed in much broader terms is that of sexual morality. "Continuing to talk as if we're in the sixteenth century isn't helping. We need to take a broad approach to the question of sexual morality—not just contraception, homosexuality, or people living together without being married, because those are specific moral issues, but actually going right to the heart of the matter, to sexual morality as a whole," he argues.

And he doesn't stop there. "When we talk about communion, we have to ask ourselves about the nature of the Eucharist. Is the Eucharist just for the elite, the saintly spiritual elite, or is it also for those who are struggling to be better people and who want to grow? Is the Eucharist only for those who are no longer sinners?"

In the twenty-seven-page interview with *La Civiltà Cattolica*, in which he speaks freely on issues formerly considered taboo, Pope Francis is firm on doctrinal matters but also makes it clear that he is seeking what Quinn is asking for—that is, to open up discussion on these matters.

Quinn also thinks it essential to reconsider the role of women in the Church, an issue that is fundamental not just in the Catholic Church but in all cultures. "On the one hand, women are being abused in many societies.

We see it in Muslim countries, but also in our own so-called free societies, and in the case of nuns: they are all under the authority of men! In 1983, John Paul II appointed me to a committee that was to review the life of men and women in religious orders within the [United States] and their relationship with bishops. I had to write a report: the Church needed to pay much more attention to the difference between men and women. After reading it, John Paul II often said to me, 'The most useful part of what you wrote was that point.' Women are different from men, they don't think like me. And I don't mean that they don't think: they are more astute, more intelligent, but they think differently, and that needs to be understood,' he says.

During the press conference on the flight back to Rome from Rio, Pope Francis said something similar when claiming that we have not yet come up with a truly profound theology of women. "A Church without women is like the Apostolic College without Mary. The role of women in the Church is not just motherhood, to be the mother of the family, but is something far stronger; it is the icon of Our Lady, the Madonna, who helps the Church to grow. Our Lady is more important than the apostles. The Church is feminine; she is a wife, a mother. The role of women in the Church can't be limited to being mothers, workers, providers. It's more than that. The Church cannot be understood without women, but women who are active in it," he says.

He returns to this idea in the interview in *La Civiltà Cattolica*: "We need to broaden the opportunities for women to have a stronger presence in the Church. We need to work harder to develop a profound theology of women. Only by doing so may we be able to better reflect on her role within the Church. The female temperament is needed wherever we make important decisions."

Although in many parts of the world there are Catholic communities that cannot attend Mass because they have no priest, until now—in keeping with the Church's rule of clerical celibacy—the synods of bishops have not yet come to a decision regarding the ordination of married men (*viri pro-bati*) who are acknowledged to be good practicing Catholics.

In this context, it is of interest to consider Jorge Bergoglio's friendship with the widow of Jerónimo Podestá, the Bishop of Avellaneda who was at the center of a scandal for the Church in Argentina in the 1970s. In 1972, Monsignor Podestá married his secretary and assistant Clelia Luro, a thirty-nine-year-old mother of six daughters who was separated from her former partner. After living in exile in Peru, Podestá founded the Latin American Federation of Married Priests and Their Wives, which fights for the Church to focus on the poor and for clerical celibacy to be optional rather than obligatory.

In the book *Jerónimo obispo, un hombre entre los hombres, su vida a través de sus escritos* (Bishop Jerónimo, a Man among Men: His Life in Writing), a biography published by his widow in 2011, Cardinal Bergoglio is mentioned in the acknowledgments. He gave the anointing of the sick to Podestá on June 23, 2000.

"Bergoglio was a true brother who came to the intensive care unit when Jerónimo was near the end of his life and held his hand. Even though he was in a coma Jerónimo pressed the cardinal's hand, his last gesture, thanking the Church that he had loved and for which he had suffered so much, for being by his side as his soul left his body," she writes.

Clelia, eighty-seven and a friend of the pope's, is the first to argue that reconsidering the issue of celibacy is not particularly urgent.

"Francis is going to turn the Church upside down, make Vatican II a reality, get people to live the gospel, and make the Church into what Jesus wanted it to be. In terms of the celibacy rule, it's not about getting rid of it. That's not what married priests are asking. I think he may decide to make it optional, but first he has to establish himself as pope. The things he has already started doing come at a cost," she says.

For twelve years, Clelia spoke with Jorge Bergoglio on the phone every Sunday. "He was always there for me after Jerónimo died, and the issue of clerical celibacy often came up in conversation. Bergoglio once said to me,

'Jerónimo left you behind so that you can help me think,'" she tells me in an interview for this book, shortly before her death.

"I don't believe that the ordination of married men and the issue of clerical celibacy are on the pope's agenda," says Cardinal Kasper. His words seem to coincide with those of Carlos Galli, former deacon of the School of Theology at the Pontifical Catholic University of Argentina. "I don't know if the issue of clerical celibacy is going to be debated. In a priest's life, celibacy signals his having offered his love entirely to the service of others, and is also a stimulus for this, which is why I think that the deep-rooted meaning of clerical celibacy will remain intact. Would it be possible to have some kind of priestly ministry that is not governed by the rule of celibacy but would instead be reached through marriage? I don't see why not; we have examples of it in the Orthodox Church and amongst the Anglicans. Might Francis bring about changes on this matter? I don't know," says Galli.

"What I do know," he adds, "is that as Bishop of Buenos Aires he showed great love toward those priests who left the ministry: he was there for them along the complex paths their subsequent lives took; he gave them financial help when they needed to reintegrate themselves into civilian life; and he helped them with the process of canonical dispensation. His fatherly and brotherly love is evident. I don't know if he is going to take that next step, but he is at least going to let the debate about it happen."

Galli continues: "In Aparecida, it was an issue the Brazilian bishops wanted to talk about. Not in the sense of doing away with celibacy or even having two sets of rules, but rather seeing how priests who have left the ministry can continue to be of service. I think that Francis will listen to what the bishops have to say and may even organize a consultation. But I don't know if this papacy, with all the challenges it is facing, is the right time to think about two sets of rules [regarding celibacy for priests]."

In the press conference that he held on the plane returning from the Holy Land on May 26, 2014, Pope Francis confirms that, yes, this theme can be discussed. When asked if he has spoken about this question with the ecumenical Orthodox Patriarch Bartholomew, he responds: "The Catholic

Church has married priests: the Greek Catholics, the Coptic Catholics; in the Eastern rite [churches] there are married priests. Because celibacy is not a dogma of faith but a rule of life which I appreciate much, and which I believe is a gift for the Church. Since it is not a dogma, the door is always open. But we didn't talk about this with Patriarch Bartholomew because, to tell the truth, it is not the most important thing in relations with Orthodox Christians."

Many people who are hopeful and enthusiastic about the revolution being carried forward by Francis—a pope who wants more than anything to be in contact with the people—are worried about something else: that he might be assassinated. Domenico Giani, head of the Gendarmerie Corps of Vatican City, which is responsible for the pope's safety, inspires absolute calm when asked about the issue. "I place a great deal of trust in the Holy Spirit, but also in the preventative action we take before any celebration or event, in the Vatican, in Italy, or abroad. Of course, as the commander of the Gendarmerie Corps, I have no choice but to ask for the protection of our patron saint, St. Michael the Archangel, who watches over us. But I don't think there are any specific threats to the Holy Father, although, given that he is a symbol, we always maintain high levels of security while aware that we are 'useless servants' who are trying to carry out their 'useless role' as best we can, allowing the Lord to lead us toward whatever is his goal."

Giani was born in Arezzo fifty-one years ago and is married with two daughters. He denies that the trip to Brazil was a nightmare for him. On the contrary, he says that Pope Francis's first international trip—during which he shunned the bulletproof Popemobile in favor of a Fiat Idea—was "an apotheosis." Nor is he flustered by the pope's unpredictability, such as his habit during the Wednesday papal audiences of suddenly stopping to greet and hug the faithful. "I like the fact that the pope is surrounded by people, as was also the case with John Paul II and Benedict XVI. It's great seeing Francis in the middle of all these people. The pope might seem to be 'undisciplined,' and thus our security force might seem to be in crisis, but in actual fact our security protocols and our essential work in collaboration with Italian and foreign police forces allow us to operate with total calm," he insists. "I'm not worried about physical contact, but I do fear excessive affection, which can become dangerous, not deliberately, but because the simple wish to hug the pope or say 'I touched him' can get out of hand."

Just as there are people who worry that Pope Francis might be assassinated because of all the tables he's overturning in the Vatican, there are also those who worry—despite the fact that he appears ten years younger since the night of March 13, 2013—that he, too, might eventually resign from the See of St. Peter if he realizes that he doesn't have the necessary energy to go on, as was the case with his predecessor.

Not long after the resignation of Benedict XVI, on February 11, 2013, the German journalist Peter Seewald, author of a book-length interview with the Pope Emeritus titled *Light of the World*, said that the last time he had seen Benedict he had seemed physically and emotionally exhausted. During that last encounter, when he asked, "Are you the end of the old order or the beginning of the new?" Pope Benedict XVI, who had yet to turn eighty-six, answered, "Both."

"I don't know how long Francis's papacy will last because I am convinced that he will resign," says Father Galli. "First, because I believe he shares Benedict XVI's feelings that the pope should govern the Church only while he is fit to do so, physically, but above all mentally. Second, because by doing so he will create a tradition. Benedict XVI's gesture in resigning is still singular, unique. But to create a tradition, someone else needs to do the same thing, and then someone else. I think that we're seeing the start of papacies with limited lengths: if bishops resign at seventy-five, and cardinals stop being electors at eighty, why shouldn't popes also think about their service to the Church in similar terms? I'm not saying that we have to make it a fixed term, just that we should think about it differently," says Galli, who believes that Francis might even end up returning to Argentina.

José María Poirier, the director of *Criterio* magazine, has similar thoughts. "Yes, I've even written about his resignation. I might be wrong, but I get the strong impression that Benedict XVI's resignation ushered in great change in the history of the Church. Considering Francis's age, and if he manages to achieve what he has set out to do and thinks that it would be good for the Church to be led by someone stronger, with another vision, it's entirely possible," Poirier argues. Cardinal Murphy-O'Connor claims to know nothing of such speculations. "I think that Bergoglio can change things in four or five years, but I hope and pray to God that he will be with us for many more years."

On the flight back to Rome from Tel Aviv, when asked if the day should come when he feels he no longer has the strength to continue his ministry, would he resign from the papacy as his predecessor did, Francis suggests that he would. "I will do what the Lord tells me to do: to pray, to seek the will of God. I believe, however, that Benedict XVI is not a unique case. Seventy years ago, emeritus bishops did not exist. Today we have many. What will happen with emeritus popes? Benedict XVI is an institution: he opened the door, the door of the emeritus popes. Will there be others? Only God knows. But this door is open: I believe that a Bishop of Rome, a pope who feels that he does not have the strength anymore—because today we live a long time—will have to ask himself the same question that Benedict did."

Some days later, however, on June 7, 2014, in a meeting with athletes in Rome, he says something that leaves many people thinking that, in truth, Francis is not thinking of resigning but of dying in office. "I pray for you," he tells them, "and I ask you to pray for me because I, too, have to play my game, which is your game, which is the game of the whole Church. Pray for me that I may be able to play this game till the day that the Lord calls me to himself."

It's the middle of August 2013. Rome is half empty, but in the Vatican things are happening—noisy things. The sound of a drum booms passionately through St. Peter's Square. It's "El Tula"—Carlos Tula, a Peronist activist from Argentina and well-known supporter of the Rosario Central soccer team, famous for his drumming. He manages to take part in the papal audience that Pope Francis holds for the Argentine and Italian national squads on August 13, the day before they play a friendly match as a tribute to him at Rome's Olympic Stadium.

"El Tula introduced himself to the Swiss Guards, who called a Prefect, and he explained who he was. 'You ask the pope if I can come in,' he said. Someone asked one of Francis's secretaries, and the pope said, 'Let El Tula in,'" recounts Ernesto Cherquis Bialó, spokesman for the Argentine Football Association in a radio interview. "Not only did El Tula get in, but he was the next-to-last to greet the pope, he kissed him on the cheek and gave him a copy of his autobiography."

This audience in the imposing Clementine Hall—marked by the euphoria and confusion of the Argentine delegation, which was incredibly disorderly when the time came to greet the pope, especially in comparison with the neat and tidy Italian group—was useful to Francis. "Now do you understand why I'm a bit lacking in the discipline department?" asks the pope, laughing, to those he works with, who can't disguise their horror at all this chaos—and the sound of the drum—amid the Renaissance marble of the Vatican.

In the context of all this "lack of discipline," several days later the pope telephones a group of thirty young people—including some non-Catholics and atheists—who have written him a letter saying that they would like to meet him after walking from Bergamo to Rome. The letter includes a telephone number.

"Hello? This is Pope Francis," he says, surprising them, and inviting them to spend an hour that afternoon in a reception room at the Casa Santa Marta. They can't believe it. They come exactly as they are, sweaty from so much walking, to talk to the pope, whom they ask all sorts of questions. Francis is delighted.

The Argentine pope feels shut away in the Vatican. "Do you know how often I've wanted to go for a walk through the streets of Rome? I like walking the streets, and now I feel a bit caged. But I have to admit that the Vatican gendarmerie are great, they let me do a few more things now, although their duty is to ensure security here. In Buenos Aires, I was a 'cura callejero'—that is, a priest who walked the streets," Francis admits during the press conference on the flight from Rio to Rome. Maybe that's why there are urban legends spreading that Francis likes to leave the Vatican in disguise to walk the streets of Rome.

"The Vatican doctors told the pope that they needed to talk with his physician to go through his case history, so he would need to travel to Rome from Buenos Aires. They called him, and the doctor set off at once. When he arrived at Fiumicino Airport, he realized that he hadn't arranged for anyone to pick him up. How would they know who he was? As he was wondering, he went out into the arrivals hall and heard someone calling him. He turned around and saw two priests in black cassocks. One of them was the pope. So he went over, all excited, and said, 'Your Holiness!' And Francis signaled to him to keep his voice down. No one had recognized him, and he had gone unnoticed in such a big crowd" according to an e-mail that's circulating in Argentina.

Although the story sounds as though it could be true—indeed, the pope's doctor from Buenos Aires did travel to the Vatican—it's absolutely false that the pope went to pick him up from the airport in disguise. But when a myth is born, it's normal for legends to propagate.

"I don't like ideological interpretations, a certain mythology of Pope Francis. When they say, for example, that he goes out at night from the Vatican to give food to the homeless. . . . It never occurred to me. Sigmund Freud said, if I am not mistaken, that in every idealization there is an aggression. To paint the pope as a kind of superman, a kind of star, seems offensive to me," Francis says in an interview with *Corriere della Sera* in March 2014. "The pope is a man who laughs, cries, sleeps peacefully, and has friends like everybody else. A normal person," he adds.

Although he goes for walks inside the Vatican (*mens sana in corpore sano*, "a healthy mind, a healthy body"), Francis makes up for being under lock and key, for not being able to wander the streets, which is his passion, by using the phone a lot. He makes many calls to his friends, but also to strangers who write him letters because they feel that the new Argentine pope is *uno di noi*, one of us, and a friend.

On Wednesday, August 4, it's unbearably hot. The phone rings in Michele Ferri's house. Michele wrote a desperate letter to the pope after his brother was shot dead, riddled with bullets by criminals in Pesaro, a city in the center of Italy, in June. The crime has destroyed Ferri. "The more time goes by, the greater the pain. I've always forgiven you everything. But this time, God, this time I can't forgive you," he writes on his Facebook wall. In the midst of this anguish, he sends Pope Francis a letter, without knowing if he'll ever receive it.

That Wednesday, August 4, the phone rings in Ferri's house, and he answers it. He hears a voice saying, "Hello Michele, it's Pope Francis." At first he thinks it's a joke, then he starts to realize that no, it's for real.

Ferri doesn't go into detail about the conversation, but he shares the extraordinary moment on Facebook. "I got an unexpected phone call today. When I picked up and said 'Pronto?' a voice answered saying 'Ciao, Michele, it's Pope Francis.' I can't describe my feelings," he writes. "He said he had wept when he read the letter I'd written him."

That's what this missionary pope is like, the pope from the end of the world.

# Essential Chronology of
# Jorge Mario Bergoglio's Life

## 1936

Born in Buenos Aires on December 17, 1936, the son of Italian immigrants. His father, Mario, is an accountant employed by the railways, and his mother, Regina Sivori, is a committed wife dedicated to raising their five children.

## 1950

He studies in secondary school as a chemical technician and also works in a textile factory.

## 1953

September 21—He receives the call of God to the priesthood when he goes to confession in the Basilica of San Josè in the Flores neighborhood of Buenos Aires.

## 1957

He enters the diocesan seminary of Villa Devoto, but soon contracts pneumonia and nearly dies. The upper part of one lung has to be removed.

## 1958

March 11—He enters the Society of Jesus at the age of twenty-one.

## 1960

He takes first vows as a Jesuit and then goes to Chile to study humanities.

## 1962

He returns to Argentina to study for a degree in philosophy from the Colegio Máximo de San José in San Miguel.

## 1964–1965

He teaches literature and psychology at the Institute of the Immaculate Conception of Santa Fé.

## 1966

He teaches literature and psychology at the Institute del Salvador, Buenos Aires.

## 1967

He begins studies in theology at the Colegio Máximo.

## 1969

December 13—He is ordained a priest by Archbishop Ramón José Castellano.

## 1970–1971

He continues his training to be a Jesuit at the University of Alcalá de Henares, Spain.

## 1973

April 22—He makes his final profession with the Jesuits.

Back in Argentina, he is named Novice Master at Villa Barilari, San Miguel; professor at the Faculty of Theology of San Miguel; consultor to the Province of the Society of Jesus, and also Rector of the Faculty of Philosophy and Theology at the Colegio Máximo.

July 31—Father Pedro Arrupe, Superior General of the Jesuits, appoints him as Provincial of the Jesuits in Argentina, an office he holds for six years.

## 1980

January—He goes to Dublin, Ireland, to study English and stays with the Jesuits at Milltown Park.

## 1980–86

He is Rector of the Colegio Máximo, as well as a parish priest, again in San Miguel, and resumes his work with the university sector.

## 1986

March—He goes to Germany to do research for a doctoral thesis on Romano Guardini, but decides to return to Buenos Aires after some months. In Germany, he discovers the image of Mary Untier of Knots.

## 1987

He teaches at Colegio del Salvador in Buenos Aires. He is elected Procurator for the Jesuit Province of Argentina and in September goes to Rome for an international meeting of Jesuit Procurators, and then goes to Japan.

## 1990

July 16—He is sent into exile in Córdoba by his superiors and serves as spiritual director and confessor in the Jesuit church there for the next twenty-two months.

## 1992

May 20—Pope John Paul II appoints him Auxiliary Bishop to Cardinal Antonio Quarracino, for the Archdiocese of Buenos Aires.

June 27—He is ordained Bishop and becomes Episcopal Vicar of the Flores district in Buenos Aires.

## 1993

December 21—Cardinal Quarracino appoints him Vicar General of the Archdiocese of Buenos Aires.

## 1997

June 3—Pope John Paul II appoints him Coadjutor Archbishop of Buenos Aires.

## 1998

February 28—Following the death of Cardinal Quarracino, he becomes Archbishop, Primate of Argentina and ordinary for the Eastern-Rite faithful in Argentina who have no Ordinary of their own rite.

## 2001

February 21—Pope John Paul II makes him Cardinal.

October—He is appointed general rapporteur to the Tenth Ordinary General Assembly of the Synod of Bishops on the Episcopal Ministry, after Cardinal Edward Egan, Archbishop of New York, has to return home.

## 2005

April—He participates in the conclave that elects Pope Benedict XVI. He is the runner-up in that election.

## 2005–2011

He is president of the Argentine Bishops Conference.

## 2007

May—He plays a key role in the assembly of the general conference of the Latin American Episcopal Conferences at Aparecida, Brazil, and is the chief editor of its final document.

## 2011

December 17—He reaches the age of seventy-five and submits his letter of resignation to Pope Benedict XVI.

## 2013

February 28—He attends the final meeting of cardinals with Pope Benedict XVI, who resigns that same day.

March 13—Cardinal Bergoglio is elected pope and takes the name of Francis.

June—He publishes the encyclical, *Lumen fidei*, "The Light of Faith." It was mostly written by Benedict XVI.

July—He goes to the island of Lampedusa, off the coast of Sicily, to mourn the deaths of African immigrants in the Mediterranean Sea. It is his first papal visit in Italy.

July—He participates in the World Youth Day in Rio de Janeiro, Brazil.

October—He visits Assisi and prays at the tomb of St. Francis of Assisi.

November—He publishes the apostolic exhortation, *Evangelii gaudium*, "The Joy of the Gospel," which is the programmatic document for his pontificate.

## 2014

February—He creates nineteen new cardinals in his first consistory in St. Peter's Basilica.

May—He makes a pilgrimage to the Holy Land, visiting Amman, Bethlehem, and Jerusalem.

August—He makes his first journey as pope to Asia, visiting Korea, for the sixth Asian Youth Day and the beatification of 124 Korean Martyrs.

# Acknowledgments

To all those who kindly collaborated with the author of this book:

Fr. Carlos Accaputo; Fr. Nicolás Angellotti; Fr. Juan Gabriel Arias; Julio Bárbaro; María Elena Bergoglio; Jorge Bergoglio (of the family in Cordoba); the family of Julio César Cantú; Fr. Gustavo Carrara; Nora Mabel Castro; Carlos Cecchi; Oscar Crespo; Germán De Carolis; Santiago de Estrada; Fr. Lorenzo "Toto" de Vedia; Celia Dalila Díaz; Fr. José María "Pepe" Di Paola; Fr. Mariano Fazio; Archbishop Víctor Manuel Fernández; Susana Fernández Pedemonte; Santiago Fraga; Fr. Carlos Galli; Manuel García Solá; Fr. Fernando Gianetti; Domenico Giani; Fr. Ernesto Giobando, SJ; Gustavo Alfredo Girard; Sergio Gobulin; Juan Grabois; Fr. Eugenio Guasta; Fr. Alberto Ibáñez Padilla, SJ; Fr. Juan Isasmendi; Delicia Juárez; Damián Karo; Cardinal Walter Kasper; Martha Laera; Ernesto Mario Lach; María Inés Lahora Carrera; Daniel López; José Ignacio López; Clelia Luro de Podestá; Mario Fabián Maidana; Fr. Guillermo Marcó; Cardinal Jorge Mejía; Ana Meza; Inés Miguens; Hugo Morelli; Cardinal Cormac Murphy O'Connor; Rafael Musolino; Pedro Nicola; Fr. Jorge Oesterheld; Bishop Oscar Vicente Ojea; Alejandro Pavoni; Fr. Ignacio Pérez del Viso, SJ; Francisco Piñón; Esteban Pittaro; Eduardo y Rogelio Pfirter; José María Poirier; Archbishop Mario Poli; Archbishop John R. Quinn; Sister Martha Rabino; Julio Rimoldi; Fr. Silvio Rivera; Mario Roldán; Pablo Romano; Fr. Ángel Rossi, SJ; Gladys Rueda; Fr. Alejandro Russo; Cardinal Leonardo Sandri; Archbishop Marcelo Sánchez Sorondo; Fr. Juan Carlos Scannone, SJ; Fr. Andrés Swinnen, SJ; Carlos Velasco Suárez; Fr. Pedro Velasco Suárez;

Gustavo Vera; Aída Vescovo; Federico Wals; Eduardo Woites; Fr. Humberto Miguel Yáñez, SJ; the authorities of the Institute of Our Lady of Mercy (Istituto Nuestra Señora de la Misericordia), where Francis attended kindergarten and received his first Communion, and the authorities of the *Escuela Pública* (Public School) Nº 8 Pedro Antonio Cerviño, where he went to primary school.

To my research team, that worked with enthusiasm and dedication: Clara Fontan (coordinator), Paula Markous, and Nadia Nasanovsky.

To the persons who helped me, but who requested that I not mention their names.

To the two books that are essential reading: *The Jesuit* (*El Jesuita*) and *On Heaven and Earth* (*Sobre el Cielo y la Tierra*), and their respective authors.

To Luz Henríquez, who had the idea for this book, for her patience and professionalism.

To Alberto Moriondo, for his invaluable assistance in the publication of this book in English.

To my colleagues, friends, and the editorial board of *La Nación*, the newspaper for which I write, for their constant support.

To my family, in particular to my parents, Piero and Ana, and to my brothers Enrico and Giacomo and my sisters-in-law, Mercedes and Angela, who took care of my children when I was engrossed in the task of writing this book, and to my nephews Piero and Guillermo. To Consuelo and Ana Luz for their assistance.

To Juan Pablo and Carolina, to Edwin and to Gerry, who helped and supported me in this endeavor.

To my Friends, who encouraged me; to Cristina, Irene and Raffa, my Roman supporters.

# About the Author

Elisabetta Piqué has been a correspondent in Italy and the Vatican for *La Nación*, Argentina's main newspaper, since 1999. She was the only reporter to write that Cardinal Bergoglio, whom she has known since 2001, would be elected pope. Born in Florence, Italy, she was educated and grew up in Argentina. After obtaining a degree in political sciences and international relations from the Catholic University of Buenos Aires, she began her journalistic career. She reported on wars and conflicts in Afghanistan, Iraq, Kosovo, the Middle East, and on major international events including the hand-over of Hong Kong to China. She has focused on Pope Francis since his election to the papacy.

# Learn More About Pope Francis and His Message of Mercy

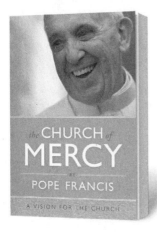

### The Church of Mercy
*A Vision for the Church*

Collected from Pope Francis's speeches, homilies, and papers presented during the first year of his papacy, *The Church of Mercy* is the first Vatican-authorized book detailing his vision for the Catholic Church. This book's deep wisdom reminds us that the Church must move beyond its own walls and joyfully bring God's mercy wherever suffering, division, or injustice exists.

Hardcover | 4168-0 | $22.95
Paperback | 4170-3 | $16.95
Discussion Guide 10-Pack | 4204-5 | $9.95

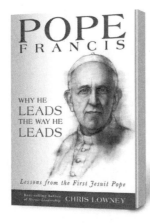

### Pope Francis: Why He Leads the Way He Leads
*Lessons from the First Jesuit Pope*

Best-selling author and former Jesuit seminarian Chris Lowney offers an in-depth look at how Pope Francis's Jesuit training has directly impacted his various leadership roles and what it suggests about how he might lead in the future. Readers will gain essential lessons to help them with their own leadership challenges.

Hardcover | 4008-9 | $22.95
Paperback | 4091-1 | $16.95

**TO ORDER:** Call 800.621.1008, visit www.loyolapress.com/store, or visit your local bookseller.